Princess

Princess

ANN MORROW

CHAPMANS
1991

Chapmans Publishers Ltd
141–143 Drury Lane
London WC2B 5TB

BRITISH LIBRARY CATALOGUING IN PUBLICATION DATA

Morrow, Ann
Princess.
1. Great Britain. Royal families. Diana, Princess of Wales
I. Title
942.085092

ISBN 1-85592-515-X

First published by Chapmans 1991

Photoset in Linotron Aldus by
Rowland Phototypesetting Ltd, Bury St Edmunds, Suffolk
Printed and bound in Great Britain by
Butler & Tanner Ltd, Frome and London

Acknowledgements

First my thanks to a number of people in royal circles for their guidance and encouragement. Also to Roger Beale, Joanna Bogle, John Boyd, Dame Barbara Cartland, Donald Campbell, Sir Hugh Casson, Marion Cookson, Dr Jack Dominian, Hilary and Robert Falcon, Brigadier Andrew Freemantle, Germaine Greer, John Grigg, Dr Jozsef Gyorke, former Hungarian Ambassador to London, Maria Giust, Rod Hackney, Tiffany Nicholson, T. C. M. O'Donovan, Norman Pratt, Claire Rayner, Bernadette Richardson, Barty Roche, Les Rudd of Turning Point, Peter Shellerd of The Royal Academy of Music, David Sassoon, Philip Somerville, Sir Roy Strong, Charles Swallow, Douglas Sutherland, Dave Tarpey, Valentino, Patric Walker, David Williamson of Debrett's Peerage, Zelda Westmead of Relate, Margaret Holder of *Royalty* magazine, the staff at the Taskiemka Archives for research; to Ralph Martin's *Charles and Diana*, Andrew Morton's *Diana's Diary*, Ingrid Seward's *Diana* and Peter Lane's 'A Study in Development'; to Bill Lewis, *Private Eye* Librarian, and to the London Library.

As always most special thanks to Mike Shaw at Curtis Brown for his encouragement and support, to Ian and Marjory Chapman who commissioned this book and who, with their zingy team, helped and sustained. Particular thanks go to editor Janice Robertson for her felicitous decisions.

Thank you to Sharon Baines and Marva Douce who worked appalling hours, to Terry Keeler for apt revisions and to personal assistant Angie Montfort-Bebb for her unique contribution.

This book is dedicated to my husband for his help and judgement but most of all for brightening all the days.

They met in a cabbage patch.
He said, 'Would it be too awful, if . . . ?'
She said, 'Well . . .'
The consequence was
They drove away in the State Landau
And the World said, 'Bravo.'
   This is their story.

Contents

Photograph
Acknowledgements

———•———

BLACK AND WHITE PHOTOGRAPHS

Section 1
Lady Diana's christening   *Associated Newspapers plc*
Lady Diana's first birthday   *Press Association*
Lady Diana aged 3   *Press Association*
Lady Diana and her brother   *Press Association*
Playing croquet   *Press Association*
At Silfield School   *Associated Newspapers plc*
On the Isle of Uist   © *PAR*
At the Young England Kindergarten   *Photograph by Steve
   Back, Associated Newspapers plc*

COLOUR PHOTOGRAPHS

Section 2
The Princess of Wales at 21   *Photograph by Snowdon, Camera
   Press*
The balcony kiss   *Popperfoto*
At Balmoral   © *Alpha*
Dancing in Australia   © *Photographers International*
Taking baby William home   © *Photographers International*

CHAPTER 1

The World's Obsession

———————◆———————

You hear footsteps on the stairs, the chauffeur's discreet, 'Ten fifteen. Right . . .' and the muffled sound of the exhaust as the black car pulls away from a deceptively shabby house in a Chelsea street. Inside all the Sloane touches are there: yellow and white striped wallpaper, little enamel boxes and bowls of fresh flowers.

The men straighten their ties, the Princess is on her way, bounding up to this first-floor sitting room, those long legs climbing two at a time. Suddenly she is there. Her layered short blonde hair looks terrific, her skin has the sheen of rose petals and her teeth are extremely white for someone once so fond of chocolate and kippers. Immediately warm, fresh, friendly and funny, you realise photographs never quite capture her; she looks even better in the flesh.

You are struck first by the eyes, vulnerable and expressive, a cornflower blue. They sparkle, shyness gone; the pink glossed lips part in laughter which is never far away, and her hair is threaded with sunny highlights. The voice, light and high, comes as a surprise, because she is so modern, yet it is predictably upper-class crystal. 'Camilla . . . Gerald;' pecks on the cheek, 'lovely to see you.'

Her movements are quick and graceful; 5 feet 10 inches tall in her stockinged feet, she has the ballet dancer's straight back and quite often stands in fifth position.

This is a rare evening for her when she is free to be with trusted friends. Even they hang back, not wanting to appear pushy, but she makes it good for everyone with a teasing laugh, a rolling of eyes on realising she is now the longest-married in the room. The aura is royal; not for one minute do you forget that this is the future Queen, though this evening she is wearing a satin jumpsuit. Another light kiss for a newlywed girlfriend as she moves round the sitting room with its photographs of glowing children in gleaming silver frames and copies of *Tatler* and *Vogue*, one featuring the Princess. 'Oh that . . . yah', an embarrassed giggle.

Cool and relaxed she sits down, legs outstretched, sipping a favourite homemade lemon drink. Good friends are all around. They had worried once that she would be ground down by the dead hand of Palace protocol. She complained then how she hated all the 'heel clicking and bowing' of court life. They feared that being Princess of Wales would change her, that she would lose her sparkle, but they say she is still the same. 'Diana has always been a fabulous girl.'

Although she is thirty on 1 July 1991, and her face is more mature and assured, the exuberance is still there. She is probably still quite capable of stunning a stuffy gala gathering at Covent Garden by whizzing down the banisters of the Royal Opera House in a fuchsia taffeta evening dress. By being herself, totally unselfconscious, good humoured and bouncy, she could make the poet Laurie Lee feel it was an honour to receive a light kick on the ankle when his speech went on too long at a Royal Academy dinner.

She holds the world spellbound. Misty enchantress of the media, Dinki-Di, Shy Di, Diana Super Star, Di-light, Di-namite, Princess of Wales, of Wiles, of Wows. There is nobody in the whole world who even begins to match, let alone outshine her. The Queen is valued, Princess Anne respected, the Queen Mother loved, but the Princess is adored.

Never childish, never petulant, though behind the scenes she can get cross, she has the highest expectations for herself and of her staff. She is never overdressed but always stylish; polished without being programmed, outgoing but not outrageous. Attractive because she is not too clever, she also has a certain serenity. To the monarchy, she has brought the glamour of youth but, more importantly, a sense of renewal.

An upper-class Alice in Wonderland, hers are the virtues of a perfect English nanny, loyal, kind, tactful, warm, discreet, firm. Still fresh and original with all the *joie de vivre* of the twenty-year-old girl who married a future king, she remains quirky, irreverent, dignified, motherly, skittish, sweet, hopeful, wistful, sexy, determined yet soft. It never seems to strike her that she is a knockout. The world's most closely watched beauty ever, and the most photographed, she has a wonderful lack of vanity.

Her marriage has had its difficulties; they celebrate their tenth wedding anniversary on 29 July 1991. The laughter has gone a little. We miss their jokes together and the occasional scribbled 'Smile Daddy' message on her upturned palm.

Prince Charles had everything to gain by marrying; his life hardly changed. She was the one making the sacrifices, losing many of her friends and much of her freedom. Dotty about babies but hating the business of having them, she bore two speedily: an heir and a 'spare'. She has looked at her marriage and decided to dedicate her life to carrying out engagements better than any other royal, sublimating any loneliness in work.

A girl who has never cared for horses, dogs, red meat, sludgy colours, serious books, hunting or shooting, she adores up-to-the-minute fashion and red, the colour of sex and power. She likes going barelegged on engagements, is not too fond of gloves or vivid lipstick, loves ballet and tap dancing and is besotted with her boys.

People are immediately at ease in her company. She has a way, shared only by the Queen Mother, of making each person she meets feel they are the only one who matters. Her smile is wonderful, her face just lights up and people are still laughing long after she has left.

She never raises her voice, talks gently; sometimes she will take a hand in hers and her interest in others is never phoney. She conveys warmth and is tactile in a way no other member of the royal family has found possible. There is a glow of royalty but never a hint of grandness. She comes across as a refreshingly 'sparky, very English young woman'.

Originally thought of in royal circles as 'a piece of funky Dresden china', this strongwilled Princess is today more in demand and more fulfilled than anyone might ever have predicted. Her working life, she tells you with breathy honesty, is 'seventy per cent sheer slog and thirty per cent fantastic'. She has learned to live constantly with danger. The day after a man lunged at her in a crowd she admitted, 'I am terrified, I never get used to it.' Her care is for the unemployed, the elderly and the homeless.

Full of fun she has a niceness which is not boring. There is also, apart from the sparkle, brightness and glamour, a quality of goodness. 'She is so full of vitamins and vitality,' says one of her advisers, 'it is hard to imagine her ever being old.'

Weep no tears for this girl. People may like the concept of her as a medieval madonna floating ethereally over a depressed nation. The reality is she is a down-to-earth well-born girl, conventional, cheerful, wanting to be liked, who has made a huge success of one of the most difficult jobs in the world. Confident, glossy and burnished, she is an aware patron of forty charities, constantly in demand for tours overseas. The hope is that she never becomes disillusioned.

Her photograph is pinned over cots, on tanks, in factories. Girls dress like her, shape their hair like her and try to become like her. Men adore her, want to look after her and protect her. She loves to flirt but it would be very foolish to take this lighthearted banter seriously. If you ask her how she sees herself, she says simply, 'I just like laughing . . . I'm a normal person, hopefully, who loves life.'

Hers is star quality. No mere decorative accessory, she has taken an ill-defined job and given it a modern twist, creating a dazzlingly effective role for herself. Brave enough to shake hands with AIDS sufferers and go into the drug haunts of the dying showing no sign of cynicism or world weariness, she has become a world obsession setting a cracking pace for monarchy.

CHAPTER 2

Ladies who Lunch

———————————◆———————————

The Princess of Wales is coming to a charity lunch at the Savoy.
Lady Rothschild has insisted on two dry runs of the menu to
make sure of a perfect Barbue à la Vapeur, Délice de Volaille au
Vin, Blanc Sorbet and Praline en Surprise. After the sorbet, the
Italian couturier Valentino will show his latest collection.

Socially mobile hostesses on charity committees know that the
very best way to raise funds is to invite along a member of the
royal family. Then you can charge the earth for tickets; and as
guest of honour the Princess is the cream.

Today's lunch is for the AIDS Crisis Trust, a chic date not to
be missed by socialites. Tickets were £175 each. Had they been
£700, they would still have been snapped up to support this trendy
cause, and as it is four hundred people were turned away from
this gathering of not exactly nouveau but show business and some
Establishment people: what was once called Café Society and
more appropriate to a give-away glossy property magazine than
Jennifer's Diary. Now, on 30 April 1989, a sunny spring day in
London, they want to do their bit for the immune deficiency
syndrome casualties.

From midday onwards, the fashionable and wealthy started to arrive at the River Room entrance. It all seemed incongruously apart from the plight of AIDS victims, often ostracised by society as if they were contagious, treated like lepers in the medieval world.

It is a day for the ladies who lunch, all suntans and highlights: women with golden skin at the end of a long English winter, sucked in cheeks, blonde bobs or sleek black hair held by grosgrain bows. Thin legs and supple shapes have been kept in trim by personal trainers, cosseted feet luxuriate in soft Italian leather shoes.

Here a touch of Chanel, a few Yves St Laurents; over there a Krizia. Like exotic birds they peck each other on the cheek, pearl and gold clip earrings almost touching as they reach out for a 'Bucks Fizz' of champagne mixed with the juice of blood oranges. Their escorts, some balding but nearly all with perma-tans, as if never a moment is spent in an office, stand by simpering as their women eye each other.

Then the Princess arrives, gilded in turquoise and white, her skin with the glow of real sunshine – she is just back from Necker – a natural glamour. Followed by two smiling detectives, there is a light touch on the hand for the little girl who gave her a posy and she is ushered into an inner sanctum where a handpicked few selected by Mrs Marguerite Littman, the principal organiser, wait to meet her.

For Patricia Flanagan, Bridget White, and Maureen North, the little team who had organised the lunch, the Princess has sympathy: 'Oh, it must have been awful getting the placements right.' But by that stage they were too excited and wondering about their curtsies to worry where to put the Bentincks, the Rothschilds or the Abbouds.

Time to go into lunch. The girls stayed behind – they were not included – and picked at the few cheese straws and from bowls of tiny yellow and red tomatoes; the invitations were bundled up. There is nothing more dismal than an empty room where there has just been a party.

A rough sign on an easel said that anyone who cared to pay £500 to the Aids cause could, after lunch, be photographed by Terry O'Neill alongside Joan Collins. Chauffeurs would wait,

6

check their Filofaxes in a desultory way or use the car telephone as their employers posed alongside the irrepressible trouper in her beige turban and short high-waisted skirt and who was now going into lunch with Lord Snowdon. He was limping and looking almost portly as he went down the stairs but a later check-up at the Cromwell Hospital revealed that he was in good condition.

His wife, the grave Lucy, followed behind chatting to Princess Margaret's great friend and lady-in-waiting Mrs Jane Stevens, in chic black and white with a four-strand pearl choker. Sir Georg Solti, the conductor, was brown and beamy; Marie Helvin, top model and former wife of photographer David Bailey, who did lots of work behind the scenes for the lunch, struck a matelot note in striped T-shirt and white jacket and was carrying a demure little basket.

Lady Carrington, wife of the former Foreign Secretary, wore a discreet blue and red silk shirtwaister, good taste for lunch or tea in the garden with the vicar; Michael Caine's wife Shakira was svelte in pale blue pinstripes; but almost stealing the show was Richard Shortway in a stunning, dazzling shocking pink jacket. Mrs Vivien Duffield was with her constant companion Jocelyn Stevens, exuding bounce in his usual red and white striped shirt. Detmar Blow tried very hard and wore a hat which had two huge wings like an old aeroplane; but it did not get her the attention expected.

Valentino sat next to the Princess. Back in Rome, he paused from work on his latest collection to recall, 'It was one of my beautiful days.' It is known that in private she likes his clothes. 'But I was quite surprised, being a designer, how we spoke very little about fashion.'

As the models pranced on-stage, the Princess whispered in Valentino's ear, 'What happens if they eat?' 'I said, "Your Royal Highness, I hate people who are not enjoying food, they are not interesting." She said she loves everything; she likes food very much.' Her presence at the Savoy would go a long way towards securing the £100,000 being raised for Milestone House in Edinburgh, a hospice specially built for AIDS sufferers.

She was far more photogenic and stunning, Valentino thought, than any of his top models. What struck him – on his own admission he can sum up women fairly quickly – was that 'The

Princess seemed such a good human being, very simple and, as a mother, her eyes are full of fire when she speaks about her children.' There is no better way to appeal to an Italian.

CHAPTER 3

Augusta had a Miserable Time

Marriages made by Princes of Wales were not always the joyous affairs of 29 July 1981 when Prince Charles married the comely Lady Diana Spencer. He is the twenty-first Prince of Wales and she the ninth Princess.

The future George IV remarked, 'I am not well, pray get me a glass of brandy,' on seeing his future bride Princess Caroline of Brunswick-Wolfenbuttel. She was not a lovely creature, unlike the first Princess of Wales, who was described as the 'most beautiful woman in England'. This was Joan, 'The Fair Maid of Kent' who married the Black Prince in 1361.

A more hapless Princess of Wales was Catherine of Aragon. Married to Henry VIII but unable to bear him a son, she fell out of favour when he became infatuated by Anne Boleyn, but at least she kept her head.

A busty blonde Princess of Wales, Caroline of Ansbach, married the future George II in 1706. Politically aware, she was witty and bright and, like the present Princess, cultivated her own satellite court. Showing a certain nonchalance over her husband's

9

mistresses, she expressed the hope that one of them, Mrs Henrietta Howard, might help her solid German husband improve his lamentable English. It seems she had little success, for when he was told in 1727 that his father had died and thus he was now king, he disbelievingly replied, 'Dat is one big lie.' Never an easy man, he shared with the present Prince of Wales a preoccupation with health and diet. In 1760 he was found dead in the lavatory after a heart attack brought on by his exertions.

He always despised his son Frederick, calling him a 'half witted coxcomb' and 'the greatest ass'. In spite of a yellowy skin and beaky nose, this Prince of Wales, known as 'Poor Fred', nearly married an ancestor of Lady Diana Spencer. However, the Prime Minister forced him into an alliance with Princess Augusta of Saxe-Gotha.

The unfortunate Augusta had a miserable time, being evicted with her husband by a jealous King from St James's because he feared that the Prince and Princess of Wales might become too popular. Their son George, who was twelve when his father died, was born in a lodging house near the London Library in St James's Square.

This future George III married Charlotte of Mecklenberg-Strelitz, a dull but decent woman who bore him fifteen children. He had been in love with Lady Sarah Lennox, a descendant of Charles II and Louise de Kerouaille, a relation of Diana's, but was told he must not marry for love but must choose a solid German princess. It was as well he had chosen such a simple undemanding soul for he later went mad, tried to smash the Prince of Wales's head against a wall and lost America as a colony. His great champion is Prince Charles who feels the excitable king has been generally misunderstood.

Perhaps because of the headbashing, his son, later George IV, married his cousin Caroline, a grossly overweight, unsavoury and lewd lady who could hardly have been more different from today's delicate Princess of Wales. Her husband was driven to keeping a string of mistresses including Mrs Fitzherbert and Lady Jersey.

Heirs to the throne often had to be chivvied into marrying suitable girls. There had been no Princess of Wales for two generations when Queen Victoria began to worry about her eldest son. He was displaying a 'sudden fear of marrying' and, above all, of siring children.

'Oh, that boy,' Queen Victoria wrote to her daughter Princess Victoria in exasperation. 'As much as I pity him, I never can, or shall, look at him without a shudder.' A determined matchmaker, Queen Victoria pleaded with her daughter to help find a wife for the future King Edward VII.

Princess Victoria sat under a tree with a copy of the Almanach de Gotha, searching in this Who's Who of European aristocrats for a suitable young lady for her brother. Royal requirements for a bride were sensible then, as now. Queen Victoria told her daughter, 'We want a girl with good looks, health, education, character, intellect and a good disposition.' But, she stressed, 'Great rank and riches, we do not want.'

A Danish princess, the enchanting and beautiful Alexandra was thought ideal for Queen Victoria's incorrigible 'Bertie'. She was summoned to the Palace, the monarch telling members of her Household quite plainly that she wanted to 'see the girl' not so much to decide upon her son's future happiness as to make sure 'she will suit me.'

Princess Victoria urged that they move quickly because the Tsar also had his eye on the Danish beauty. 'It would,' she thought, 'be too dreadful if this pearl were to go to the Russians.'

Even the Prince of Wales, when consulted, grudgingly admitted his family's choice 'charming and very pretty'. But the Queen grumbled about his lack of enthusiasm and wondered about his capacity to be in love. Prince Charles himself has questioned the whole state of ever 'being in love'.

Married in 1863, Alexandra had the same generous instincts as the present Princess of Wales and carried herself with the same grace. She was marvellous with the sick, the handicapped and, at Court, bubbled with gaiety and wit. Her sister Dagmar went to Russia in her place and was the mother of the last Tsar, Nicholas II, assassinated in 1918. Although elegant, playful, charming and skittish, hiding her grandchildren's nightdresses and pyjamas, Alexandra was not encouraged to be anything more than a decorative, forbearing and tolerant princess of Wales.

Even her mother-in-law, the Queen, commiserated: 'I often think her lot is not an easy one.' And she was not referring to the cruel twist of fate which left her daughter-in-law deaf from rheumatic fever, putting the final seal on this pretty woman's loneliness. The Queen knew of her son's philandering; he had several dalliances with feathery lovelies, among them Lillie Langtry and Mrs Alice Keppel, who was invited to his death bed by his devoted wife. Far from being ascetic like our own Prince of Wales, he ate five ten-course meals a day and had a forty-eight-inch waist.

His second son, Prince George, became Prince of Wales. His elder brother, Prince Albert, died of influenza in January 1892, only days after celebrating his twenty-eighth birthday. George would marry his dead brother's fiancée, Princess Mary of Teck.

In monarchy there are harsh necessities. It had been difficult finding 'a good sensible wife' like Princess Mary of Teck for Albert, so she was asked if she might be available for Prince George instead. They married on 6 July 1893 after a courtship that was hardly impetuous but rather touching in the sensitivity shown by the Prince, who apologised in a letter for appearing 'shy and cold'.

In its way it was a love match. Although you would never find Queen Mary jumping into her husband's lap and giving him a decent kiss, she could show concern. Once when the Prince of Wales had been inspecting a submarine at Portsmouth and seemed to be underwater for an unconscionable time, his anxious wife muttered, 'I shall be very disappointed if George does not come up again' as she peered at the gloomy waves.

As Princess of Wales she could be soft hearted and humorous beneath a stern exterior, but she was never cosy or motherly. She had a weakness for Floris chocolates, liked singing 'Yes, We have No Bananas', doted on small antique *objets d'art*, usually other people's, and loved a pudding called 'Rod Grod' made with raspberries and sago. In common with the next Princess of Wales she preferred fish, chicken and asparagus to meat and root vegetables. She was kind to her staff, always choosing their one hundred and twenty Christmas presents herself.

Her eldest son, the superficially glamorous David, the future Edward VIII, avoided all efforts to get him married to a flower of the English or Scottish aristocracy. He lost his virginity to a prostitute in the summer of 1916 in Calais. This introduction sparked off an obsession with sex and in particular with a prostitute called Paulette found for him by an equerry. His sexual appetite could hardly be sated and he seemed to 'fall in love' with almost every woman he met, causing the royal family endless anxiety.

He fell for the brittle chic of an American divorcee called Wallis Simpson and gave up the throne. A second brother again succeeded; the slight Duke of York and his wife who never wanted to be royal became King and Queen. George VI and his wife, today our Queen Mother, would save the throne after the dreadful feeling of disillusion created by the Abdication in December 1936 when more than half the population believed that Britain should become a republic.

The Queen Mother was generous and affectionate to Edward VIII though his decision catapulted her physically frail but mentally strong husband on to the throne in 1937. 'I am terrified for Bertie,' she said, 'but for God's sake don't tell him.' To the king who was leaving she wrote a tender letter: 'We want you to be happy more than anything else . . .' The bitterness said to have been ingrained in the Queen Mother at this time was directed more towards Mrs Simpson than her brother-in-law.

Most of his servants despised him and refused to join him in exile. 'Your name's mud. MUD!' Fred Smith, who had been with the King since 1908, said angrily. 'Oh Frederick, please don't say that. We've known each other for so long,' the departing king replied. A junior piper was appointed as a last resort but he said his parents would be shocked. Later Edward wrote to Queen Mary that he would never forget how they 'let me down.' With 'craterous' haunted eyes, the Duke of Windsor moved from spas to nightclubs, a thin, sad and permanently tanned man living an aimless life.

When George VI died in 1952, worn out by war and the 'intolerable honour of monarchy', the Queen Mother's message on her white flowers at his funeral was, 'To a dear husband, a great and noble King'. Their daughter the present Queen was crowned on 2 June 1953.

If anyone could epitomise the importance of the Queen Consort, it is Queen Elizabeth the Queen Mother, who turned the role into something unique. She paid a huge price but today ninety per cent of the British are pro-monarchy and filled with optimism about the Princess of Wales, this girl who has already brought an aura of unprecedented distinction to her delicate role.

CHAPTER 4

The Family is Quite Extraordinary

———◆———

A friend of the Princess's says, 'You come into a room and you see the Queen standing there and she is your mother-in-law; well, you have to behave, right?' A wise daughter-in-law, the Princess has a delicate relationship with the Queen, not rompingly warm but politely dutiful, admiring her as she might a fine headmistress.

The Queen is far too subtle ever to be dictatorial. However, if an M.O.T.G., 'morally obliged to go' invitation wings its way to Kensington Palace, in the words of the Mafia, this is something even a princess of Wales cannot refuse. Always pleasantly worded, she may hear about it first from Sir Robert Fellowes, her sister Jane's husband, who is the Queen's Private Secretary. 'Diana, the Queen thinks it would be marvellous if you could be at the Trooping, the Cenotaph, the corgi flypast,' whatever . . . bang go the Princess's other plans. It is said that the Princess was rather surprised on her first Christmas with her mother-in-law to be given a present with a stilted greeting 'From Her Majesty the Queen to the Princess of Wales'.

As the Princess's confidence has increased, any nervousness 'in the presence' has disappeared, especially as the Queen has so clearly begun to rely on her. In October 1990 the Princess helped entertain the Italian President Francesco Cossiga while Prince Charles remained at Balmoral nursing a shattered arm. The Queen Mother, aged ninety, was understandably forgiven for not appearing at yet another royal banquet. The Italian visitor was delighted with the decorative substitute.

In the way she has approached all hurdles, the Princess trod softly from the beginning, always careful not to overstep the mark though she has known the Queen since childhood. It had been one thing seeing this family friend over the years with her cheerful 'How's Johnny?' piping royal inquiries about Earl Spencer's health, and quite another for this warm, sunny, uncomplicated girl to live as a bride-to-be with her future mother-in-law.

A gregarious and highly social member of the royal family laughs: 'The family is quite extraordinary. Prince Charles, Prince Andrew and Princess Anne all still have sets of rooms at the Palace but the Queen never drops in on them. She goes straight to her chilly sitting room, with its pleated paper fan in the empty fireplace, presses the bell and up come the lamb cutlets. There they are in Buckingham Palace all having dinner alone, each in different rooms. You'd think sometimes they might like to sit round and have a chat.'

This apartness treasured by Prince Charles, made life difficult at first for the newlywed Princess. 'I couldn't believe how shy she was with them,' a courtier observed critically, 'even though they are an extremely relaxed, friendly family.'

On the rare occasions when the royal family eat together they use only one set of eating irons: simple silver knives and forks with George III stamped on them, wiping them on their bread between courses, and they talk seriously. Diana was not bookish or travelled and if occasionally they lapsed into French or German, she was embarrassed; languages have never been her strong point.

The Queen was quite stunned when the Princess ran round the dining table and jumped into her husband's lap to give him a smoochy kiss. This was very disarming; it really did not matter that the Princess had no view about nuclear warheads.

Today, a mature Princess finds being with the royal family easy but suffocating. Often after the first curtsy and social 'kiss' on her mother-in-law's extended cheek . . . 'mm, so lovely to see you,' she is impatient to be off. More than a match for them, she is stronger than they imagined and jokingly is compared to Queen Victoria.

In the home, Prince Philip is very much the 'boss'. The Queen fusses round him, being personally 'very attentive' though he may be quite unaware, steeped in a study of the Malaysian Orang Asli tribe. Early on in family discussions, he enjoyed changing the Princess's mind, she has always had a little stubborn streak, but nowadays he thinks this wilful, pretty daughter-in-law has had too much influence on Prince Charles. However, with her sense of fun the Princess can very often defuse a potential flare up between her husband and Prince Philip with a little gentle teasing and flattering of her volatile father-in-law. Prince Philip's arthritis may often contribute to his irascibility. The staff have often wondered if something could be done about this when they see him wincing in the stable yard and resting his hands against the wall. 'It is no wonder he is full of painkillers before he goes on these coach and four events,' they say.

Princess Anne could never be classed as an ally. There has been no pretence that the Princess and her husband's forty-year-old sister could become bosom friends. But as they mature, they appreciate each other; there is a growing mutual respect, and the Princess of Wales is amused by her sister-in-law's comment that in her experience dignitaries generally come covered in grass – thrown up by the visiting helicopters.

In the past, Princess Anne has behaved in public as if surrounded by wild animals who if given encouragement might leap up and tear down her sternly upswept hair. Now this second hardest-working member of the royal family after the Queen, nominated for a Nobel Peace Prize for her work as President of the Save the Children Fund, has proved herself and can afford to relax.

'I was never a fairy-tale princess and I never will be,' Princess Anne once snapped, exasperated by the adulation shown to her soft-hearted, beautiful sister-in-law. It is true the two have little in common, certainly not horses. A superb horsewoman, Princess Anne says self-mockingly, 'When I appear in public, people expect me to neigh, grind my teeth, paw the ground and swish my tail – none of which is easy.'

Ironically since her marriage break-up, the no-nonsense Princess Royal has a new-found serenity. Her parting from her husband, Captain Mark Phillips, after sixteen years, followed the revelation that love letters had been written to her as 'my dearest' by one of the Queen's equerries, the thirty-four-year-old Commander Timothy Laurence. It was the Princess of Wales who comforted him during the public uproar, lunching in Mayfair with the handsome naval officer. Rumours spread about the suggestion of a £250,000 royal payoff being made in June 1992 to Captain Mark Phillips in return for his silence after what looks like an inevitable divorce from Princess Anne.

Warm and loving, the Princess finds the Queen's two eldest children tend to suppress emotional feelings and have that 'cold egotism' spotted by Lady Ponsonby, wife of Queen Mary's private secretary, which, she thought, 'seems to chill you in all royalties.' Prince Charles is often on a spiritual quest but rarely at church on Sundays; nor could he find much time to be at home with Prince William for his first half-term.

Princess Anne's father-in-law Major Peter Phillips, might, after the death of his wife, have relied less on the whisky bottle and avoided a stroke had there been some cheering practical visits from his royal daughter-in-law. But she was busy doing good round the world while he was only twenty miles from her own home. The practical and motherly Princess of Wales, remembering her own lonely childhood, made a point of keeping an eye on the Phillipses' children Zara and Peter during their parents' difficulties and absences.

The Queen is full of praise for the Princess of Wales but really finds the uncomplicated Duchess of York with her love of horses a much easier daughter-in-law. The Queen dotes on Prince Andrew with his fine record as a helicopter pilot during the Falklands war. Even with her finely honed sense of propriety, she was indulgent when he gauchely admitted on a television chat show, 'You know, the one thing I can never possibly imagine is my mother and father making love.'

When Prince Andrew married Sarah Ferguson, daughter of Prince Charles's polo manager, Major Ronald Ferguson, the

Princess of Wales was delighted and welcomed her into the royal family. But there is a difference between the two daughters-in-law that is highlighted by a simple thing. The Duchess still feels a little excitement about the perks of being royal but it is the Princess who feels entitled to use the Palace pool every morning without checking first. The Duchess of York always puts in a respectful call. However, the Duchess, who may soapily gush about how thrilled she is to be a royal daughter-in-law, does excellent impersonations of the Queen behind her back, even when courtiers are watching.

When the Duchess first leapt on the royal carousel, for a time the Princess was slightly swept along by her sister-in-law's zest for japes. Prankishly they dressed up as policewomen and raided Prince Andrew's stag party at Annabel's the night before the wedding on 23 July 1986. Nicknamed the Merry Wives of Windsor, they went in for a little horseplay at Ascot, prodding top-hatted friends with umbrellas but greatly displeasing their mother-in-law.

With that unerring Cancerian instinct, the Princess pulled back after a few tacky incidents. She was appalled by the Duchess's decision to take part in the television programme 'It's a Royal Knockout', thought it greedy of her to keep the royalties on her Budgie book when Prince Andrew's Civil List payment is £155,400, and was shocked by the Duchess's clowning in America when she pretended to knight her host's dog with a kitchen knife.

A friend of the Princess's from school days sounded slightly shocked. 'Frankly I have been taken aback by the bitterness with which she has spoken about the Duchess. Diana feels betrayed about the way Fergie has behaved on a number of points.' 'The girl lacks judgement,' another friend suggested. She is 'forever doing the wrong thing', and drove her forty-five-year-old private secretary and equerry Lieutenant-Colonel Sean O'Dwyer into resigning.

However, the Princess remains ostensibly friendly, tapping the Duchess's tummy when she was pregnant in 1990 and teasing, 'I know it's going to be a boy called Elvis.' The Duchess was always convinced her second baby would be a girl, but the Princess insisted, 'You're carrying the baby way out in front and that's how I looked when I had both my boys.' After the birth of a second daughter she helped the Duchess to become svelte, trotting her along the banks of the Dee and keeping her away from the traditional mutton puddies at the royal picnic lunch.

There is something touching about the Duchess's new strained pale attractiveness; the chubby cheeks and hips have gone and so has the gummy game smile. In Argentina they admire her 'chispa', meaning sparkiness, and in 1990 she won full marks as 'The Most Inspirational Female Personality' for her self-discipline in losing weight. Anxious to keep Prince Andrew's interest, meeting his former girlfriend, the actress Koo Stark, she wore a thigh-high skirt and showed a bare midriff while Miss Stark wittily wore virginal lace. The Duchess tries hard, is good natured and willing. The Queen wants to find her a worthwhile job and consulted Mrs Thatcher in the hope that, fully occupied and fulfilled, she is less likely to do silly impulsive things or enjoy too much lavish hospitality offered by sheikhs and American millionaires.

In the meantime, the Duchess is settling down in her £5 million American ranch-style house built on the edge of Windsor Great Park. Nicknamed Tesco Hall, this 'monstrous great place' has been built in the walled garden of the lakeside house given to the Queen and Prince Philip by King George VI when they married in 1947. It burnt down mysteriously before they could move in and to this day villagers stay mum. 'Nobody knows, tiddly pom,' says Mrs Jan Robertson, a colonel's wife living nearby.

It is hard to know what the Victorian historian Walter Bagehot, who cautioned that the magic of monarchy was its mystery, would make of the Yorks. There is a cynical theory that they are part of a clever Buckingham Palace ploy to make the family attractive to the average video-owning 'new Briton'. If they can see this royal couple as 'just like us . . . not a bit stuck up,' the Prince and Princess of Wales can go on being tastefully remote.

While most of the royal family are more than capable of looking after themselves, the Princess feels protective of Prince Edward, her youngest brother-in-law. She has always had a soft spot for him, partly because he thinks of Prince Charles as a hero. Affectionately calling him 'Scooter' after a cuddly, likable, woolly puppet in the Muppet series, she took his side when he had the courage to opt out of the Marines and was enduring a chill in the family especially from the Queen. Prince Edward has gone in quite a different direction from his brothers, but has had the spirit to form his own theatrical company and owns a greyhound which has run well at White City.

The royal net spreads wide but it is to the Princess, this comparative newcomer, that everyone turns when in trouble, because she is gentle and has a listening ear. The men in the family enjoy the sympathy of this decorative in-law and the women know her advice will be kindly.

When Princess Alexandra's sweet-faced daughter Marina Ogilvy rebelled against her parents, resenting their anxious correctness as fringe royals, and announced that she was pregnant, it was the Princess of Wales who helped the family. Thoroughly conventional herself, she still understood the girl's point of view.

Married now, Marina poses in rubber tights and black mini skirt for Paul Mowatt her photographer husband. She enjoys her baby and finds the Princess of Wales easier than her own mother. 'My parents have been horrible to us,' she says, and alleges that they wanted her to have an abortion rather than bring disgrace on the family. When the Queen finally gave grudging permission to their marriage in her customary handwritten consent the words 'my trusty and well-beloved cousin' had been chillingly deleted. There can be no greater disapproval.

The Princess of Wales gets on easily with the principal members of the royal family, but there is a little competitiveness with her Kensington Palace neighbour. Princess Michael, six feet tall, forty-five years old and with a beauty which makes sophisticated men crumble, says correctly of herself, 'I may be a lot of things but I am certainly not boring.'

A bit too soignée and worldly for the Princess of Wales she is refreshingly honest about her distaste for 'kissing babies and cutting ribbons', two things, she admits, 'which bore me rigid.' Frank about the trivial demands of royal duties, she says, 'You don't need an O level to shake people by the hand.'

There is a great deal of support from, of all unlikely people, Princess Margaret, who also lives in Kensington Palace. Prince Charles calls it the 'Aunt Heap'. They share an interest in music and the Princess has always been sympathetic about her sixty-year-old aunt-by-marriage's ill-fated romance with Group Captain Peter Townsend, one of King George VI's married equerries, and also about the end of her marriage to the photographer Lord Snowdon.

In the late 1940s divorce was unthinkable in the royal family, and for this reason the Princess could not marry Townsend. But ironically she was divorced when her once 'highly physical, intensely passionate' relationship with Lord Snowdon ended. Prince Charles tells his wife this is a chastening example of what can happen if you break the royal rules.

It was Princess Margaret's daughter, Lady Sarah Armstrong-Jones, a girl of unassuming easy charm 'adored by the Queen', who was instrumental in helping to bring her friend Lady Diana Spencer to the attention of Prince Charles at Cowes.

Always tinglingly aware of being the Queen's sister, Princess Margaret can be fearfully haughty. An art dealer recalls accompanying her round a gallery and saying as he excitedly pointed out a particular painting, 'Look, Your Highness,' only to be given a withering look as the Princess added with icy sangfroid, 'Royal,' and made him jump. The young Waleses, however, are allowed to call her 'Margot'. They enjoy her delicious food and, as both Princesses are abstemious – Princess Margaret now drinks only barley water – evenings do not go on as once they used. In the past it was often three in the morning, and nobody could leave, until the Princess asked, in her throaty imperious way, 'Who's going to take the dawg out for its last walk?'

Nowadays the Princess of Wales thoughtfully brings her little punnets of raspberries and other organically grown delicacies from Highgrove. And since they share a mutual distaste for hearty countryside pursuits but a love of dance, Princess Margaret is happy to pay the Princess the greatest compliment, trusting her with the treasured mantle of patron to the English National Ballet.

In the royal family, it is the Queen Mother you need as a friend. Everybody adores 'Ma'am Darling'. 'May I pop round?' the Princess will ask if she has a free afternoon in London. The Queen Mother, who can be lonely – not all her relatives are so attentive – replies, 'Oh, that would be such fun.' Over tea and chocolate cake in the Garden Room at Clarence House there is such merriment and understanding in a sweet hour together that both feel elated and surprisingly cheerful about their destinies.

CHAPTER 5

He Was All Sport

If you stand in the room where the Princess of Wales was born on 1 July 1961 it helps explain why she has been chosen as future Queen. Views from the sunny double bedroom with its old-fashioned twin marble washbasins and huge taps are straight across to Sandringham House, the Queen's Norfolk home.

Prince Charles first set eyes on her at the time of her christening. 'I have known him all my life,' the Princess says, adding with a slight smile, 'a lot of nice things happened to me when I was in nappies.'

As a child she fondly recalls racing half a mile across the parkland to Sandringham House. When asked later if she ever felt uncomfortable with the Queen, the Princess looked faintly puzzled. 'No, why should I be?'

'We are not,' her mother once declared, 'at all grand,' with a hint of tongue-in-cheek. To the children, the Queen, their nearest neighbour, was simply 'Aunt Lilibet', someone who gave good children's parties. Though once, in a fit of pique, Diana refused to go to a royal nursery party and could not be cajoled into changing her mind, showing an early stubborn Spencer streak.

From her earliest years, being with the royal family has seemed natural. After all, jelly and custard tastes much the same in an aristocratic nursery as in a caravan. The great fun at royal birthday teas was seeing Prince Edward covered in honey and, for Diana, even better, was a game of hide and seek with the Queen and Prince Andrew in the long Sandringham House corridors.

Today the Princess has bitter-sweet feelings about the out-wardly gloomy looking, ten-bedroomed Victorian Gothic house where she grew up. Traditionally on loan to the Fermoys from the royal family, her earliest memories are the happiest, when her parents appeared well suited and she received loving attention from a graceful, sparky mother and a cuddly reliable father.

Trees and shrubs encroached from the Royal Park making it an ideal secret playground for the Althorp children. They raced about the sweeping lawns and the heated swimming pool was appreciated by the royal children, especially Prince Charles.

Originally, Park House was for extra guests from Sandringham, until it was rented from George V by the 4th Baron Fermoy, who was forty-six when he married the Princess's maternal grand-mother, Ruth Gill, a twenty-year-old colonel's daughter from Bieldside, in Scotland in 1931.

Coming from a family dedicated to military service she has always been a woman of the utmost propriety, as you might expect of someone brought up as an Aberdonian, a people who pride themselves on being forthright and rather despise the Celtic winsomeness of other parts of Scotland. She is a talented pianist and the couple met in France where Ruth Gill had been a promising pupil at the Paris Conservatoire. Now a close personal friend and Lady of the Bedchamber to the Queen Mother, Ruth Lady Fermoy has never been especially intrigued by the interest-ing foreign blood brought by her great-great-grandmother, who lived with Theodore Forbes, a Scottish merchant, who worked in Bombay for the East India Company.

Forbes found the average, well-bred white woman could not endure the heat of the colonies for long, so he took in a local Armenian girl, Eliza Kewark, for comfort in the monsoon. He never married her, though he had children by her and left her a legacy of one hundred rupees a month. David Williamson of Debrett's Peerage found that Eliza Kewark communicated with her lover's executors in Scotland after his death at sea in 1820. Letters written on her behalf had her distinctive signature 'arsayber', Armenian for Mrs Forbes. Their illegitimate daughter Katherine was sent home to Scotland to be educated.

The Princess's American family connection began with a Mr Frank Work, a shop assistant in Ohio who later became extremely wealthy. He had a beautiful daughter called Frances, known affectionately as 'Fanny', who married the Princess of Wales's great-grandfather, James Boothby Roche, later 3rd Baron Fermoy, and it was their son Maurice who was to marry Ruth Gill.

However, Frank Work, who had become a stockbroker and adviser to the Vanderbilts and many of America's distinguished families, was unimpressed by the impoverished Lord Fermoy. He thought any marriage with a foreigner a 'hanging offence'. It was nothing to him that the Fermoys, originally a Norman-Irish family, owned several properties in Ireland, about 19,000 acres in County Cork alone. However, his Fermoy son-in-law loved to gamble and sold the family seat, Trabolgan, a handsome Georgian house overlooking Cork harbour. Today it is a holiday camp. Freckled children called Siobhan and Seamus jumping in the swimming pool shouting 'janey mac' when the water is cold, are unaware that they are in the home of the Fermoys for one hundred and eighty years. But they marvel at the fanciful Arc de Triomphe, 'an exact copy' they say of the 'wan' in Paris, a fine resting place for dead Roches.

The family simply moved on to another handsome Fermoy property. This was Cahirguillamore House at Rockbarton overlooking a deer park and rewarding pastureland in Limerick. They enjoyed the leisurely life of the Anglo-Irish, the seasons in Dublin and London, playing croquet on the lawn, lolling in wickerwork chairs drinking cocktails at sundown and house parties. There was always lots of laughter and special celebrations when a Fermoy daughter, Sybil Roche, married Nigel Baring, one of the banking family, in London in 1908.

With the acceleration of the Troubles the Fermoys were advised to stay away from Ireland. The great house was dismantled, commandeered by the IRA in 1921 and later used as a barracks by the Irish army. All that is left today is a ruin, a symbol of the family's decline in Ireland. Behind the tall black gates of what was once a handsome 37,000-acre estate in Golden Vale land, there is a straggly farm and a sign on the rusty ironwork says, 'These lands are preserved for Fur and Feather.' In the field behind a black horse lies dead.

Living in a tumbledown lodge in the grounds at Rockbarton Stud is one of the last of the family, Barty Roche, a resilient old character. He is much loved by the locals, who respect him for his knowledge of horseflesh rather than any connection with the Princess of Wales. Although one of the Roche clan, he never had a privileged start in life. 'I went to the local National School where,' he boasts, 'one year I was the most backward in the school, the next the best.'

Just out of hospital recovering from a battering by thugs who repeatedly beat up this seventy-five-year-old bachelor, he has the Fermoys' merry blue eyes. His dressing gown held by a safety pin, he gave a toothless grin as he recalled the Princess's great-grandfather. 'He was all sport. He'd bet on flies up the wall, ah he was terrible well liked, very good-looking, a head of curly hair and round face, he was always having parties, a grand man.'

Kilshannig near Fermoy in Cork is an appealing eighteenth-century crumbling manor house with a mezzanine entrance thought to be based on Blenheim. Although it was lived in by the Princess's great-great-grandfather, Edmund 1st Lord Fermoy, MP for Cork and Lord Lieutenant, until 1855, it only ever rated as a second home. When his childless heir died, the younger son, James Roche, who married the flighty Fanny Work, succeeded as 3rd Baron at the age of sixty-eight.

Like so many old houses in Ireland, Kilshannig has a depressing granite face. Weeds creep up the walls, panes of glass are cracked in the windows; it is gaunt without soft lawns or groomed drives. But this Fermoy ancestral home is typical in that the grey outside hides a luscious interior with a quite perfect curled-end Christopher Wren inspired balustrade and Kilkenny marble fireplaces for log and peat fires. After a day's hunting, tall mahogany doors opened to the salon where Fermoys had their crystal glasses re-filled with champagne before an excellent dinner. The dining room has an extravagant rococo ceiling, an almost edible riot of cherubs, lions, dolphins and eagles by the celebrated Italian plasterers, the Francini brothers. The locals in the predominantly Catholic village of Fermoy say of the bacchanalian satyr, 'It's the devil.'

In 1960 the house was bought by a Captain Douglas Merry. 'It was,' said the gregarious former English sea captain, 'a wreck.' Merry, who runs a 250-acre stud farm and was just back from Hawaii attending horse syndicate board meetings in a swimming pool, has spent a fortune on Kilshannig. He was very touched when the Princess of Wales's uncle the 5th Baron Fermoy came to visit in 1982. He was full of praise and particularly admired the restoration of the original Georgian colours, strong mustards, berry reds and vivid blues.

Not long afterwards the Fermoy family were shocked when the Baron committed suicide in 1984 in the stables of his Berkshire home. This stocky, charming man who often expressed a wistful interest in his Irish roots, was succeeded by his seventeen-year-old son Patrick Roche who was still at Eton.

With its meadows dotted with Kentucky Derby winners and graceful thoroughbreds, it is like a Stubbs painting showing enchanting views over wooded acres and fields nestling under the Galtee and Knockmealdown mountains. As it is unlikely with the present tension in Northern Ireland that the Princess could visit Kilshannig, the Fermoys have thought about commissioning a painting of the house as a gift for her. When Prince Charles was asked outside Sandringham church by an Irishman in a wheelchair, sixty-five-year-old Bernard Cullen, if he might ever visit Southern Ireland, the Prince replied: 'I would love to. But do you think I would ever get there? Perhaps if I did they would blow me up.'

The Princess's American links have been the most lucrative. When the naughty Fanny Work's marriage to the third Lord Fermoy failed, she returned to New York in 1891 a wilful daughter begging her father's forgiveness. The old man relented but on condition that she should never go back to Europe, changed her name back to Work and become an all American girl again. However, he was enraged when he discovered in 1907 that with the spirit which seems to go with the name Frances in that family, this wayward daughter was in love with a Romanian who worked with horses, Auriel Botanyi, whom she later married. She left a nice fortune which was inherited by her great-grandchildren, including the Princess of Wales.

Her sons, Maurice and Francis George Roche, inherited £600,000 each from their grandfather on condition they became American citizens and never visited England. They went to Harvard and spent early years in America, but found the lure of Europe too much. The courts upheld their claim to the money, and it was on a bit of a spree that the thirty-five-year-old twins sailed to England on board the *Lusitania* to attend the Coronation of George V. Maurice had succeeded as 4th Baron Fermoy in 1921.

Their mother disobeyed her late father again and returned to Europe, the forbidden continent, for Maurice's wedding in Aberdeenshire to Ruth Gill.

A responsible Norfolk landowner and for a time a Conservative MP, Lord Fermoy was a reliable and frequent companion of King George VI. He played tennis and ice hockey with him and was with him on a February shoot in 1952 the day before his death at Sandringham. The Fermoys had three children.

Their son Edmund succeeded in 1955, and their eldest daughter Mary Roche married Anthony Berry, a Conservative MP who was killed in the Brighton bomb disaster in 1984. His widow remarried, a teacher called Dennis Geoghegan, but he went into a monastery after three years.

The bond with the royal family was such that Queen Mary speedily related the news of the birth of the Fermoys' younger daughter Frances to the dying George V in the hope it would cheer him up. But sadly he died next day, 20 January 1936.

Frances Roche would make the marriage of the season, to Viscount Althorp, affectionately known in royal circles as 'Johnny' and heir to the Spencer earldom.

CHAPTER 6

The Spencers Were in Sheep

The Spencers have no murky history, just beautiful women who seemed to catch the eye of future kings. It is an honour to be a King's mistress. Three were the paramours of Charles II and one of James II. The men were statesmanlike, valiant and loyal to the crown.

Lady Diana Spencer is better born than her husband, which helps explain her easy transition to princess. At the time of their engagement Prince Charles grumbled, 'I am getting fed up learning all about her past. I am beginning to think she is more royal than I am.'

This worthy, aristocratic, landowning family with its phlegmatic attitude and lack of flamboyance has always been attractive to the monarchy. They have been reliable courtiers down the ages, with few hints of scandal. Dependable, solid, conventional, they were unexciting but sound.

The first recorded Spencer became one of the wealthiest men in England by slyly taking the meat and wool from his flock of 19,000 sheep straight to London, cutting out the middle man. Money resulted in power and good connections. In time the

Spencers became earls, belonging to that happy breed valued by any ruling King and officially called 'beloved Cousins'.

Althorp came into the family when John Spencer bought this pleasant moated house in Northamptonshire in 1506, but it was never thought grand enough for the family who preferred Wormleighton, Warwickshire. Henry Spencer, who had heroically supported Charles I in the Civil War, was made Earl of Sunderland in 1643, but was killed in battle that same year. In reduced circumstances, his widow was forced to move with her four children from the Warwickshire manor house to the less desirable Althorp.

Her eldest son Robert, the 2nd Earl Sunderland, a buccaneering opportunist, redesigned Althorp, creating much of its present-day elegance. His son Charles married the Duke of Marlborough's daughter Anne Churchill in 1699 after much parental scheming. But she died of consumption at the age of thirty-two leaving her capable mother Sarah, Duchess of Marlborough, coping with her children, among them a six-year-old daughter, Diana, a task relished by the formidably ambitious matriarch.

As soon as this granddaughter, her 'dearest Di', was old enough she tried to get her married to the Prince of Wales and even offered him a £100,000 dowry, which he found very attractive. But the Prince, known as 'Poor Fred', was forced to marry the seventeen-year-old Princess Augusta of Saxe-Gotha, who arrived at her wedding clutching a doll. This Princess of Wales never became Queen as her husband died before his father George II. She was, however, the mother of a king, George III. Meanwhile Diana Spencer had to make do with a Duke, but one with a good title. She became the Duchess of Bedford.

The 1st Duke of Marlborough had no sons, so Diana's eldest brother Charles Spencer inherited his grandfather's title and Blenheim Palace, that grand house built at Woodstock in Oxfordshire in honour of a ducal victory. Her other brother John unexpectedly became heir to Althorp. The old Duchess was fond of him and, not caring much for Charles, left him all her *objets d'art*. As a result, the Princess of Wales grew up surrounded by handsome paintings, porcelain and ornate furniture at Althorp which might as easily have gone to Blenheim or Woburn. Amongst them is a rather macabre portrait of Sarah Duchess of

Marlborough with a shock of spidery short hair. She had chopped off her hair after a row with her husband, to spite him, but was full of remorse when after his death she found it tied with ribbons in his desk.

The title Earl Spencer was given to John Spencer's son by George III. In celebration he built Spencer House in London's prestigious Green Park; it is used by the family still for parties. In the eighteenth century this house was known as a phoenix because of its Roman style decoration. For nearly a century it fell into dilapidation but in 1985 Jacob Rothschild leased it from the Spencers and in return spent £16 million on the restoration. The Princess attended the opening in November 1990 looking very confident and pleased in her short black glittery skirt. The 1st Earl Spencer had a stunning daughter, Georgina Spencer, better known as 'Duchess of Dimples'. At seventeen she married the Duke of Devonshire, giving the Princess of Wales more ducal links. Her relations already included the Bedfords and the Marlboroughs, some of the realm's premier families.

Flirtatiousness is nothing new in the Spencer family. The Duchess of Devonshire was notorious. Cheating quite blatantly on her amiable husband with 'Prinny', the Prince of Wales, one of her pregnancies caused speculation at court and sympathy for her husband who could not be credited seriously with being the father. For three centuries every Prince of Wales had been a friend of the Spencer family.

The 2nd Earl, George Spencer, married Lavinia Bingham, daughter of the 4th Earl of Lucan, the disastrous military commander nicknamed 'Lord Look-On' who helped to lose the Light Brigade at Balaclava in the Crimean War. Their eldest son John, 'Honest Jack', the 3rd Lord Spencer, was so inarticulate it was unkindly suggested he had been taught to read by a Swiss footman.

Neither witty nor polished enough for court circles he was considered a 'complete zero' by his aristocratic relations. However, this apparently slow-witted man became Speaker of the House of Commons and was admired for his sound judgement. He had a genuine social conscience and helped to pass the Reform Bill of 1832. But he was still sarcastically described by Queen Victoria's Prime Minister, Lord Melbourne as 'This tortoise on which the world rests.'

His mother never hid her contempt for this uninspiring heir who was too shy to propose to Esther Acklom, the Yorkshire woman she had chosen for him, so she popped the question. The marriage was a surprising success, though short-lived. Lady Spencer died four years later when their only child was stillborn. Her husband wore black for the rest of his life. Eventually he retired to Althorp to his hounds and the cultivation of Swedish turnips. His relatives complained he only became animated when 'rubbing down horses or feeding the dogs'. Every time he had a fall in the field, a servant was standing by to snap any dislocated joints back into place.

The Spencer line came to a temporary halt when the 4th Earl's wife, the delicate and pretty Adelaide, nicknamed 'Spencer's Faerie Queen' failed to produce an heir. Once when asked why his wife seemed to stay in bed all morning and lie about in the evenings with her feet up, Lord Spencer replied 'I suppose she's trying to make a little Spencer.'

The title then passed to his half-brother, Charles Spencer, whose eldest son Jack fell in love with Lady Cynthia Hamilton, a serene, melon-mouthed beauty. This ravishing daughter of the Duke of Abercorn was hotly pursued by the Duke of Windsor when he was Prince of Wales. She was never interested however and married the Princess's grandfather, the 7th Earl Spencer.

Their son, the present Earl Spencer, was his mother's darling; she constantly tried to protect him against the irascibility of his clever and cultivated father. The Princess is thought to resemble this grandmother in looks and sweet personality and this is perhaps one of the reasons why her father so adores her.

Viscount 'Johnny' Althorp was always popular in royal circles. His bluff, easygoing geniality made him an acceptable escort for Princess Margaret, making up foursomes with Princess Elizabeth and her husband. He was personable enough to be a natural choice as Master of the Queen's Household when King George VI died, making him even more eligible.

A good-looking man and unlikely to offend with acerbic comments in a Sandringham drawing room, he was always at home with royalty, so he was not particularly overwhelmed by his daughter's engagement to a future king. 'Some of my family,' he said matter-of-factly, 'go back to the Saxons. Diana had to marry somebody, and I've known and worked for the Queen since Diana was a baby.'

Born in 1924, his godmother was Queen Mary. After Eton and Sandhurst he joined the Royal Scots Greys and had a gallant World War II. After the war he spent three years in South Australia as ADC to the Governor before becoming equerry to George VI in 1950. He was the catch of the season; so too was Frances Roche, Baron Fermoy's pretty daughter. She played the piano well – they are a musical family – and after a spell in Paris spoke French. She enjoyed a little dilettante studying of History of Art in Florence and, like her daughter Diana, never came out, sharing a distaste for the snobbish aspirations of life as a debutante.

When she was eighteen she developed two passionate loves, for serious classical music and Viscount Althorp. He, however, was unofficially engaged to Lady Anne Coke of Holkham Hall, daughter of the Earl and Countess of Leicester. Even so he lost no time in proposing to Frances Roche, this enchanting but unworldly girl, and jilted Lady Anne, causing rather a scandal at the time. But when she recovered from the humiliation Lady Anne fell in love with Colin Tennant and theirs has been an enduring marriage.

Soon after Frances's engagement to Viscount Althorp, he had to leave her to go on a six-month tour of Australia with the Queen. Royal duty came first. Life in a royal household is no respecter of romance, motherhood, marriage or even death; the momentum is remorseless. The besotted Frances went on board the SS *Gothic*, the royal liner, before it sailed and presented her bemused fiancé with a life-sized head of herself done in imperishable red oxide by the fashionable portrait artist of the day Nicholas Egon. It had been commissioned at high speed and for sittings she wore a white embroidered dress and demurely listened to the *St John Passion* on the gramophone.

This touchingly obvious ploy would ensure the amiable equerry did not succumb to some sun-kissed antipodean debutante. It also showed a streak of determination in this young woman with her deceptive heart-shaped face. Already she was getting a reputation in the flat lands of Norfolk for being 'rather fast', which in those days implied perhaps heavy flirting rather than today's full commitment.

On 1 June 1954 Frances Roche, with her quick strides and blonde head held high was at eighteen the youngest girl to be married in Westminster Abbey this century. Together they seemed an ideal couple. An ethereal bride, she wore a camellia-coloured faille dress with peach blossom embroidery in silver crystal and diamante and carried lily of the valley. The Queen, Prince Philip and Princess Margaret were amongst the 1,700 guests attending this fashionable wedding of the year.

A verger commented on the scent worn by the women guests. It was so expensive and delicious, he boasted, 'I could pick up a scent at twenty yards and I've only been wrong once today.'

No bad fairy could ever have predicted the sadness in store for this couple who appeared so perfectly matched. Wedding photographs often have such poignancy. They seemed blessed by the gods as the crowds admired the good-looking pair passing under the raised swords of the Royal Scots Greys and on to their wedding reception for nine hundred at St James's Palace. It was a real Norfolk gathering of royals and landowning friends.

Nine months later, their first child, Sarah, was born. The Queen Mother was a godparent to this lively redhead who has the Princess's good looks but a mouth which is not as soft. Two years later a second daughter, Jane, arrived. This time the Duke of Kent was a godfather and she would marry the Queen's Private Secretary, Sir Robert Fellowes, maintaining the family tradition of royal service.

When her husband died in 1955, Ruth Lady Fermoy happily handed Park House on to her daughter Frances and her son-in-law, who gratefully took over the lease for their growing brood and nannies. Lady Fermoy dedicated the rest of her life to being a companion to the recently widowed Queen Elizabeth the Queen Mother, a close bond formed by their widowhood and shared love of classical music.

The Princess of Wales has always been devoted to her maternal grandmother, who has a caustic wit. The two share style and dauntingly high standards. It is unwise to disappoint Ruth Lady Fermoy, as her daughter Frances would find to her cost when her mother gave evidence against her in a messy divorce.

Lord Althorp desperately wanted an heir so neither parent was overjoyed when a third daughter, Diana, was born on 1 July 1961. They had been so sure this baby would be a boy, they had not even thought of a girl's name. But a doting father from the beginning, Viscount Althorp was exceptionally proud of this serene new arrival, describing the 7 pound 12 ounce baby as a 'perfectly magnificent physical specimen'. Her nurse Joy Hearn recalled gratefully, 'Diana never woke at night.'

Lady Althorp breastfed her baby, often daydreaming as she looked south across the parkland from the great windows of the airy bedroom in which she herself had been born. A television was installed in her bedroom the day after Diana's birth. Lady Althorp was already getting a little bored with life in Norfolk and did not share her husband's love of country pastimes.

Ironically, Diana was the only one of the four Spencer children not to have a royal godparent. In a simple ceremony on 30 August 1961 in a pretty local church, St Mary's Sandringham, she was christened Diana Frances by the Rev. Percy Herbert in a baptistry decorated with gilded trumpeting cherubs. Her godparents included John Floyd, chairman of Christie's, the auctioneers, Viscount Althorp's sister Lady Mary Colman, wife of the Lord Lieutenant of Norfolk, and his cousin, Alexander Gilmour.

The longed-for second son, Charles, finally arrived on 20 May 1964, born in the London Clinic. Another son, John, born on 12 January 1960, had died on the same day. Having produced the heir, Lady Althorp began to be restive, friends thought she looked a little strained.

Originally her love for the Queen's equerry was fairly simple, based on overwhelming physical attraction. Now weary after the birth of five children, the sad fact was that they found they had little in common mentally. This cultivated woman with a love of the arts was now bored by her stolid, uncomplicated, country-loving husband, who was so fond of cricket he once offered £5 to anyone who could hit a ball through one of the Park House windows. The more she got to know him, the more he irritated her. Capable herself, she had little faith in the Viscount's determination to be a farmer and thought he lacked direction. But he went to the Royal Agricultural College at Cirencester in Gloucestershire before buying a 250-acre farm at Ingoldisthorpe.

Right: Diana at 8 weeks old with her parents, Viscount and Viscountess Althorp. She was christened Diana Frances on 30 August 1961 at St Mary's Church, Sandringham.

Below: Lady Diana Spencer on her first birthday, 1 July 1962.

Above left: Diana, aged 3, at Park House, Sandringham.

Above: Diana with her beloved young brother, Charles, Berkshire, 1968.

Left: The barefoot croquet player, summer 1970, at Itchenor, West Sussex.

Above right: Diana (*circled*) and her classmates at Silfield School, King's Lynn.

Right: On the Isle of Uist, Western Isles in 1974.

In 1980 Diana was a helper at the Young England Kindergarten in Pimlico.

The children were well behaved if slightly subdued, trained to answer well, be aware of their place and always polite. 'My sisters and I were brought up not to be snobby.' Viscount Althorp, the Princess's adored young brother, is glad of this sensible upbringing which helped his television career in America. The little girls were very pretty with shiny hair and bows holding back side partings.

As Diana has been painted as such a paragon of virtue over the years it is a relief to find she could be as tiresome as any other small child, locking nannies in bathrooms and throwing their clothes out on the roof. She hated walks and having her hair washed. 'Oh, not hairwash time again!' she would moan, but Nanny Janet Thompson found a way. 'My method was to lay her down in the bath leaning her on my arm with her hair trailing in the water. But it was always a bit of a struggle.'

Her bay pony, Romany, threw Diana when she was eight, breaking her arm; a couple of years later the pony caught its foot in a rabbit hole and she had a second bad fall. Only the Queen has been able to persuade her to ride again, but seldom. But Diana loved being out with her father and his gundog, Bray. She had a cat called Marmalade and a spaniel named Jill, but says today, 'I'm just not an animal person. I am instinctively wary of them and they sense it which makes them a bit afraid of me.'

In the summer there were picnics at Brancaster where the Althorps had a beach hut and the children built sandcastles. They went shopping in King's Lynn for birthday treats, had tea at Sandringham, helped at Park House garden parties, but most of all enjoyed visits from 'Daddy' to the nursery. Twenty-five years later, Earl Spencer still smiles as he remembers: 'We played bears in the nursery on our hands and knees.' 'My father,' his son tells you with pride, 'is brilliant with people.' He certainly found more affection and uncritical acceptance in the company of his children than with a dissatisfied wife and disappointed father.

The 7th Earl, a brilliant, bearish man was happiest in the famous Spencer library with its 70,000 books, 3,000 of them priceless rarities which had been printed before the start of the sixteenth century. He had nothing in common with his outdoorish, bland, easy-going son and despised his ambition to be a farmer. He was cranky and loathed smokers. When Winston Churchill, a distant relative, was researching a book on their common ancestor the Duke of Marlborough, the old Earl was enraged when he saw his cigar and recalled jubilantly, 'I ripped it right out of his mouth and stamped it on the floor.'

However, another side to his churlish nature was revealed when his beloved Cynthia died of cancer and he wrote tender, understanding letters to his grandchildren which amazed the adults in the family. He had a mischievous humour which has been inherited by the Princess of Wales and also Prince William. 'Excuse the wart,' he would say, shaking hands with his thumb doubled inside his palm to nonplus guests.

When he died in 1975, the young family moved to the big house in Northamptonshire and Norfolk lost the company of the popular, likable Johnny Althorp who became the 8th Earl Spencer.

Long after the family had gone, the Queen kept a tender interest in Park House but it remained empty and neglected for ten more years and was used only occasionally for royal shooting parties. It was a relief when the Queen decided in 1983 to present it to Group Captain Leonard Cheshire, someone she greatly admires. A local beet farmer said of this once happy family house, 'It was in a shocking state, nobody seemed to want to live in it.'

Now comfortably restored in soft pastel colours as a Cheshire Home holiday hotel for the disabled, in the pretty dining room there is a painting donated by Diana's mother. The room in which the Princess was born is now called the Royal Air Force Room and is the first you come to at the top of the stairs. Some of the old Althorp retainers now look after the guests and amongst them the Viscount's former valet, Derek, is barman. Inga Crane, who was an au pair, still remembers how 'Diana danced as a little girl in a fantasy world of her own.'

Today when the Princess of Wales is staying with the Queen in Norfolk she leaves Sandringham House and nips across the wooded fields to Park House, where she pops her head round the door and says, 'Hello . . . I was just passing.' Leaving her blue wellingtons in the doorway as she did as a little girl, she pads through the house in stockinged feet.

'She was a bit upset the first time she came back,' a member of staff thought, 'seeing what had become of the old house.' But the Princess's generous nature meant that she was glad it was giving so much pleasure to others. 'Ah, we used to have a piano over there,' she remembered as she stood for a moment in the sitting room. 'It's a bit sad,' she said, turning away. Then, stifling any waves of regret or nostalgia, she sat on the floor downstairs in guernsey and cords.

On her second impromptu visit, Ian Phipps, a boy from Cheltenham who had been blinded and brain-damaged in a car accident, did not recognise her soft low voice until she squeezed his hand, saying with a big grin, 'Ian, it's me, Diana.' She held people's hands, listened to them and laughed with them, creating in these fragile lives the most memorable of holidays.

CHAPTER 7

She Upped and Off

'Suddenly one day she wasn't there any more,' lamented a Spencer family friend long after the divorce. For some time, the marriage had been lacklustre, with few shared interests. But in his amiable way, Viscount Althorp thought it happy.

In 1966 he and his wife met an avuncular naval veteran Peter Shand Kydd and his wife Janet at a dinner party. Shand Kydd was everything Viscount Althorp was not, flamboyant, extrovert and gregarious. A graduate of Edinburgh University, this Marlborough-educated farmer could make people laugh. He was never afraid of taking a risk and has often been described as 'a bit of a gipsy'. He likes moving on and has just done so, leaving his second wife, the Princess of Wales's mother, alone near Oban. At the age of sixty-five the restless Mr Shand Kydd had fallen hopelessly in love once more, this time with a Frenchwoman in her forties, the mother of three children. At the time of the breakup with the Princess's mother he protested that no other woman was involved but was already making secret trips to Provence and now wants to marry for the third time.

Back in 1963 Shand Kydd had given up all interest in the family wallpaper business, leaving it to his brother Bill Shand Kydd. Bill's wife Christina is a sister of the hapless Lady Lucan whose husband disappeared after the murder of their nanny at their house in Belgravia on 7 November 1974 and has not been heard of since. Bill Shand Kydd was one of the last people to see Lucan when his brother-in-law, who is a distant cousin of the Princess, called on him in Sussex on the night of the murder. Peter Shand Kydd emigrated to Australia attracted by the hearty abrasive outdoor life. He bought a thousand-acre station called Murrumbidgee. It was here near Yass, an outpost south-west of Sydney and not far from Canberra with nothing but two pubs and two shops, that Diana found peace and time to think about her proposal of marriage unbothered by prying eyes except those of a few friendly 'roos'.

Shand Kydd tired of Australia, returned to England and bought a farm in Scotland on the island of Seil. He was forty-two and would virtually sweep thirty-one-year-old Lady Althorp off her elegant feet. On the face of it, both marriages were stable and content. The Shand Kydds had married in 1952 and had three children, Adam, Angela and John. But now his wife Janet, who was thirty-two, watched helplessly as a good marriage disintegrated beneath the intolerable strain of this unforeseeable passion, which accelerated when the two couples went skiing.

A leggy blonde, 'Yes, I've got good long legs like my daughter,' Lady Althorp was excellent company with a lively mind and shrewd intelligence. She is an indemnity member at Lloyd's. Her husband was used to men finding his wife attractive, and it was not in his nature to be jealous. However, he had not appreciated the strength of the physical attraction between Shand Kydd and his wife. Blandly unaware of the threat to his marriage, which in 1954 had, ironically, been hailed as 'the hope of the nation', he spent the *après ski* hours swopping skiing stories with a subdued Janet Shand Kydd.

The Althorps had a close friendship with the royal family; the Queen was godmother to their son Charles. Lady Althorp was seen as an excellent wife and mother who sometimes looked after Prince Charles at children's parties. However, soon after the skiing holiday, when the Althorps and Shand Kydds were back in England, the erring pair were unable to live without each other and eloped. The girl who had been called Bride of the Year became The Bolter.

That summer the Althorps agreed to a trial separation. It was decided that Diana and Charles would be in London with their mother where they would both go to school in September. The other daughters, Sarah and Jane, were already at boarding school. It was the end of any real family life, though it had long since stopped being cosy at Park House where the atmosphere was often heavy with the tension of incompatibility.

After a few rather strained family holidays for half-term or Christmas at Park House, the marriage, Mrs Shand Kydd explained, had 'completely broken down'. In the way children can be acutely aware of unhappy undercurrents Diana became more withdrawn and spent a lot of time dressing her teddy in her brother's baby clothes.

Viscount Althorp, realising that a breakup was inevitable and that he had lost the delectable Frances, now took a stern line. He also had the invisible but powerful support of the Establishment. He insisted that Diana and Charles should go to school in King's Lynn and live at Park House with him. He was adamant in his refusal to let them anywhere near his wife and her lover in London.

Their thirty-one-year-old mother, in her own words, 'strongly objected to this,' took a court action in June 1968 and lost custody. Six months later, Lady Althorp with her demure manner was named as 'the other woman' in the Shand Kydds' uncontested divorce.

In the hope of keeping her children, the Viscountess sued for divorce alleging cruelty by her husband, which he denied. In April 1969 he was granted a decree nisi because of her admitted adultery at Queen's Gate in South Kensington in April 1967. She was not helped by Ruth Lady Fermoy, who, shocked and disapproving, gave evidence in court against her. Lord Spencer was even seeing eye to eye with his son, since both were outraged and humiliated by the scandal.

It was a particularly bitter divorce full of salacious revelations which found their way into the papers. It brought a surge of sympathy for the Viscount, who was seen as a wronged man by the whole of Norfolk. There was not much feeling for his sensitive wife who had been unhappy but enduring until she produced the longed-for heir. It was seen as a disgrace because the woman had run off. Had Viscount Althorp gone away with another woman, he might have been viewed admiringly as 'a bit of a flier, old Johnny'.

After the divorce became absolute in 1969, Lady Althorp became Mrs Shand Kydd four weeks later at a quiet registrar's office wedding. She was blissfully happy with her new husband and moved to a large house with a garden in Sussex near Ichenor.

Years later, after her daughter's marriage to the Prince of Wales, she would talk openly about the hurt. Cooking bacon and eggs in Scotland for her husband and guests in 1982, Mrs Shand Kydd bridled at any suggestion that she was a 'bad mother' who had 'upped and off' uncaringly abandoning her children. She had always been confident that she would be allowed to keep her two youngest, Diana six and Charles four, at the time, but she had not allowed for her husband's sense of outrage and wounded pride. He in turn dismissed her revelations as 'cheap and unkind'. And really all they did was to remind everyone of the events which had such a profound effect, particularly on Diana.

After the divorce Diana kept a photograph of her mother next to her bed, but found any mention of her was frowned upon. 'Seriously affected' by the breakup, she confided in a nanny, 'I'll never ever marry unless I really love someone. If you're not really sure you love someone then you might get divorced. I never want to be divorced!'

As always it was the children who suffered most although their mother had tried to explain things before she left. Their grandmother Ruth Lady Fermoy tried to be with them at Park House as often as possible. She tended to indulge her grand-children, bearing even with the wilful Sarah leading her pony into the drawing room.

Viscount Althorp was shattered and roamed about disconsolately. The children now saw their father alone, brooding and still puzzled by his loss. The task of bolstering them was left to the nannies and the children helped one another. Diana tended to be solitary and had unusual poise and grace for a child of her age. Subconsciously she was almost becoming châtelaine at Park

House, a little mother figure, obsessively tidy, cosseting her brother but bossy and making sure he put his toys away.

This prim Diana was so exceptionally neat and perfectly turned out she was nicknamed 'the Duchess', shortened later to Duch or Duchy by her friends. Not for her the sort of rebellion which makes everyone's life hell when a child is angry and blames itself for the parents' divorce. Instead she was quiet and obedient, learning always to sit up straight, speak only when spoken to and shake hands when introduced. There were occasional lapses when she would slide down stone steps on a metal tray, a custom she has never been able quite to give up.

After her mother's departure she became even more reliant on her father, often wistfully asking 'When's Daddy coming home?' Her father tended to over-compensate. For her seventh birthday he hired a camel named Bert from Dudley Zoo. Diana and nineteen friends took turns riding the camel, but really she would have preferred a hug from Mummy. When she returned from seeing her mother in London, her father found she was 'always awkward' and unmanageable for a few days. The nanny would complain that she was making unfavourable remarks about her father.

At first there were stilted, uncommunicative meetings in the nursery at teatime. Viscount Althorp got only the briefest replies as he asked about pets and lessons. He had found it much easier to be close to them when they were small. Nanny Mary Clark who presided over these agonising sessions and could see 'he wasn't very relaxed' suggested the children should be allowed to join him in the dining room for lunch, and this became easier for all, more of an adventure.

It was at about this time that Diana developed the slightly imperious manner which masked agonising shyness. More than ever she tended to look down at her feet when people spoke to her, even if it was 'Aunt Lilibet'.

Her father doted on her and hated the moment when he decided, for her own good, that she must join her sisters at boarding school.

CHAPTER 8

The Fur and Feather Section

At a dinner party in Sydney, Australia, when the Princess was asked what she thought about Red China, she replied, 'Oh, I think it is awfully pretty with a blue tablecloth.'

This story and another suggestion that her only prize at school was for the best-groomed guinea pig underestimate her. It is true that if you ask whether she would like to have gone to university she gives you a look of bemused disbelief. She has done very nicely on the minimum of academic achievements and has understandably no wistful longing to be an undergraduate nor dreams of overthrowing society.

Palace mandarins say her slim education was a bonus. It has been much easier to shape a receptive young mind. Had the Princess gone to a competitively academic school like St Paul's, opinions and political attitudes might have formed which the Palace would have found deeply unattractive. Instead she was pliable and open to ideas. Her bright, quick mind impresses charity fund-raisers and she has a good grasp of financial issues and priorities. She has proved very nicely that academic laurels are no indication of future human development.

In those hunting and shooting circles in which she spent her childhood Earl Spencer, in common with other old-fashioned aristocratic fathers, never considered sending his daughters to university. On a weekend visit to France, the Prince of Wales complimented his hostess on her elegant English. She replied, 'My father believed in educating girls,' at which he sighed, 'I wish that had been the philosophy in my wife's family.' According to Earl Spencer, rather than studying at a British college girls should be finished in Switzerland, marry well and be decorative accessories to their husbands, model wives and mothers, remaining dutifully at home. His first wife was perfect in every respect except she wanted to be an accessory in someone else's home. As a result the routine of bricks and plasticine by day and then being tucked up and kissed goodnight by 'Mummy' had come to an abrupt end. They missed their mother terribly, this lively figure, all grace and light charm, springing through the nursery green baize door like a well-bred filly to release them from a firm 'nanny routine' or take them out on treats.

The effect on Sarah was to make her openly rebellious and at sixteen she was expelled from school though she had passed six O levels. Later she admitted, 'I used to drink because I was bored, I would drink anything: whisky, cointreau, sherry or, most often, vodka because they couldn't smell it on my breath.' The Spencers were sad when Sarah was asked to leave the school but not outraged like the legendary Irish couple affronted by any suggestion that their daughter could not hold her drink.

Diana would be taken on a rare outing by her mother, who by now was living in London, to buy her uniform in Harrods for Riddlesworth, a school which always put a child's feelings first. Parents grumble that the children are almost too happy at this preparatory school near Diss in Norfolk.

The Queen's great friend the Duchess of Grafton is a vigilant governor of Riddlesworth (£2,155 a term) which is like a big old family house with clanging gongs and cheerfulness. The girls are neat, well behaved and many titled. One new arrival when asked 'Are you an Hon?' replied defensively, 'Yes, I can't help it.' An Honourable is not rated highly at Riddlesworth.

'It was dreadful losing her,' Earl Spencer now recalls, 'a dreadful day' for both father and daughter. Riddlesworth was only forty miles from Park House, but this was small comfort to Diana as her father drove through the flatlands, past ochre, pink and sage-green houses and fields which in summer she remembered being full of lavender.

When they got to the gates, this child with her solemn eyes and vulnerable mouth, a tear not far away, sat holding tightly on to Peanuts, her white and brown guinea pig, so recently leading the field in the Fur and Feather Section of the Sandringham Fair; in the boot was her school trunk marked 'DF Spencer'. The car bumped slowly over the lazy policemen past homely crops of beet with large green spinachy leaves almost as high as the low white wooden fence until they reached the sandstone Georgian house. In the cobbled courtyard pretty with geraniums and blue-framed windows, new girls disgorged from Mummy's Volvo stand around today eyeing one another. The school has a rustic charm; children are woken by a cowbell at 7.30 a.m. But to a nine-year-old this tall, elegant house with its high ceilings and great mahogany, wooden-seated 1892 lavatories, seemed enormous.

'It's funny,' a senior teacher remarked, 'we have no memory of the mother, but he was marvellous.' They say of Diana's father, 'Such a nice man, so caring and so anxious to know she was happy.' Against all advice, he insisted on visiting her when she had mumps. He had not had them himself but arrived with a huge basket of fruit for all the children, making them laugh in the sick room; they adored him.

Before Diana came home to Park House, Viscount Althorp could be seen shopping alone for treats for her in King's Lynn. He loved the fun of children's parties, letting off fireworks and being boisterous. Diana was particularly close to him, the one who always put another log on the fire and was the first to draw the shutters on cold nights.

Her tuck box, which she keeps in her study in Kensington Palace with its initials D.S., would contain after a weekend at home 'Big choc cake, ginger biscuits, Twiglets'. Chocolate has always been her weakness and her comfort. Her great friend Alexandra Loyd, whose father is the agent at Sandringham, recalls, 'Diana once gave me a massive box of chocolates and we sat and ate them all on the school lawn. She said she gave me the box because she adored those chocolates and could share the present with me.' Her favourite breakfast was baked beans and she always asked for more.

When Diana first arrived she was a little withdrawn but, as they say in the lower fourth, never 'boo-hooed'. Miss Elisabeth Ridsdale, the headmistress, since retired and known as 'Riddy', thought her 'rather unhappy', and in common with other children from broken homes, her work had suffered, so she was put in a very small remedial class for children with slight learning difficulties. That classroom still has the same few old-fashioned desks and a peachy orange ceiling which struck one of today's pupils, little Milly Thomas aged eleven, as 'rather vulgar'. Typically Diana would turn her own misery into something useful. 'She was awfully sweet with the little ones.'

Joan Wilkins, 'Old Wilkins' to the children, is everyone's idea of an old-fashioned physical training mistress. Today whitehaired but with the clearest blue eyes she exudes good health. Now retired, she coached Diana's swimming as one of the team winning the Parker Cup, and Miss Wilkins thought her 'very biddable but not a goody goody'. She also taught the 'Little Dots' calligraphy so shaped Diana's writing now used for effusive 'thank you' notes. Nowadays there is an indoor heated swimming pool, but in those days, 'the little darlings had to change in a whipping wind in the rhododendron bushes' before diving into the outdoor pool.

Dutifully Diana appeared to settle down, winning the Legatt Cup for helpfulness. She ran, she jumped and walked in crocodile past Goose Girl's Cottage on One Tree Hill, played tennis well but deep down perhaps was not as happy as the other children.

As Princess of Wales, she visited the school with Alexandra Loyd and admitted that on the way from London they had dreaded coming back. But the headmistress, Mrs Patricia Wood, a delightful and amusing doctor's wife, knew the Princess 'had been pretty apprehensive and assured her she would not have to stand in a corner.' The visit went well, with lots of laughter when the Princess heard how at the time of her engagement the Head asked the children to surrender any textbooks with Diana Spencer's name in them. Enterprisingly, all the seven- to twelve-year-olds immediately got busy forging royal signatures in the hope that, without these books, they could do no work.

The Princess asked to see round some of her old haunts. A couple of girls in their summer pink striped dresses took her to Dormitory 3 with its teddies and greying woolly toys on beds. The Princess remarked, 'Still the same hundred-year-old paper I see,' glancing at the pink wallpaper with tropical green flowers and blue birds of Paradise.

Walking to the window overlooking vast green acres, she laughed about the bed called 'the water jump', making light of a child's incontinence. Then she was dragged off to see the furry-animal hutches, scene of her triumph when she won the Pets Corner Cup. Solemn little girls with navy blue velvet Alice bands held out their guinea pigs, pet mice and rabbits. 'She spoke to me as I was holding my rabbit but I am afraid he died three days later,' one said miserably.

There is a portrait of the Princess looking very regal in the corridor near the school mascot, a large bear called Rodney. Dressed in a pair of underpants, a note is attached to his neck which says, 'Rodney needs washing'; he is taken to hockey matches and gets covered in mud.

At school Diana was teased about the size of her nose, but what really hurt was the unconscious cruelty of older girls who had picked up intriguing gossip about her parents and their divorce. Even so, whatever unhappiness she felt deep down, she passed her Common Entrance to her mother's old school, £3,000 a term West Heath, an all-girls public school. Despite her stepmother's cruel comment, Diana was never 'thick as two boards'. Countess Spencer has asserted that 'having a conversation with Diana and not talking about clothes . . . was a crashing bore.'

West Heath, founded in 1865, is in the heart of Kent near Sevenoaks. She slept in dormitories called Delphinium and Cowslip and was in a form called Poplar. Its other most famous old girl had been Princess May of Teck, later Queen Mary, a role model for the school with its emphasis on proper behaviour.

Never a tearaway, the most outrageous thing Diana might do was to join a midnight feast in the dormitory. Under a solemn poster portrait of Prince Charles over her bed, savage pillow fights took place and custard pies sailed past the future King's nose. To avoid games she put blue eyeshadow on her knees, pretending they had been badly bruised. If you really mis-behaved, you had to do the weeding. If you were untidy, your cardigan was confiscated and you had to pay a fine to get it back.

Although her sister Jane, quiet and steady with eleven O levels, was head girl, after only six weeks Diana returned home unhappy and tearful. But she was persuaded to go back and responded to the coaxing of the Australian headmistress, Miss Ruth Rudge, who cajoled her into learning to 'develop her own mind and taste'. It was a regime based on gentleness and incentives, just what this sensitive child needed as she came to terms with her parents' parting, a time when children are full of self-reproach.

Here Diana would form some of her best and most enduring friendships, Carolyn Pride, who would be one of her flatmates at Coleherne Court, a student at the Royal College of Music and Drama, and Caroline Harbord Hammond who worked in the press department of Conservative Central Office. But the headmistress did not encourage the 'best friend' principle so popular in girls' schools. Knowing so many of her pupils came from broken homes, she felt that their reliance on each other could mean another trauma when they left to go their own way.

Diana did social work and won a 'special award for service' for her care of an old lady whom she visited regularly in Sevenoaks, making her tea and cheering her up. Miss Rudge remembers how, even as a schoolgirl, she had a strong sense of colour and 'dressed often in bright red dungarees'. She was meticulous about the way she looked, fastidiously wangling a bath a night when other girls managed only three a week.

Good at sport, lacrosse and tennis, though never in the same league as her mother, who qualified for junior Wimbledon in 1952, she captained the swimming team. Diana's swallow-dive was called the Spencer Special; there was not a ripple in the water as she plunged in. It was just as stylish many years later off the King of Spain's yacht in Majorca. A leader at netball, Diana was dismissive, 'It was much easier for me to get the ball in the net because I was so tall.'

When she failed her O levels a second time, except for one in Art at Grade B, her father was disappointed that she insisted on leaving school. She invited twenty-four friends to a farewell lunch in a field near Gracious Lane Bridge, where they picnicked on cold pheasant, game chips and biscuits. Her friends gave her a gold chain hung with the letter D.

CHAPTER 9

Ready for Agincourt

There were nine monarchies left in Europe when Prince Charles, Duke of Cornwall and Duke of Rothesay, Earl of Carrick and Baron Renfrew, Lord of the Isles, Great Steward of Scotland and heir to the throne, was born on 14 November 1948, a foggy, raw Sunday evening, at 9.14 P.M. in the Buhl Room at Buckingham Palace.

When his mother, a delighted Princess Elizabeth, had recovered from the anaesthetic, her husband Prince Philip – they had married in Westminster Abbey on 20 November 1947 – was grinning at her from behind a huge bouquet of carnations and roses. The King smiled and asked a Palace footman to bring champagne to celebrate the birth of his first grandchild.

The Queen kissed her son-in-law, who was dressed in a rumpled sweatshirt and tennis shoes. Prince Philip had been playing squash to work off fatherly anxiety during the comparatively short delivery. Trying to hide emotion as he watched his 7 pound 6 ounce son being breastfed, he remarked gruffly that he looked 'rather like a plum pudding'. The Princess thought the infant Charles had hands like no other baby, 'such long fine fingers'.

Bells chimed 5,000 times from Westminster Abbey for this small noisy bundle who already aroused more interest, even gurgling under white muslin, than his father ever could, even if he vaulted into space. 'Constitutionally,' he once joked, 'I don't exist.' Quite soon this baby would get used to the Palace's two hundred footmen and three hundred clocks. Later at school when, during a history lesson, a boy suggested some of the monarchs of the past had behaved badly, 'Oh, but they're different nowadays,' Prince Charles replied, already confident.

For a few days after the birth Prince Philip had supper in his wife's bedroom. Reluctantly the mother would hand over the baby to his Scottish nursemaid, Helen Lightbody, a firm believer in the nanny maxim 'Regular habits make happy babies,' who would settle him in the nearby dressing room.

Princess Elizabeth doted on her firstborn and he still has that special place in her heart. But then Prince Charles has always appealed to the women in the family. The Queen Mother adored him, calling him 'my gentle little boy'. She remembers how he tried to comfort her when he found her in tears on the day of her husband King George VI's death, 6 February 1952.

After the King's death, when she succeeded as Queen, Elizabeth II knew intuitive feelings of motherhood had to be stifled; duty to Crown and Commonwealth came first. Attempts at truly intimate family life became virtually impossible. So palace protocol began for Prince Charles when he was four and moved with his parents to Buckingham Palace. But the Queen was unhappy about her children, Prince Charles, and Princess Anne, born in August 1950, having to curtsy to her and the formality was abandoned. No longer would the British monarch be greeted by curtsy or bow over the cornflakes or schoolroom desk.

The Queen inherited a fairly elderly, stuffy and unbending Household, so although Prince Charles shared with Diana a typical upper-class childhood, his was lonelier. The green baize door opened at fixed times to admit parents, but rarely together. 'My father sent me notes,' he recalled sadly. Prince Philip had been at sea for his first five birthday parties. He adored this loving but stern father, copied him by holding his hands behind his back and sat fascinated watching him dress in naval uniform.

The poignancy of this small boy's isolation would be dramatically highlighted when with a soulful look he asked a servant who the Queen might be and was crisply informed, 'Your mother.' Once when the young prince asked her if she would read him a bedtime story, she replied softly, 'I only wish I could.'

Very early on his father also taught him that he must never run towards his mother in public or shout 'Mama': 'Remember always who you are.' This lesson was well learnt. Prince Charles lined up with the officers on board the Royal Yacht *Britannia* to greet the Queen back from a 162-day trip abroad and stretched out a pudgy hand. 'Oh no, not you!' The Queen, aghast, quickly led him to her private sitting room for a proper hug.

Prince Charles's solitude as a child is one of the reasons behind the Princess's determination to give her children as much loving and as normal an upbringing as is possible. A lack of cuddles and warmth in his formative years, his wife believes, helps to explain his remoteness in the marriage. But she agrees that the idea of thrift should be instilled into Prince William and Prince Harry as it was in their own father. Prince Charles remembers being told by the Queen, 'Dog leads cost money,' and spending forlorn hours in the grounds of Sandringham trying to find a leather corgi strap he had lost.

Prince Philip, as a typical naval officer, worried about the warm, softening influence of the Queen, Queen Mother and Princess Margaret in Prince Charles's formative years. So he chose manly pictures of minesweepers for the nursery, bought his son a tiny red electric car and gave him a miniature cricket bat. The Prince was too young for polo, definitely a 'man's game' and riding horses, so father and son played this dangerous game using bicycles and tennis balls.

Drilled by his father always to look people straight in the eye, he soon learnt to stand during lessons so he would be able to bear hours in the hot sun later at Independence celebrations in the colonies and to be meticulous about timekeeping. Told to meet his parents by the Palace staircase and to be there one minute before they arrived, the flustered Prince rushed in to hear a disapproving, 'Fifteen seconds late, old fellow' and looked up to see a grim-faced Duke of Edinburgh leaning over the balustrade. As a father, however, he was not so irritable as Peter the Great, who became so enraged by his heir's unpunctuality, he chopped off his head.

Today, in his own strong position, Prince Charles no longer tolerates his father's short-tempered asides. When Prince Philip says, 'What bloody rubbish you talk,' he will merely walk away or coolly remind his father that he is speaking to the future King. But he likes to poke fun at the Duke affectionately, once saying slyly, 'Wherever I go in the world, I find trees planted by my parents before me, and I notice that while my mother's seem to flourish, my father's tend to droop rather wearily. This leads me to assume that trees must be snobs.'

On his desk Prince Charles has a photograph taken with his father and he has scribbled on it, 'I was not meant to follow in my father's footsteps.' He has never been able to turn easily to his own father and instead confided in Lord Mountbatten. After his death in 1979 he leant on the more intellectual Sir Laurens van der Post, who said of his royal disciple, 'He is following his own star.'

Lord Mountbatten provided a good listening ear and loved the link it gave him with the inner sanctum of the royal family. This relationship and a hint of the resentment felt by Prince Philip that his uncle should have taken his place with his son was evident after Mountbatten's assassination in Northern Ireland. Both men who loved the man known as 'Uncle Dickie' by the royal family, had escorted the body back to Broadlands.

Before the funeral at Romsey Abbey, father and son were having lunch, neither with much appetite, when Prince Charles suddenly rushed from the table. After a while, Prince Philip looked at his watch and testily asked where his son was, adding impatiently, 'We are supposed to leave soon.' The manservant nodded and later returned saying, 'I have been unable to find him, Sir.' Prince Philip was very irritated.

The reality, John Barratt, a Mountbatten aide, explained later, was that when he found Prince Charles he was standing on the river bank where his father could not see him. His head was bowed, and he was so 'obviously in anguish . . . I couldn't disturb him.' The royal family is blessed in many ways, but privacy is a privilege often denied.

Sir Hugh Casson, who was often at Windsor when the Queen's

children were small, recalled how even at an early age Prince Charles was aware of his destiny, while Princess Anne had much more fun, jumping over chairs, carefree and high-spirited. Soon he would have his first experience outside the royal cocoon, at Hill House School in a leafy Knightsbridge square near Harrods, where the emphasis was on character. This suited rich parents too busy to have much influence on their children's lives. For the Prince it provided a taste of ordinary life but he also had to get used to tittering tourists nudging one another as the Hill House boys, looking like billowy Lord Fauntleroys in rust-coloured corduroy breeches, trooped along the King's Road, Chelsea for gym and games at the Duke of York Barracks. Considered a slightly snooty sulky little boy, in reality he was solemn and shy.

Cheam, a prep school dating back to 1646, had a reputation for happiness rather than high achievement, and was ideal for this introspective child who seldom smiled and was a thumb-sucker.

'Hey Fatty, get off my foot,' shouted an exasperated boy at the future King during a soccer game. In the way that children can be cruel to each other, Charles was also known as 'mealy-eye' because of his keen appreciation of any movement towards the dining room. In fact the school had been told that he must be taught to observe as much as possible.

Prince Philip had been a laurel-leaves athlete at Cheam, captain of the cricket and hockey teams and winner of the silver medal for all-round ability at running, swimming, sailing, jumping and javelin throwing, a depressing litany for a son who was happier in the pottery class. 'His tea set,' observed the headmaster Peter Beck encouragingly, 'was rather nice.'

Royal training teaches you to overcome most physical diffi-culties; mental anguish can be a bit more difficult. Eventually Prince Charles became good enough to captain the soccer team in his last year, though the school lost every game that season.

The Queen and Queen Mother wanted Prince Charles to go to Eton but Prince Philip disapproved of this elitist school and the predictability of the product. Some of the old-fashioned courtiers thought it monstrous to send the Prince of Wales away to boarding school at all, many still believing the best education was to be had in one's own library or perhaps travelling with a tutor to Florence.

By 1962, Prince Philip felt his son was ready for Gordonstoun, his own public school with a reputation for toughness but also an element of classlessness which could never be said of Eton. Here in northern Scotland, bright fishermen's sons, crofters' children and the aristocracy learnt to live up to the school motto, 'There is More in You.' In preparation for Gordonstoun's tough regime Prince Philip had sent him to stay with his falconing chum, James Robertson Justice, the bearded actor who liked all the supposed manly pursuits: deep-sea fishing or plunging into icy-cold lochs.

Although there was always great sympathy for Prince Charles from the women in the family he has never complained about being sent to this 'awful place', never a word about the constant pressure to do the impossible, like leaping over 8-foot walls in one bound. In those days if you were frightened of heights, you were encouraged to climb mountains; if you hated exercise, you went yomping across the bleak terrain above the Moray Firth. It was a junior commando course.

'My only recollections are of complete horror,' Lord Rudolph Russell, the Duke of Bedford's son, says of his Gordonstoun schooldays. When asked how Prince Charles was getting on, Prince Philip shrugged, 'Well, he hasn't run away yet.' Lord Rudolph made the attempt twice and failed, which makes this famous school sound more like Stalagluft III.

Once again Prince Charles had to bear with the galling record of his father, the golden-haired star athlete of the school. However, one of the masters who had taught Prince Philip was comforting. 'I prefer teaching Prince Charles literature, trying to teach Wordsworth to Philip was pure loss.'

Much to his grandmother's dismay, Prince Charles started the day at 7 o'clock with a cold shower and a run without a vest even in winter, just shorts and canvas shoes; then he raced back for bed-making. In between waiting at table, he gulped his own breakfast before clearing the dishes for the other boys' next course.

He was also rather lonely but remembered Lord Mountbatten's warning about the difficulty of making true friends. 'It's always the undesirable types who try to make up to you; the ones you really like tend to steer clear in case they are accused of being snobs.' So, carrying his books in a leather case and followed by a detective, the Prince was glad of some relatives at school for company – two European cousins and Mountbatten's grandson, Norton Knatchbull, now Lord Romsey, who values this schooldays connection highly.

The Prince's thoughtfulness and integrity are personal qualities which have nothing to do with spartan schooldays in the uncompromising glens. But Gordonstoun must be given credit for moulding the character of 'the young man', as the courtiers used to call him.

A much-needed dent was made in his image of conformity when the world heard he had been sipping cherry brandy in the bar of the Crown Hotel at Stornoway on the Isle of Lewis. He and some classmates were going to see *It Happened in Athens*, starring Jayne Mansfield, just like any other schoolboys except the Prince's detective was sent to buy the tickets. While they waited, Prince Charles was spotted from the street and thought, 'I can't bear this any more,' panicked and fled into the bar.

The Prince's version is that, 'Never having been into a bar before, the first thing I thought of doing was having a drink, of course. And being terrified and not knowing what to do, I named the first drink that came into my head, which happened to be cherry brandy because I had drunk it when it was cold out shooting. Hardly had I taken a sip when the world exploded around my ears. I wanted to pack my bags and go to Siberia.' It was a harmless enough incident for any ordinary boy but already the Prince knew he had to set an example.

Before his final year, Prince Charles had the happiest time of his young life in Australia at Timbertop, two hundred miles from Melbourne and part of the desirable Geelong Grammar School. At weekends he stayed in casual unpretentious style with a discreet landowning couple Geoff and Kay Ritchie at their property Delatite in Victoria. 'I went out there with a boy,' said David Checketts, his equerry, 'and returned with a man.'

The Prince had fun. Meeting for the first time the delectable Dale Harper at a school dance, he nicknamed her 'Kanga'. Later she came to England, designed frilly frocks and married his friend Lord Tryon. He invited her and the Ritchies to his wedding in 1981.

Cambridge proved to be the next real turning point. Prince Charles arrived at Trinity, founded by Henry VIII in the sixteenth century, with A levels in History and French and five O levels, getting through maths at the fourth attempt. One of two hundred and twenty undergraduates, his talents were not for science but geared to the arts. He came under the sphinx-like but enlightened eye of the Master of Trinity, Lord Butler. The Prince's mind would develop under 'Rab' Butler's guidance. Tricked out of becoming prime minister, who better to teach his royal charge about Machiavellian practices at the Palace of Westminster? 'I told him who was a bloody fool and who wasn't . . .'

Most evenings they had a talk and Butler gradually became impressed. 'The boy,' he announced, 'has great gifts.' Charles began with 'ark and anth', archaeology and anthropology, topics which genuinely interested him, but after the first year troubled by that old royal conscience and sense of duty felt compelled to change to history, though Lord Butler felt he could easily have got a First in these subjects still so dear to his heart. When Butler remonstrated, his pupil explained, 'I need to study the British Constitution because I'm probably going to be King. I feel history. It fascinates me. I don't know whether it's me, or being born into what I am.'

When a group of undergraduates were talking about the future, the Prince suggested wryly, 'I want to be King of Europe.' It seemed outlandish then, but now, with the trade barriers to be demolished in 1992, not such a wild proposal after all.

He was lucky in his supervisor, Peter Laslett, Reader in Politics and Social Structure. Concerned that the heir to the throne was surrounded by 'a kind of sycophancy', and out of touch with real life, he lent him a copy of Herbert Marcuse's *One-Dimensional Man* in an effort to bring his royal charge up to date. The next term, he was eager to hear the Prince's view on this philosopher who endorsed upheaval and student riots. 'I read it with father,' the Prince replied primly, 'while on tour in Australia.' Laslett shrugged and decided there was little point in much more discussion.

Prince Charles's heroes were the Goons, a comic group on radio. Cambridge would unleash his talent for comedy, and he wrote several funny sketches for the *Footlights* revue. He can still be amusing and full of self mockery about his image in popular newspapers: his need for solitude, the 'a loon at last' headlines and the belief that he does nothing but talk to flowers or crouch over a ouija board.

However, Cambridge was not all academic discussion or lonely hours spent leafing through Gibbon's *Decline and Fall*. Half the enjoyment of these three unfettered years, the Prince found, was to climb in at all hours of the night. 'It is a great challenge, has been going on for years and what does it matter really?'

But to the other undergraduates he always seemed apart. A fellow student John Molony said, 'He seemed an easygoing sort of chap, superficially easy to know. But deep down he's a very private person. I don't think anyone gets to know him really well.' They were prophetic words.

A late developer, Prince Charles was the first heir to the throne to get a degree: a 2.2 in Anthropology and History. Lord Butler thought it a good degree considering all his other duties, a pleasant euphemism for his close friendship with the luscious Lucia Santa Cruz. Initially Prince Charles thought girls who stayed over with their boyfriends at Cambridge 'not quite nice'. But that was before he fell under the spell of Lucia, a dark-eyed beauty and daughter of the Chilean Ambassador. Lord Butler who had employed her to work as a researcher on his autobiography watched with approval as a romance flourished with the Prince, who had asked if he might stay in the Master's Lodge for privacy. It was 'a request which we were very glad to accede to,' the Master recalled.

If university is about teaching you to think, then Prince Charles would benefit and approach his role as no other Prince of Wales. On the morning of his 21st birthday he had knelt and prayed in the Chapel of St John in the Tower of London for the strength 'To give and not to count the cost, to fight and not to heed the wounds.' That night there was a party for four hundred at Buckingham Palace to celebrate his Coming of Age. Unlike his contemporaries who preferred Beatles music and busty blondes leaping out of surprise birthday cakes, the Prince listened to the aesthetic violinist Yehudi Menuhin accompanied by a chamber orchestra.

All early gaucheness gone, Prince Charles was now an engaging young man, already a Privy Counsellor and King in his own right if anything should happen to the Queen. He had been influenced at Cambridge by Hugh Anderson, left-wing president of the Union and no supporter of a static monarchy. He qualified as a jet pilot, was a Royal Marine Commando, became a high-altitude skier, a parachutist, commanded HMS *Bronington*, a 360-ton minesweeper, in North Atlantic gales, rode steeplechasers, played polo and learned to parachute, but still he felt driven to prove himself. He became an immensely considerate young man, but also could be selfish.

He was versatile, one minute playing the cello or painting gentle watercolours, having intense and lively conversations on the meaning of life, the next entertaining pretty women at the Palace. The loneliness of monarchy has made him self-reliant. He can lose himself totally in classical music, admitting, 'I'm reduced to tears every time I hear a certain passage in "L'enfance du Christ" by Berlioz.'

At his traditional Investiture in 1969 he made an important impression as the first English Prince of Wales in nearly seven hundred years to take the trouble to learn Welsh. His speech so impressed the people of Caernarvon that the Mayor, lyrically Welsh, declared, 'You could have put a suit of armour on him and sent him off to Agincourt.'

CHAPTER 10

Raine, Raine, Go to Spain

———— • ————

'Where's my Daddy?' and the slight figure of the Princess waltzes into the shop at Althorp with its display of flashy jewellery, seahorses, copies of her engagement ring, pearl chokers and mock Dresden porcelain on sale. Homely women from the village straighten up and smile; many remember her as a young girl dancing and skipping along Wooton Hall, the handsome entrance to Althorp. It was here with its black and white marble floor that Diana learnt to become a confident dancer. Plugging in her record player and making sure all doors were shut and that she was completely private, she whirled and pirouetted in a dream world under the sombre gaze of generations of Spencers. She was always fascinated too by the Oak Room where the first Earl was secretly married while a party went on downstairs.

The Princess has a quick appreciative glance at the home-baked lemon sponge and chocolate cake once made for the family, now for visitors' teas, and smiles at fake daffodils and tulips on the tables. They are new. Mrs Rose Ellis remembered Diana as a little girl, in the kitchens as cakes were being baked. 'She would run her fingers round the pudding bowl licking the sugary icing.'

None of them had even so much as bothered to look up as the Princess's helicopter landed on the lawn. They are rather used to it. 'A great red monster', blades still whirring, it looked incongruous in this almost medieval landscape where deer grazed near parkland and a cricket ground. Everywhere the touch of Le Nôtre, the master gardener who created the formal gardens at Versailles. Diana remembers whizzing round the tranquil wooded acres in a pale blue beach buggy, or sometimes on her bicycle.

Now the grounds are a bit arid, no flowers and a bit weedy. White blinds pulled down at the tall Georgian windows to protect the Rubens and the Lely portraits give a touch of Bleak House; bay trees outside are like sentinels and a standard flies over the grey stone. It is not a warm mellow house, or a place to be sad or lonely.

Prince William and Prince Harry have come separately by car, driving through Nobottle with its snug little red stone houses, some thatched, and past the Haddon Pytchley Inn where the detectives like a beer. Spencer Court sounds like a dower house, but this area also has its inevitable new houses: 'an outstanding village designed for modern needs' implying Elizabethan charm and not the modern and intrusive reality.

Mrs Stephanie Wilson has been at Althorp for ten years now and remembered, 'Just before her engagement Lady Diana came home; tea was served in the long study and she was very quiet. Then suddenly there was a wonderful sound; she was playing the piano . . . lovely classical music.'

Now it is a dull, grey day in June, when Northamptonshire can look surprisingly stark. Lord Spencer explains, 'I say Althorp, not Althrup; it's easier,' and is very cheerful. Lonely chimes from the clock in the stable block with its pretty blue wooden doors, modelled on Inigo Jones's church in Covent Garden, signal it is two o'clock and time for the courtyard gates to swing back; Althorp, teenage home of the Princess of Wales, is open to the public.

Not a lot of visitors bothered about Althorp originally but since Lady Diana's marriage to the Prince of Wales the Americans and Japanese have been pouring in: all helping the Spencers recoup some of the £2 million spent on the house putting it right after the 7th Earl's death in 1975.

'We have,' said the present Earl, 'a large group of Japanese pyjama makers from Osaka; if they have made enough in the year they come here for a huge party. I don't speak Japanese, but my wife does.' Here the self-deprecatory chuckle. 'They might commit *hara-kiri* in the yard if I even tried.'

He prowls about. 'Any sign of the coaches?' he asks Mrs Sue Ingrams. A squirearchical, rubicund figure in his check cap, striped shirt and flannels, he chuckles. '. . . Oh good, it's a cold day for June . . . it brings them out.'

In the wine shop an American is buying a bottle of Althorp Mead. 'Is it our own honey, goodness no, it comes from Liverpool.' Another chuckle. He has an appealing vagueness about the prices: 'I can't add up.' Leaning over to put his signature on the label showing Elizabeth I, he says, 'I'll sign on the ruff.'

He is good with people. 'One woman said to me, "Oh you're Diana's brother," and that made my day.' Just then a teacher with spectacles tapped him on the arm. 'I'm from Cheshire and I just wanted to tell you how much I have enjoyed myself, how nice it's been.' He was very touched. 'I have to go now,' she said, as if he might be asking her to stay. 'I have the dog in the car.'

The people who do stay are wealthy Americans and Japanese who pay handsomely £1000 to £2000 for the privilege. The week before a production team of two hundred had been filming one of Barbara Cartland's novels, *Jewel of Love*. Lord Spencer made it plain that if it had not been for his ninety-year-old mother-in-law, he would not have allowed such an upheaval of the stately home.

'There were wires everywhere. Then, as the men were carrying out a table, I heard one of them saying, "Is this theirs or ours?" A small difference between a table three centuries old and one made in the television studio's carpentry shop.'

A group being taken round the house admired the same long table and the guide explained helpfully, 'We hire out some of these rooms you know.' But a small compact body with grey hair said shrewdly, 'Not to the likes of us but to the gentry.' They all crane forward to listen as the guide lowers her voice conspiratorially. 'Mrs Shand Kydd never became the Countess,' and everyone inscrutably admires the ceiling with one hundred and ninety-eight different flowers, the ormolu gold on the mahogany doors, the lavender blue porcelain, and stands back for the Aubusson carpets and the Waterford glass chandeliers.

Viscount Althorp sidled out from the lift with the slight girl, his wife whom the staff call 'Lady Victoria'. The young couple had hoped to be invisible. 'Was she in jeans again?' the staff ask each other. A plaintive, 'yes' and another replies, 'Plainly dressed . . . mmh and she's such a nice person.' They like the young Lady Althorp, the future châtelaine, but wish they saw more of the Princess. One of them confided, 'She sees her father usually in London, you know, at Spencer House near the Ritz,' implying that the Princess does not want to spend time with her stepmother.

The family moved from their rambling country house to Althorp in the windy reaches of Northamptonshire when the 7th Earl died and Diana was fourteen. The old man had been happier and more preoccupied with his collection of some of the rarest books in Europe than the running of the estate. The place was dusty and dirty, though he always inspected visitors' shoes before he allowed them into the house. But after his wife Lady Cynthia died in 1972 when Diana was still at Riddlesworth, the old house became even shabbier and more dilapidated, the estate went into greater decline.

For the children, Diana and her brother particularly, the move to Northampton was a fresh beginning. Not all the staff moved from Park House. 'Collie', Mrs Violet Collison, the housekeeper, who now does gate duty at Sandringham, went with Mrs Shand Kydd. Rose Ellis, the kindly cook at Althorp, remembers a girl with '. . . pleasant ways and down to earth attitudes'. Today the remaining staff are still very jolly, laughing with Lord Spencer about 'open days'.

Albert Betts, the butler, would bring Diana chocolate cake with butter icing. 'She had a weakness for raspberry and strawberry ice-cream and lemon soufflé,' he recalled. 'A neat little girl,' he added. 'She was the kind of child who never forgot to send birthday cards on the right day.' She went for long walks in the grounds, tap danced on the parquet floors and did ballet in the 115-foot gallery under portraits by Sir Joshua Reynolds.

Loving the history of her family, Diana asked questions about the luscious porcelain and played with the Victorian tea set. The homecoming to Althorp was a happy one and compensated for the anguish of the parents' divorce. But for the children soon there would be a ripple in their new contentment in the shape of

their new stepmother, the Countess of Dartmouth, a divorcee
who had fallen deeply in love with and married their father.

She was formerly married to the Earl of Dartmouth, by whom
she had three sons and a daughter. When the marriage broke up
in 1976 Lord Dartmouth sued for divorce and cited Earl Spencer
for adultery. Her children were: William, thirty-one; Rupert,
twenty-nine; Charlotte, eighteen and Henry, twelve. The Spencers married very quietly that same year and none of the children
attended the ceremony.

Experienced as a member of the British Tourist Authority and
once very active on the Greater London Council, getting lots of
publicity when she complained about dirty teacups at Heathrow
Airport, the new Countess Spencer, Raine, was well aware of the
commercial potential of Althorp and set up a shop selling gaudy
costume jewellery. The staff at Althorp, who had been leading
fairly independent lives, suddenly had to come to attention, and
her stepdaughters agree that the place is more efficiently run
now. 'It never Raines but it pours,' the servants would remark.
A couple of kitchen hands were briskly described by the new
châtelaine as a 'pair of sluts'.

In the climate of horrified disapproval, even her enemies
acknowledge that she has probably saved Althorp from crumbling
ruin, but at a cost. Home life is now different. In 1986 entrance
to Althorp cost the public £1 a head, contributing to the £80,000
cost of running the house for a year; now it is £2.75 but the
running costs have also increased.

The house was run down. With no wife to help him the
dispirited Earl had no heart for Althorp. His new Countess had
immediately arranged to have eleven of the twelve Van Dycks
sold, though the Gainsboroughs and the Rubens and family
portraits by Joshua Reynolds remained, perhaps slightly startled
to find themselves on walls newly painted lurid pinks, greens and
blues. It cost a great deal to clean up the walls, the Countess
Spencer explains, because 'They were all painted with Woolworth
paint . . . A hundred years of gravy have come off . . . That's
why it cost so much, getting that muckage off.' The colours, she
explains, are 'truly Georgian' and 'will mellow' to more subtle
tones with time.

Where once there had been a distinguished Old Master, there

is now a large painting of the present Countess in shocking pink looking rather chocolate-boxy. 'We had to sell. We had no money, just a huge overdraft,' Earl Spencer says almost apologetically, explaining the departure of Andrea Sacchi's picture 'Apollo Crowning the Musician Pasqualini', bought by the first Earl in 1758, and sold to Wildenstein the art dealers for £40,000. It was subsequently sold on to the New York Metropolitan Museum of Art for £230,000. This was done to cope with swingeing death duties at the death of the 7th Earl, when his son inherited two and a quarter million pounds of debt.

An extrovert, in the public eye for years, the Countess was the opposite of the children's mother in every way. Her own mother, Dame Barbara Cartland, the ninety-year-old prolific ist, says, 'My daughter has a sparkle about her which makes everyone in the room attentive to what she is saying, and in the early days Diana . . . was shy.' Her first impression of Diana, then about sixteen, was of a very quiet, gentle and extremely pretty girl who found her stepmother overbearing. A bit plump and not a great conversationalist, she nevertheless endeared herself to her step-grandmother by shyly confessing she smuggled Barbara Cartland books to school. However, Miss Cartland did not realise that this girl, who could look very serious one moment, could be doubled up with quiet laughter the next.

The Princess was the gentlest in her reaction to her father but there is still no great bond between herself and her ebullient stepmother, who once caustically remarked, 'If you said Afghanistan to Diana she'd think it was a cheese.' The Countess confided that in her opinion her husband was the only Spencer 'with any grey matter at all'.

Her honest view is, 'Sarah resented me, even my place at the head of the table, and gave orders to the servants over my head. Jane didn't speak to me for two years, even if we bumped into each other in the passageway; it was bloody awful.' Even today Lady Spencer finds it difficult to talk about her truculent stepdaughters and says with feeling how difficult it was to have a conversation with any of them. The girls were deliberately mulish. 'But,' said a member of the Countess's family, 'Charles was always nice to Raine.'

Even the dutiful Diana, whom she called 'Pigeon toes', when

telephoned once by her stepmother and instructed to wear something suitable, 'preferably black', for a memorial service, deliberately wore a bright outfit bought specially from Miss Selfridge to annoy her. But typically Diana was kind to her stepmother's youngest son Henry. Barbara Cartland recalls how her grandson, who was feeling rather lost and uncertain at Althorp with his mother's new husband, 'found a friend in his stepsister Diana. She devoted herself to him in a very touching manner. There are very few teenage girls who would have been so caring.'

According to one of the family, their mother Mrs Shand Kydd was not at all pleased when her husband remarried though she had been the one to run off. Countess Spencer says defensively, 'I didn't break up their parents' marriage.' She also got her own back on her three stepdaughters by describing Jane as 'Only good for producing children,' Sarah as 'Okay while she sticks to hunting and shooting which is all she cares about,' and, about Diana: 'How can you have a conversation with someone who doesn't have a single O level? It's a crashing bore.' Prince Charles, however, is reputed to like his stepmother-in-law, admiring her intelligence and dynamism.

The children may have resentfully muttered 'Raine, Raine, go to Spain,' sulked and made things difficult, but she wrestled with the crippling death duties which threatened to bankrupt her husband. Three years later she would achieve something even more astonishing when she virtually saved his life, and this the children could never deny.

Lord Spencer was fifty-five, a little overweight but with a good health record, when he collapsed with a brain haemorrhage, ironically at a party to celebrate Althorp's coming out of the red. The prognosis was gloomy and doctors all agreed that the Earl could not survive. But his second wife, with that persistence and determination which makes her so effective, vowed she would do 'the only thing' she could, 'to use my life and energy for his life.' 'If you sit down and cry,' she added, 'you cry for yourself.'

'She will stop at nothing,' says her husband. The Countess rushed him down the M1 to London, scorning the local Northamptonshire hospitals. She remembered hearing about a German drug called Aslocillin which had hardly even arrived in Britain and persuaded a family friend, the Duke of Portland, to get hold of this drug which was being tested at a laboratory in

Haywards Heath. He put it on a train to Victoria. It was not legal to sell Aslocillin in England but she persuaded doctors to try it on her husband, who was now also suffering from double pneumonia and a burst lung abscess.

Although he was in a coma Countess Spencer kept on playing *Madame Butterfly*, Puccini's opera, to the recumbent Earl, refusing to allow him to slip away. The combination of this emotional favourite, the drug and her cheerful determination helped to save her husband's life. 'Suddenly he just opened his eyes and was back.'

'My miracle', he calls his wife, and tells you, 'we are still passionately in love. But sex isn't the overriding thing in marriage is it? I have seen Raine without her make-up. I have even seen her with her hair dead straight in a gondola in Venice, in the rain. I liked it better that way. That doesn't stop her re-curling it. I'm happy for her. I don't mind how she is as long as we're together.' The slight hesitancy in speech from his illness is always there.

'Without Raine I wouldn't have lived to see Diana married . . . she . . . sat with me for four solid months, holding my hand and even shouting at me that I wasn't going to die because she wouldn't let me.' Now everyone celebrates the Earl's tremendous recovery and the fact that he enjoys doing his bit around the place and helping in the wine shop.

Raine is adored by her husband, whom she calls 'Johnnikins', a nickname always loathed by the Spencer children. They were also dismayed by the acquisition of a new step-grandmother, the publicity-loving Barbara Cartland, so different from the stately, blue-blooded Ruth Lady Fermoy, their maternal grandmother.

'My fault is I fell madly in love with a man when I was forty-five,' the Countess explains with a wry glance aside. 'Most women turn to good work when they are over forty, but I'd done mine.' When she met her second husband she recalled how he struck her as 'a very lonely and unhappy man'. It was a case, says Spencer, 'of two very lonely people who found each other and found happiness together.'

Bubbly and ebullient, people feel very positively about Countess Spencer, while she believes herself lucky that she has had 'two wonderful marriages', but recognises, 'I suppose people resent it.'

Lord Spencer says it was fortunate that 'She came to me as an older and wiser woman.' Rather touchingly he likes to tell you, 'I had my chances.' He is still an attractive man. 'I took out one or two girls, but in London, not at home.' He has a rather appealing slightly dated way of referring to all women as girls; but he found that, 'Somehow they didn't seem, well, suitable.'

There was a price to pay in his remarriage. He does not see enough of his royal grandchildren. The Spencers are rarely invited to Highgrove. Earl Spencer adores the princes and before Christmas gives them a party when a dog-cart is dotingly filled with presents. He says proudly, 'William lectures me.' The little boy orders his grandfather to climb over farm gates. His wife usually contrives to be in London for these visits.

Today Lord Spencer still has his youngest daughter's infectious giggle and is easily convulsed with laughter. 'Loons are all attracted here, they come in buses, they like this place.' It is hard to know whether they are coming to see the Princess's father, the Flanders Mirrors or the two statuette slaves rescued from the river Tiber 2000 years ago.

Chuckling about the pressures of being married into the royal family, he gives the distinct impression that he considers the Windsors just a bit 'nouveau'. But in the early days he had to live with 'we do not approve' rebukes from the Palace.

Well matched with his showy Raine there was a certain flamboyance about his choice of a gold Rolls-Royce as he arrived at Buckingham Palace to celebrate his daughter's engagement on 24 February 1981. He appeared on television outside the Palace and because of his stroke sounded a tiny bit slurred; he has a guileless tendency to talk a little too freely about his daughter. 'Don't you ever do that again, Daddy,' the Princess telephoned him crossly.

After the royal wedding, Barbara Cartland chortled, 'I shall invite Americans to tea and give them meringues; they have never seen them you know.'

As the day ends and the visitors are whisked away in their coaches, Lord Spencer climbs the wide staircase, rests on the bronze of an orange setter called Forager and looks with a pleased smile at his walking stick engraved 'Earl Spencer – HRH Prince of Wales'.

CHAPTER 11

A Lot of Fun in the Chase

It was time Prince Charles started thinking about a suitable wife. One of the Queen's favourite ladies-in-waiting, Lady Susan Hussey, a good friend to the Prince, was with him in a theatre one evening when he sighed, 'Will I ever be able to choose the girl I want to marry?'

It had always been assumed that his wife should be a 'pure young girl'. Actually discretion rather than chastity was required by the Buckingham Palace 'selection board' as they reached for the magnifying glass and studied the field. Experienced courtiers believed a track record of virginity was important, but less so than the prurient imagine. They would find a unique girl with all the qualities.

Prince Charles was enjoying a perfectly satisfactory bachelor life, but publicly being compared unfavourably with his great-uncle Edward VIII who fell in love with an American divorcee, Mrs Wallis Simpson, and gave up the throne in 1936 to marry her. Prince Charles was the oldest unmarried Prince of Wales since the Old Pretender in 1718 and royal advisers feared he might be following in the Duke of Windsor's self-indulgent footsteps.

Like Henry V and Charles II before him, Prince Charles would remain unmarried until the age of thirty-two. He began to resent his image as an ageing playboy. 'I work bloody hard right now,' he said in 1978, 'and I will continue to do so.' He wanted to be the unofficial ambassador for British industry and proved his worth in 1977 when he raised £16 million chairing the Queen's Silver Jubilee Trust. If nothing else this was his turning point; on his own admission he had been a slow starter.

'This falling in love at first sight,' he said once, 'is not the way royal marriages are made.' Prince Charles never felt the need to get seriously involved. There was a string of 'suitable girls' until he got bored and struck them from the royal address book.

The Prince was unperturbed by being unmarried at the age of thirty. 'After all, many people nowadays do not marry at an early age,' he argued defensively when pressed about finding a future Queen. But heirs to the throne are not like 'many people' and have a duty to provide the next generation of princes.

An early low-key romance developed with a Welsh girl, Janet Jenkins, who worked as a receptionist at the British Consulate in Montreal. The Prince took her out to dinner and, she remembered, sent his beef back because it tasted of garlic.

A great favourite and serious runner was Davina Sheffield, a girl approved of by the Queen and the Queen Mother. A granddaughter of Lord McGowan, not only was she glamorous and bright, but seemed to enjoy hours of fishing and watching the Prince play polo. He took her on a romantic expedition to a secluded bay in the West Country. They went round with a local fisherman to the tiny private beach and the publican in the little hamlet remarked that Prince Charles's father must have told him about this trysting place.

Blonde, buxom and bright, Davina Sheffield did refugee work in Vietnam. She was devastated when her mother was murdered at her house in Oxfordshire, and it was Prince Charles who gave her affectionate and strong support. The romance was nipped in the bud, however, when a former boyfriend, James Beard, talked about his relationship with her and how they had lived together in Fulham. Beard, a powerboat designer, died a few years later, but his laddish indiscretion ruined Miss Sheffield's chances of being a princess.

It was expected that Prince Charles should have a track record with women. But he complained on a royal tour to a group of media men, 'You can live with a girl before you marry her, but I can't. I've got to get it right from the word go.' But he seemed to enjoy the test runs.

Much more than a passing flirtation was his affair with Anna Wallace, nicknamed 'Whiplash' and the 'Ice Maiden'. She was the daughter of a Scottish landowner whom Prince Charles had met when out hunting with the Quorn and he was passionately attracted to her. But on the evening of the Queen Mother's eightieth birthday party, she flounced out of Buckingham Palace ballroom in floods of tears. Highly attractive with good cheekbones, a personal assistant to an extremely wealthy Iranian, Homayoun Mazandi, she was not used to being neglected, so was furious when Prince Charles disappeared, leaving her to chat with dowagers.

When the Prince eventually returned to her she asked for champagne but he brought back a glass of brown ale, saying sheepishly, 'Mummy has the keys to the drinks cupboard.' Tongue in cheek and having fun at the volatile beauty's expense, he was not even around when she stamped her feet in annoyance and stormed out. 'I can't even find him to say goodbye,' Miss Wallace complained as she left the Palace.

Prince Charles was distinctly shaken by this experience but the Queen and royal family were relieved. Anna was devastatingly seductive, an outspoken young woman, and one of the few to be honoured by a private tour of Buckingham Palace. Prince Charles had undoubtedly been very attracted by her but she would not have been a suitable Princess of Wales. In September 1982 the satirical magazine *Private Eye* ran an extract from *Time*, the responsible American news magazine, about a study on herpes. It suggested that this was now officially considered a venereal disease and that at least two of Prince Charles's girlfriends had suffered from the complaint but mentioned only Miss Wallace by name.

Women have always found Prince Charles appealing with his quizzical smile and lithe, horseman's body without an ounce of spare fat. In common with men who enjoy this sort of success, he never felt the need to talk about his conquests. Indeed, he would go to endless lengths to protect a girl's reputation. But mostly they were only too happy to be identified, even if inevitably discarded later, as the relationship seemed to improve their chances of marrying well.

The Prince cynically kept a large chocolate box of photographs sent to him by hopefuls from all over the world and, once a year, handed these round to the men on his staff, saying, 'This is the pick of this year's crop.' Whenever he was seen with a new girl, he was pursued unmercifully by photographers and once held up a stuffed pigeon wearing a wig of yellow hair. 'Here's one of your mysterious blonde birds,' he said to reporters at Nairobi airport. He had been chased round Kenya and was now boarding a plane home, chuckling at his elaborate little joke, while the girl had tactfully disappeared.

But there was a lot of fun in the chase. On another occasion when the Prince was on board HMS *Jupiter* the press crowding round were approached by a young lieutenant who confided, 'You are wasting your time, he is very pompous, not very likeable and he isn't very bright either. I am quite sure he won't see you so you had better go away and not waste your time.' It took them a second to realise that they were talking to Prince Charles.

The Prince's girlfriends tended to be blonde, long-legged and fun. A royal adviser described his taste in women, for example the Duke of Northumberland's blonde daughters, Lady Caroline and Lady Victoria Percy, 'rosebuds of England rather than the tiger lilies of the tropic south'. One faintly exotic girlfriend, however, was Georgiana Russell, daughter of Sir John Russell, the British Ambassador to Spain. 'Gorgeous Georgia' liked to wear see-through dresses and followed the fashion of the times by letting the tail of her silk shirt hang out over black trousers. She had inherited her good looks from her mother, a beauty queen who once won the 'Miss Europe' title. When the Prince tired of her and was shown her wedding picture, he was genuinely surprised, exclaiming, 'Good God, her hair is black – she is not a blonde after all!'

He liked actresses because they were chatty and not self-conscious. 'My father told me if I ever met a lady in a dress like yours, I must look her straight in the eyes, otherwise someone might take a photograph of me in what might appear to be a compromising attitude,' the Prince told actress Susan Hampshire who was wearing a very low-cut frock. Miss Hampshire thought him charming and archly pretended to use her hands as a cover-up.

Susan George, another blonde actress, was invited to the Prince's thirtieth birthday party at the Palace. The darling of a host of interesting men, including the singers, Jack Jones and Rod Stewart, she finally married Simon MacCorkindale. Fun and sexy, she too was smuggled out of the Prince's quarters in the early hours of the morning. It was a short fling but they remained friends.

There were other more serious liaisons. He became involved with a string of women all over Europe, not all of impeccable Debrett background. Fiona Watson, daughter of Lord Manton, once appeared in *Penthouse* magazine proudly showing her 38–23–35 assets which the heir to the throne had thought for his eyes only.

Of the earlier romances, Jane Wellesley, the Duke of Wellington's daughter, was possibly the brightest of the lot. Not at all attracted by life at the Palace she hated the remorseless royal spotlight. While holidaying on the Wellington family estate in Spain, she was upset when photographs appeared showing her in suggestive Sloane horseplay throwing melons at the Prince and ruffling his hair.

Once seen as an ideal Princess of Wales, this small, dark, contained girl has remained unmarried. Her work in radio and television assisting Melvyn Bragg on his Arts programme is fulfilling. Any romance with Prince Charles ended in the early seventies. The Princess of Wales later threw a severe tantrum at the suggestion of a holiday at the Wellesley hacienda. They had been married for a few years at the time and she is believed to have felt uneasy about this intelligent girl who had eluded the Prince.

Prince Charles would have done almost anything to please Lord Mountbatten, even marrying his granddaughter, Lady Amanda Knatchbull, who read Chinese at Peking University and Anthropology, History of Art and Philosophy at Kent. A girl who worked with her on a charity committee recalls that she was 'an unobtrusive sort of person, very nice, very efficient, not glamorous. She had long brown hair; don't ask me what she wore.' Her clothes made only the slightest impression on this friend.

Amanda became a social worker with Hammersmith and Fulham Borough Council. One teacher thought that this was to compensate 'for the privileges she was born to but which she feels she has not earned'. It was she who stayed with the Prince the evening before Mountbatten's funeral; her training was invaluable and she was one of the few people really to understand how he felt and be able to comfort him.

It was never a romance which took off although they were together in the Bahamas, having companionable times, walking, waterskiing and deep-sea fishing. Then although she was considered suitable by the royal family, it was discovered she had secretly been seeing someone else.

Prince Charles seems to have a fatal charm for extrovert women like Margaret Trudeau, who at the time of their meeting was married but separated from her reclusive husband, the Canadian Prime Minister, Pierre Trudeau. Swearing she could make the Prince fall in love with her, she thought up a simple enough strategy. 'I rarely wear a bra and, since the buttons were undone, the Prince deliberately peeked down my blouse,' seeming to forget his father's earlier advice. 'He didn't blush in the slightest. He told me I was pretty enough to be an actress,' she said triumphantly. However, when she pursued him later, telephoning his private number, Mrs Trudeau was glum when a sleek manservant told her, 'His Royal Highness has gone to Scotland.'

The Prince could leave girls hanging by the telephone for weeks while he got on with his life, flying planes, doing parachute jumps, playing polo and meeting world leaders at Buckingham Palace. For the girl the most exciting event in her entire life had been one call from the Prince of Wales, but no matter how long she waited there might never be another.

Rather like some sheikh, the Prince might telephone quite late in the day, but would never be refused. Flattered by the invitation to Buck House, the girl would trot along at once, thrilled by the royal summons. Arriving at a side door the policeman on duty, sometimes giving an approving beam, would tick her name off a list, allowing her to slip discreetly into the Palace's gloomy bowels.

'I'm fed up coming in through the janitorial entrance,' complained outspoken Laura Jo Watkins, an American admiral's daughter. But English girls quietly accepted that it was honour enough to be allowed into the Palace and were perfectly happy to call Prince Charles 'Sir' even in moments of high emotion.

A royal flunkey walking briskly through the labyrinthine ways would lead her to the Prince's sitting room where she would be given a fairly simple meal, served by a footman. This was hardly the picture of the glamorous, candlelit dinner enviously imagined by her girlfriends. Late at night, she quite often had to make her own way home.

Whenever things got too fraught for the Prince, he relied on the experienced and decorative shoulder of Lady Tryon, enjoying the peace of the Tryons' seven-hundred-acre estate in Wiltshire or their fishing lodge. This is near the Hofsa River in north-east Iceland – a rather desolate place called Vopnafjordur, but to Prince Charles 'it's heaven . . . it's so remote, just you and nature,' and lots of excellent salmon. 'Kanga' Tryon and her husband Anthony, a director of Lazard Brothers and chairman of a finance company, have been enduring friends.

'Dale's not a beauty, but she attracts men easily. Dustmen whistle at her, so do schoolboys, and she loves it,' a friend says of Lady Tryon. This uncomplicated, bright, chocolate-boxy blonde also has a shrewd business sense. She created the Kanga label for a range of frilly, slightly fussy, dresses and also has a shop in London's highly fashionable Beauchamp Place in Knightsbridge.

'Kanga', short for Kangaroo, Prince Charles's pet name for her, dates back to their first meeting in Australia in 1966. After that evening, every time the Prince was in Australia, he contacted her. He was delighted by her marriage in 1975 to his old friend, the heavy-featured but witty aristocratic banker Lord Tryon, whose father was Keeper of the Privy Purse, Treasurer to the Queen. Lady Tryon is discreet, devoted to the Prince and asked him to be godfather to her son, Charles.

A member of the Prince's staff explained this much-talked-about friendship with Lady Tryon. 'He likes a woman he can have a fairly earthy conversation with over the dinner table. He never did like shy, shrinking violets.'

Mrs Camilla Parker-Bowles is another bright, pretty, blonde whom the Prince has always found attractive. A niece of builder Lord Ashcombe, she was not interested in him romantically and had already fallen in love and married a young army officer, Andrew Parker-Bowles, who once fancied Princess Anne.

If Prince Charles had his way, the ideal wife would be a stunning shapely blonde with the mind of his mentor van der Post. But his father took a more pragmatic view and chivvied him about his dilatoriness in getting married. 'You'd better get on with it, Charles, or there won't be anyone left,' was the Duke's gruff and peremptory advice.

Lady Tryon and Mrs Parker-Bowles now headed an unofficial committee of close friends who vetted girls likely to have princess potential. No wonder the Princess has never been madly keen to see these two ladies at her dinner table. They know a lot more about the Prince's past than she does and that has always been galling. There had, too, been something primitive about their mission, with its overtones of the harem. Outwardly sophisticated and delightful, it seemed almost distasteful for these two married women to so enjoy the selection process.

CHAPTER 12

'Perfect for the Job'

———————

The romance really began in a ploughed field in November 1977. Diana's sister, Lady Sarah Spencer, not the easiest person in the world but never dull, and attractive in a slightly hard way, had invited Prince Charles to a pheasant shoot at Althorp. It could not be bettered in one of the Princess's favourite Mills & Boon love stories.

Diana had worn a brace on her teeth briefly, but now had her ears pierced and wore two little gold studs. On her wrist she had a silver bracelet with hearts and a gold Russian wedding ring on her little finger. She was sixteen, still a schoolgirl; he was twenty-eight and heir to the throne.

Like all daughters of hunting, shooting and fishing families, she would follow the guns with the other women. Nowadays you rarely see the Princess on a shoot. 'She cannot bear to see a living thing being killed,' a beater explains at Sandringham. But in the early days of the romance, she was besotted, ready to follow the Prince anywhere.

'You remember Diana?' Sarah had asked, and the Prince, surprised by this tall, nubile girl being introduced to him, was instantly struck by her freshness. His taste had been for fairly sophisticated, worldly, fast numbers; now he found this shy teenager enticing. In that masculine way, the Prince remembered her only vaguely from nursery teas.

Lady Sarah noticed his eyes straying towards Diana again and again. Afterwards the Prince would recall, 'I remember thinking what fun she was – what a splendid sixteen-year-old . . .' 'I thought, What a very jolly, amusing and attractive girl, great fun, bouncy and full of life.' Later these characteristics would help her survive in the Palace.

Earl Spencer knew something was up. 'They were in a huddle all weekend. I was not a bit surprised when Diana later told me she was in love.' This was very perceptive of him because Prince Charles had been seeing his older daughter for months.

After that meeting at Althorp all parties went back to their routine: Lady Diana to school, Lady Sarah to her job with Mayfair estate agents and the Prince to his Palace to take out lots more girls.

In 1978 Diana went to her sister Sarah's finishing school in Switzerland. But she hated being at the Institut Alpin Vidamanette at Château d'Oex, Gstaad and was constantly homesick. She learnt the minimum amount of French, though there were stern reprisals if girls spoke English, and found it a rather frightening regime. One girl recalls, 'She was terribly shy, a bit of a nonentity really, a rather overgrown schoolgirl who was not very sure of herself. I remember once one of us complimented her on a cashmere twinset she was wearing and she blushed and said, "Mummy buys them for me." God, at that age – we were about seventeen or eighteen – you hated anything Mummy suggested.' The only thing Diana enjoyed was the skiing. She stayed for just a few months and then flew home in floods of tears.

In London she signed on with several agencies: Universal Aunts, Knightsbridge Nannies and Solve Your Problems, for a string of 'genteel' jobs as cook, nanny and kindergarten teacher. 'I was hopeless at sauces.' Her first job as a nanny was in Hampshire for Major Jeremy Whitaker and his wife Philippa. They thought her delightful, taking their six-year-old daughter Alexandra strawberry picking and cooking occasional suppers.

Other fairly mundane jobs included serving cocktails at parties and even being a scrubber for a time, cleaning floors at £1 an hour. A serious career never crossed Diana's mind and despite failing her driving test first time, she was getting around London and socially having a very good life.

It was this lack of dedication which prevented her having a serious career though she toyed with the idea of becoming a dance teacher. Soon after she left school Diana approached the legendary Madame Betty Vacani who had presented prizes at West Heath and taught most of the royal family to dance. Tentatively Diana inquired: 'I wonder if you remember me; I used to take your Pekinese for a walk in the garden.'

Diana asked if she might come and train with her as a teacher, but she only stayed one term. She taught little ones to dance to the tune 'Hickory-dickory' at the Vacani School in South Kensington. But she quickly realised that it was not all tap dancing and pirouetting and called for dedicated hard work, self-discipline and exams.

Now eighty-two and living in retirement in Sussex, Madame Vacani says she felt the course was a little too rigorous and 'interfered with Diana's social life'. The school was then in Brompton Road, Knightsbridge, and the shops were too tempting. Diana had perhaps not realised that she should dedicate the whole day every day to the training and then, when she qualified, would be expected to go off round the country catching trains to go teaching. 'Being a dance teacher,' Madame Vacani says, 'is not an easy job.'

After that first term, Diana never came back. 'That was it,' Madame Vacani explained, and added, 'We got a postcard saying she had gone skiing in Switzerland and broken her ankle.'

But she was astonished later by the poise and confidence of this uncertain girl when she danced with Wayne Sleep at Covent Garden. It was as if Diana was determined to show Madame Vacani that she had the makings of a fine performer.

Madame Vacani, who taught Prince Charles the Highland Fling, was not invited to the wedding. When Prince William was born, she sent the Princess a gossamer white shawl for the baby but received only a thank-you letter from a lady-in-waiting in return. This saddened the elderly teacher who has a handwritten letter from the Queen thanking her for her contribution to the 'Happy

Birthday, dear Ma'am' sixtieth-birthday celebratory programme. Now that is something to treasure along with wonderful memories of teaching the Queen and Princess Margaret, Princess Anne, who 'was like a bomb' and Prince Charles, a favourite pupil, a shy child who touched her heart: 'I'll do it, Madame Vacani, if you hold my hand.'

Each of the Spencer children had been left a substantial amount of money by their American great-grandmother, Frances Work, to which they became entitled on their eighteenth birthdays. Diana bought a flat in Earls Court, a raffish part of London, once a mecca for Australians, now filled with Asian supermarkets and video shops. Number 60 Coleherne Court was in a pleasant mansion block and she paid £50,000 for it in 1979.

Lady Diana now enjoyed racing around London in her roofless sports car, cycled to work, went to the theatre, gave supper parties, giggled with girlfriends and 'broke dozens of young men's hearts,' among them perhaps that of Old Etonian James Boughey.

'Diana was a fabulous girl,' one admirer recalled. Many tried to win her, sending flowers and begging for a date, but she always politely declined though would occasionally go and eat at the Poule au Pot in Pimlico or the Santa Croce in Cheyne Walk. The doorbell was always ringing and there would be another bunch of flowers for Diana Spencer – never taken seriously until the day red roses arrived from a man called Renfrew, the secret name Prince Charles often used.

Even though she was the one to liven up parties and bring out the best in people, she was also the girl who did the washing up while everyone else was sprawled on sofas. This passion for neatness is not always the sign of a tranquil mind.

A friend of her sister Jane offered her a job which made her really happy, working as a helper in the Young England Kindergarten in Pimlico, a tumbledown old school in St George's Square.

'Please, Miss Diana, Jeremy is pulling my hair.' She loved it and they loved her. She helped them with cuttings and paste and got the glue off their overalls. But she damaged her back lifting and cuddling her charges and still has to sleep on an extra-hard mattress.

Although skittish and flippant, Diana also had sensitivity so everyone told her their troubles. She made them laugh, mopped their tears and might impulsively take off a favourite bit of jewellery and give it to a friend.

Like a thousand other girls from privileged backgrounds she owned a decent flat in London, had a dress allowance at Harrods, a new car, a Honda Civic later replaced by a sky-blue Volkswagen Polo, and went skiing every year. Weekends were spent in the country at her own stately home or with friends.

Diana, who had a special charm, shared confidences with her three flatmates and inspired a loyalty which will last till they are all old ladies. 'A super girl,' says the musical Carolyn Pride; this is echoed by Virginia Pitman who was a china restorer and brought a goldfish called Battersea with her to the flat, and confirmed by Ann Bolton, an estate agent's secretary.

Little mother, châtelaine, she organised the entertaining and cooked nice suppers featuring borscht and bread and butter pudding. Diana was not a smoker nor a drinker and the evenings were hardly wild, they bopped gently to the music of pop singers like Neil Diamond and Abba. Had Ruth Lady Fermoy popped in she would not have been dismayed; it could have been one of her own little supper parties with the Queen Mother, the place would be so neat. Everyone expected that Carolyn, one of the most attractive and assertive of the trio, might be chosen as a lady-in-waiting because she was closest, a special friend from West Heath schooldays, while Ann Bolton tended to speak up on behalf of the three flatmates and was rather protective. But not one of the girls was considered suitable to work for the Princess. A lady-in-waiting must not be too opinionated, too forceful or too attractive.

Flirty, leggy, Lady Diana told friends she thought Charles was 'altogether pretty amazing'. It is hard to reconcile this uncomplicated girl with the schemer portrayed by her step-grandmother, the novelist Barbara Cartland, who swears that, 'She went after the Prince with singleminded determination. She wanted him and she got him.'

Nobody quite understood why the excitable and outspoken Lady Sarah Spencer should suddenly make an unsolicited announcement, protesting to the world after a skiing trip with the Prince of Wales in Switzerland, 'I'm not in love with Prince

Charles. I wouldn't marry anyone I didn't love, whether it was the dustman or the King of England.' She had once been considered an ideal future Princess of Wales but the relationship was cooling. Smartly anticipating developments in her youngest sister's life, Lady Sarah added, 'I'm a whirlwind sort of lady as opposed to a person who goes in for slow-developing courtships,' gaily justifying any indiscretion.

In May 1980 Sarah married twenty-eight-year-old Neil McCorquodale, son of a printing millionaire and a cousin of her stepmother. Her life with this ex-Guards officer and her three children would give her the stability and happiness she craved.

In January 1979 Lady Diana and her sisters were invited to join a royal shoot at Sandringham. The Queen was fond of this family and wanted to help the girls who were desperately worried about their father who had been seriously ill in hospital. None of Prince Charles's previous girlfriends had grown up close to the royal family, so had not the confidence to entirely relax in his presence. Lady Diana would treat him, from the very beginning, as just another young man and this was irresistible. During another weekend at Sandringham the Queen was surprised to see her son being taught to tap dance on the terrace.

That summer during the Duke of Richmond's Goodwood House ball at the end of the July 1980 race meeting week, Prince Charles and Lady Diana had a close special dance together, but nobody took much notice because she had been so much part of the charmed inner circle of the house party scenery for years. Lady Diana was then invited by Prince Charles to Cowdray Park to watch him play polo, the sure sign of approval for any girl.

By August, Lady Diana was having fun on the Royal Yacht *Britannia* at Cowes, invited ostensibly by Lady Sarah Armstrong-Jones who had casually mentioned that 'the Prince of Wales would be on board.' A windsurfing expedition on the Solent gave her an opportunity to show off a good body as she gracefully darted through the waves, not altogether unaware that the Prince's eyes were on her. Later she ducked him by tipping over the mast of his windsurfer.

Although still sad about his acrimonious parting with Miss 'Whiplash' Wallace, friends noticed how he 'kept close to Diana

. . . lost his gloomy look and became bright and cheerful' as they sang songs round the piano.

A few months later the telephone rang in Coleherne Court, and there were girlish shrieks from the flatmates of, 'Can you get it?' 'I'm in the bath . . . washing my hair.' It was Prince Charles inviting Diana to Balmoral. She scurried round borrowing clothes from her flatmates for this important date.

When the new favourite flew up for a weekend in Scotland in September 1980 tongues began to wag. This gentle girl with a penchant for watercolours, flower arranging, cooking and dancing to Abba had suddenly caught the attention of a capricious man who bored easily, but now was intrigued by the fresh cheeky charm of a girl he had known all her life.

In the apparently easygoing atmosphere of the traditional Scottish royal family holiday this nineteen-year-old girl would be scrutinised, not unkindly but for her own sake for the future. Her bearing was right. At 5 feet 10 she weighed almost ten and a half stone, had a shape more womanly than model material. The world saw a delightful girl with a classic English complexion, a way of moving with grace and singular appeal. Girls all over England would begin to copy her simple, brushed to one side hairstyle, wear frilly tight blouses, woolly cardigans with reindeers on the front and back and flatty shoes.

No matter how intense the pressure, Lady Diana showed a resilience, a smiling distance. She was pleasantly aloof, rarely flustered, merely a hint of blush and that sideways look from underneath her fringe. It was not easy to get away from her flat in a vast mansion block right beside the busy Earls Court Road. Huge lorries trundled by but she handled her VW with élan and would shoot off to shop in Knightsbridge or visit her grandmother in Eaton Square.

What made Lady Diana so ideal, as a Buckingham Palace official suggested, apart from being immensely attractive, 'a girl of charm and sweetness' who could make even Prince Philip laugh, was that as the romance began to blossom there was no string of former boyfriends to spring up like 'jack-in-the-boxes' and tell all. At nineteen, Lady Diana Spencer was inexperienced. Her uncle Lord Fermoy embarrassed her when he took it upon himself to declare, 'She, I can assure you, has never had a lover.' And as if that were not indelicate enough, Barbara Cartland, Lord Spencer's mother-in-law, announced, 'Prince Charles has got to have a pure young girl. I don't think Diana has had a boyfriend.'

Of course Lady Diana had plenty admirers. George Plumptree, six years her senior who writes gardening books, and Simon Berry, an Old Etonian who worked in the family wine trade, were both impeccable young escorts. They would eat in and have quiet suppers. Diana had attended a cordon bleu cookery course but usually made scrambled eggs. The closest to any intimate revelation was that her nannying instincts prompted her to take away and wash dirty shirts belonging to the Scots Guards officer Rory Scott. She still has a passion for ironing and folding.

Royal matchmaking is a professional business. Lady Diana fitted in perfectly. It was not so much snobbery but that a girl brought up in the orbit of the royal circle knows the rules; the impositions and the need for formality come naturally.

But Lady Diana was refreshingly irreverent, doing an excellent 'Miss Piggy' impersonation, though that would not be well received at the Palace, since the Queen's glummest expression in public is known in the royal family as her 'Miss Piggy' face.

Simon Berry remembered a holiday in the French Alps in 1979. 'I was skiing down an icy slope and heard the strident tones of Miss Piggy in my ear informing me, "You're treading on thin ice, frog." In the next instant Diana was hurtling past, a big grin on her face.' This future Queen would capture the hearts of the cynical, even the anti-royalists. Berry specially recalled a chat he had with Diana after her sister Sarah's wedding in May 1980. Idly she had talked about the future, saying, 'I would love to be a successful dancer . . . or maybe Princess of Wales. When I marry it will be in Westminster Abbey.'

Prince Charles could not find a more ideal partner, or a more delightful girl. However, the romance remained delicate and understated until the Queen became grumpy about her son's apparent dilatoriness. For her, Diana would be 'perfect for the job'.

Diana was as much a thoroughbred as one of the Queen's valuable fillies in the stud at Wolverton. Palace mandarins thought this young woman had the makings of a future Queen and already showed surprising maturity and discretion. In their opinion Prince

Charles had remained a bachelor too long. The message was simple: 'Get on with it.'

In October she watched Prince Charles finishing second in an amateur riders' three-mile race at Ludlow and squealed with excitement every time he cleared another of the eighteen fences.

At the end of the month, Charles and Diana had stayed at the Parker-Bowles' home near Highgrove in Gloucestershire, the Prince's country house. The two men went out hunting and when they returned Diana impulsively ran towards the Prince but, seeing photographers, hesitated and quickly went inside. Spontaneity is not part of being royal. It was here, in a cabbage patch, that Prince Charles first spoke in a convoluted way about marriage. In his earnest fashion he tentatively proposed with much nervous twiddling of the gold signet ring on his little finger and that little grimace, both marks of slight unease. 'If I were to ask you,' he said to Diana, 'do you think it would be possible?' Diana thought the whole business rather comical and told friends later that the Prince had seemed 'strangely stifled'. Being invited to become a future Queen in this manner left her convulsed with giggles at 'the immense absurdity of the situation'.

The secret meetings were the most fun. Diana and Charles would go to his hide-away house right beside a pub in Church Street, Kensington aptly called the Windsor Castle. They were following the path pioneered by Princess Margaret and Lord Snowdon who used to nip off to Rotherhithe on his motor bike. Sometimes they took the Queen Mother along, too, but she would travel more conventionally.

They took such care, but a huge mocking scandal broke about a romantic tryst late at night on the royal train. The Queen was livid when one of the tabloid newspapers printed a lurid 'under cover of darkness' story about how her virginal future daughter-in-law had been ushered by police to a siding at Holt in Wiltshire on 5 November, fireworks night, after a hundred-mile dash by car from her home in London to the murky shadows of the shunting sheds. The Prince was furious and Diana herself, appalled, completely denied that she had ever been anywhere near the train, let alone in the middle of the night. 'I don't even know what it looks like,' she remarked. She complained that she was victimised because she had no past of 'leaping in and out of bed with someone . . . I mean, I haven't had a chance to have had a background like that. I'm only nineteen, but people are longing to dig up something.' She admitted feeling 'miserable' because of all the attention, and 'sort of fed-up, partly because it makes everyone else's lives so bloody, particularly for the girls who share my flat. It's just not right at all.'

The editor of the newspaper, the *Sunday Mirror*, Mr Robert Edwards, was given a rocket by the Palace. The Queen was so angry that she demanded a retraction, which is very rare for the royal family. But the editor refused to budge on his 'Love in the Sidings', confident of a story which did wonders for circulation.

An insouciant character, Edwards held the view that when the royal couple had access to so many houses, and as both were living at Buckingham Palace, why would they choose the relative discomfort of a train for lovemaking surrounded by the Wiltshire Constabulary with their walkie-talkies, dogs and sophisticated listening devices? The truth was that Prince Charles spent the night on the royal train alone in the sidings before an early morning public engagement. Rather touchingly, however, Diana had been prepared to drive through the night to see him.

It was unfortunate that he had to go to India in November, almost immediately afterwards, another little endurance test for Lady Diana. Before his three-week tour she said, 'One thing I don't want is a postcard from India saying "Wish you were here".' But he did wish that she could be with him to see the Taj Mahal, where he stood for ages, saying, 'What love this man must have had for his wife. I know what that means now.' Letting down his guard, he admitted, 'I am missing Diana like you wouldn't believe. We telephone every night and I've got letters she gave me.'

Admiring the white marble glowing in a pink sunset over Agra he avoided all the clichés like 'wonderful', 'marvellous'. He thought the Moslem faith rather attractive as it allowed a man to have 'plenty of wives; much more encouraging; lots of fun'. The tour was often running late because 'His Highness is having a quiet lesson on the tabla.' The visit made him think he ought to do yoga each day . . . the trouble was to find half an hour to read the papers.

Nor did Diana feel much better when Prince Charles decided

not to hurry home but to go on a simple, peaceful trek to the foothills of the Himalayas. A messenger was sent to the base camp at Pokhara in Katmandu to obtain sausages and bacon for the Prince, and the result of the Oxford and Cambridge rugby match. Out of touch for three days, 'It has been absolutely wonderful,' he said, looking back at the Annapurna range. 'I became rather attached to the hills.'

He had a look of peace about him and it was clear that sitting over camp fires eating freshly caught carp from the lakes cooked by the Sherpas had helped him to make up his mind about marriage. He was garlanded with frangipani and a gossamer-thin shawl was put round his shoulders, the Buddhist token for 'farewell' and 'goodbye'.

Meanwhile Diana went about her daily life as best she could, posing innocently in a see-through skirt of Tana Liberty heart print called Vivaldi at the Pimlico kindergarten, clutching chubby small children in each arm. Those celebrated legs, inherited from her mother, would flash around the world, but Diana merely remarked that the picture gave her 'legs like a Steinway piano'. Hardly. 'I don't want to be remembered for not having worn a petticoat,' she moaned. An admiring Prince Charles teased her. 'I knew your legs were good, but I didn't realise they were that spectacular. And did you really have to show them to everybody?'

On 27 November 1980 Diana admitted wistfully, 'I'd like to marry soon.' The next day she was in tears and denied that she had ever made such a wishful naïve remark. Her mother, the strong and spirited Mrs Shand Kydd, now moved in, perhaps feeling secretly that the Palace had been rather inept about protecting Lady Diana. She was aware of the fragility of the relationship between the young couple and how damaging this could be for her daughter. Through years of being close to the royal family during her first marriage, she knew that Diana's slight indiscretion could be enough to finish the royal romance. With them you only get one chance.

'Fanciful speculation, if it is in good taste, is one thing, but this can be embarrassing,' she wrote in a letter to *The Times*, adding '. . . lies are quite another matter, and by their very nature, hurtful and inexcusable.'

When Prince Charles got back from India, a member of the Household remarked on the change in him. 'It was as though a great weight had been lifted from his shoulders.'

The Queen left a message that she wanted to see him immediately on his return, but for once Prince Charles ignored his mother and went to Highgrove. He would tell his parents over Christmas about his plans to marry.

The Queen had been urging him to make his mind up. 'The idea of this romance going on for another year is intolerable for everyone concerned,' she commented. But though now sure of his own commitment, Prince Charles displayed a mature and careful consideration for his future wife, believing that she would need to be doubly sure in her own mind. He was concerned about the sacrifice for Diana to be 'in the goldfish bowl' – a royal euphemism for the constant scrutiny and loss of personal freedom.

On 14 January 1981, there was an important family gathering at Sandringham. The Spencers were invited by the Queen to talk over the possibility of the royal marriage. Prince Charles invited Diana to go skiing in Klosters. She refused as she wanted him 'to be left in peace for a while.' On 3 February Prince Charles returned from Switzerland and two days later he proposed, properly this time.

He had arranged a specially romantic supper, not their usual eggs and spinach eaten at a card table. He thoughtfully organised flowers and candles in the bachelor blue sitting room with its washed out blue curtains and leather chairs. His rather gloomy set of Victorian rooms at the Palace were comfortable rather than smart, full of old-fashioned mahogany furniture, with a dark brown study and green dining room. Specifically he requested no interruptions from the Palace servants, who with their usual exquisite tact absented themselves. After supper the couple sat cosily together on a tiny yellow sofa.

The proposal was simple and so was her answer – 'Yes.' And then, because he is such a caring man, and much more aware than perhaps many royal princes, his concern after the prompt acceptance from Diana was that she might bitterly regret the whole thing. Years of training made him suggest to her gently that she must take a couple of weeks to think about it, which was ideal because she was going to Australia to stay with her mother.

He thought the imposition of public life might be almost too much for her to bear, and asked her to reflect whether 'it was all going to be too awful.' But smiling, those blue eyes large and round and shining, she nodded, agreeing to think about things, but felt quite certain. 'I never had any doubts,' she said afterwards.

Then, behaving impeccably, though perhaps he should have been asked first, Prince Charles telephoned his future father-in-law, who was delighted to say 'yes'. Mischievously Earl Spencer could not help wondering what the heir to the throne might have thought 'if I had said no.'

That night, a breathlessly excited Diana tiptoed back to her flat, unable to resist telling her flatmates the news. One of them, Carolyn Pride, was in the lavatory, and recalls 'Diana told me through the door. I just burst into tears.' Virginia Pitman joined the others. 'We started to squeal with excitement and then we began to cry.'

'Keep your traps shut,' Diana begged, but the caution was unnecessary with these trusted friends. 'It wasn't hard to keep the secret. We never dreamt of telling anyone. That's the way we were brought up,' said Carolyn, and Ann Bolton added, 'It's like protecting your sister. We would simply never let Diana down.' Wonderful public school loyalty.

There was a hilarious celebratory breakfast the next morning. Lady Sarah McCorquodale popped in to see Diana at Coleherne Court and immediately sisterly intuition told her that the engagement was on. 'When I saw her face . . . she was totally radiant – bouncing, bubbling – and I said, "You're engaged" and she said, "Yes."'

'I'm Cupid; I introduced them. They just clicked; they are totally compatible. He met Miss Right and she met Mr Right,' Sarah chortled, declaring them to be a perfect match. 'She is very giggly; he is very giggly;' which is hardly the impression the Prince gives today as he frowns over the latest architectural digest.

Prince Charles still seemed stunned that he had been accepted, but Lady Diana, full of naïve youthful confidence, remarked: 'Oh, I never had any doubts about it.'

It began to be obvious that something was afoot when she went to Australia for twelve days' gentle reflection about her future in February 1981. During this time the couple managed lots of laughs by telephone. When he finally got through to her mother's station in Australia, as Prince Charles recalled later, 'There had been so many calls from the press that when I gave my name somebody said, "How do I know that you *really* are?" "But I am," I retorted, definitely in a rage.'

When she got back to London's Heathrow Airport, Diana was given special VIP treatment and whisked off to a meeting with the Prince. The romance was destined to be the most public courtship ever. This shy girl's ability to endure intrusion with a graceful silence made her immediately attractive to the royal family. She was discreet, able to keep quiet – unlike her sister, Lady Sarah, who earned royal disapproval by being a compulsive chatterbox. Nevertheless her breezy style and extrovert nature – for she does like sometimes to shock and startle – could send a few shivers down the spines of the Old Guard in Court circles. This spirited independence was evident as she cheated the media 'paparazzi', not letting their presence interfere with her life as she went shopping, lunched with her girlfriends or zipped off at the wheel of her car to meet the Prince.

The Queen was overheard saying in a matter-of-fact way of the press coverage, 'Well, she's going to have to learn to get used to this sort of thing. At least it's useful in that respect.'

Quite early on Diana showed inner resources far deeper than any portrait of her as a sweet and simple country girl would suggest. At first light, still tanned from her trip to Australia, she left London and drove the sixty miles in her new Mini Metro, with its double silver stripes and tinted sun roof, radio blaring, to meet Prince Charles in Berkshire at trainer Nick Gaselee's Lambourn stables. She was not totally unsympathetic to the Prince's passion for horses, her fear dating back to the time her pony Romany took a sharp turn and threw her, breaking her arm and concussing her badly.

This dawn rendezvous with her fiancé and his horse should have been full of old-fashioned romance. The Prince, who had planned to ride the £15,000 Allibar at Chepstow, had been out on a seven-mile workout along the Berkshire Downs and galloped towards a waiting Lady Diana fresh and happy.

But to her horror, she saw the horse collapse under him and in minutes die of a heart attack. The Prince held Allibar's head in his arms and Diana, with 'tears streaming down her cheeks' turned to go. Then the couple walked away . . . 'comforting each other'. Prince Charles had been 'besotted' by the horse.

There is nothing like a little shared tragedy to bring a couple even closer. This one brought out all Lady Diana's tenderness and made the Prince realise how much he needed her; he had felt extremely isolated after Lord Mountbatten's death. Not that you can compare the death of a distinguished mentor with that of a horse, although in hunting circles the comparison is pretty close.

CHAPTER 13

Your Philandering Days are Over

———————◆———————

The engagement was announced at 11 A.M. Early that morning Lady Diana had been to her hairdresser at South Kensington, to have a wash and blow-dry and to 'show off her ring'.

There was a telephone call to the Principal of the kindergarten in Pimlico, Victoria Wilson, saying Lady Diana would not be returning. 'We shall all miss her very much,' she remarked. Later she would go to a party to say goodbye and was presented with a collage made by the children. 'It was lovely,' she said later. 'I had so many children crawling on top of me. I've got more bruises on my bottom . . .'

After the Changing of the Guard at the Palace, the band of the Coldstream Guards played 'Now Your Philandering Days are Over' from the *Marriage of Figaro* as they marched up the Mall, a humorous tribute to Prince Charles as the notice of the engagement had been posted on the Palace gates.

Perceptive members of the Staff had hints of a royal engagement long before it was announced on 24 February 1981. It was not so much that the Queen and Parliament had agreed to it in accordance with the Royal Marriages Act of 1772 but that the royal fridges were brimming with champagne.

The band was playing softly in the Palace ballroom at the start of an Investiture. Suddenly the music stopped, the Lord Chamberlain stepped forward, one or two thought perhaps they had got the wrong day.

'It is with the greatest pleasure,' he beamed, 'that the Queen and the Duke of Edinburgh announce the betrothal of their beloved son, the Prince of Wales, to Lady Diana Spencer, daughter of the Earl Spencer and the Honourable Mrs Shand Kydd.' The Queen looked unusually smiley and happy. It had been her idea to share the news as it was being flashed round the world from Buckingham Palace so that the people she was about to honour should hear first.

In another part of the Palace, Prince Charles and Lady Diana Spencer suddenly appeared in his office looking 'astonishingly happy'. Surrounded by young secretaries and aides, they all had a glass of champagne. Like every young girl, Lady Diana showed everyone her engagement ring, a large sparkling oval sapphire surrounded by fourteen diamonds and set in eighteen-carat white gold. When Garrard's the royal jewellers sent round a tray of eight possible rings, Lady Diana had chosen this stunning £28,500 rock. 'It was the biggest,' she laughed.

Today Countess Spencer's shop sells copies of her royal step-daughter's engagement ring, a snip at £5.

'I can't get used to it,' the newly engaged Lady Diana glowed, looking at her ring and stretching out her left hand with all the telltale signs of a girlish inability to grow her fingernails, and a tendency to nibble them indicating a highly strung temperament.

Complimenting the ring was a very pretty diamond and emerald pendant in the design of the feathers emblem of the Prince of Wales. This was a present from the royal family. It had once belonged to Queen Mary. Now her great-grandson's wife would wear it on a velvet ribbon.

It was a bitterly cold day but this did not deter huge crowds from queueing hopefully for a glimpse of the royal couple on the balcony. But balcony appearances are rationed and usually occur only after an Event, 'something spectacular like the Queen's Birthday Parade or a royal wedding,' a Palace spokesman explained. The newly engaged couple were on the lawn. Today a svelte and glamorous princess looks back with a shudder at that engagement day family album photograph showing her looking positively chubby in an unflattering, mumsy blue suit.

The trouble with being royal is that everything you say and do remains with you forever. Whether you were gauche or winsome at twenty, there will be photographs to remind you in newspapers and magazines till you are ninety. Television preserves the simplest words in aspic. The Queen was said to be anxiously behind a curtain in the drawing room as the couple posed and answered questions.

'Are you in love?' Prince Charles supposed he was: 'Yes,' but then, with an apologetic shrug, added, 'whatever that may mean.' There are those who believe that left to his own devices he might have followed the footsteps of his great-uncle the Duke of Windsor and married an older sophisticated woman, if at all.

The twelve-year difference in age meant nothing at all; she actually emphasised it by saying, 'I have never thought about the age gap. I always ganged up with Prince Andrew.' The Prince said, 'Diana will always keep me young; you are only as old as you think you are.'

'She wanted him – and she got him!' said one of the few disgruntled and unmarried members of the Prince's staff, convinced that Lady Diana Spencer had gone determinedly after the Prince. Hating the end of his employer's bachelor days, he would insist, 'She went after the Prince with singleminded determination.'

This bubbling, inexperienced nineteen-year-old *ingénue* at the Prince's side hardly seemed a *femme fatale*, though she has always had her mother's strong will. But when asked about being in love, she had no hesitation in replying, 'Of course.' And, full of unquestioning enthusiasm, described herself as 'thrilled . . . blissfully happy'.

Forgotten now were the strain and the spotlight: how once she had wept on a bench in Berkeley Square and had to be comforted by a friend. Behind that soft smiling evasiveness and putting her head down in a protective stoop she was learning all the time, an unexpected cameo of grace under the media pressure before the engagement which had not failed to impress the Prince.

You felt that for Prince Charles, marriage was not terribly exciting, more a case of it seeming a good idea at the time and something to be got on with in view of the shortage of suitable girls predicted by his father. At the same time, 'Marriage,' he insisted, was 'much more important than just falling in love . . .' It was about 'creating a secure family unit in which to bring up children, to give them a happy secure upbringing – that' in his view – was 'what marriage is all about' and 'it would be good to have support'. At that she gave him a metaphorical nudge, as she whispered, 'Better like it.'

Lady Diana Spencer spent the night before the engagement was announced in her Coleherne Court flat, a last time of real freedom and girlish giggles with flatmates. They pretended that everything would stay the same, reassuring one another with hugs, tears and high-pitched squeaks.

Like an operatic heroine, Lady Diana had called out, 'For God's sake ring me up. I'm going to need you,' as she left the Earls Court flat. It was a lighthearted plea, but her words would be prophetic. Really good friends would be too reticent to ever dial that 930–4624 Buckingham Palace number.

Everything would change. In twenty-four hours their 'sweet' landlady Lady Diana would be moved out by royal decree. That night she would go by Rolls-Royce to dinner with the Queen Mother and her own grandmother and move into Clarence House. Here Diana would learn, 'simply by being around her', an old friend of the Queen Mother's confided. However, after a few days of the Queen Mother's warm feathery custodianship Lady Diana was on the move again. Sensibly the Queen thought that she should move into Buckingham Palace and gave her a small suite of rooms on the same floor as Prince Charles.

'Life in Buckingham Palace,' she wrote to her friends, 'isn't too bad . . . but there are too many formal dinners, yuk!' Yuk has remained a favourite unsophisticated term of disapproval and it is now Prince William's. It was a lonely four months before the wedding, though the world outside imagined a fairy-tale princess. She hates that label; in reality life was not all that magical, and she was rattling around alone because Prince Charles was away so often on engagements.

The Queen was on the floor below; Prince Andrew was away

in the Royal Navy and Prince Edward was at Gordonstoun. Diana thought wistfully once or twice about the snugness of Clarence House where she had spent only two nights with the Queen Mother and the sleek servants in black velvet who anticipated every whim.

Now Diana was in the Palace nursery wing, originally lived in by the governess. Simple and chintzy, there was a television set and lots of fresh flowers from the Palace gardens. Even when the Prince was around, very often he would be summoned to the Queen. 'Darling, I am going to have lunch with Mummy,' he would explain. There was no question of Diana being invited to this businesslike lunch where mother and son would talk about speeches, engagements and prime ministers.

One of the royal servants felt very sympathetic. 'In all the months Diana stayed there I don't ever remember her dining alone with the Queen. Or even lunch. I think she was a little afraid of her. I think one of the reasons Diana was so shy of her was that the two didn't have much to talk about.' The reality of monarchy was beginning to dawn on this girl who often affectionately referred to Prince Charles as 'Fish Face', and it was daunting.

Prince Charles knew about this painful adjustment and would say to his staff, 'Keep an eye on Diana for me, will you?' But as one nursery footman remarked, 'She never seemed to want anything. As long as there was plenty of yogurt in the fridge and fresh fruit, she would say cheerfully, "No, I'll be all right."' Her days were spent doing tapestry, skimming through the Palace corridors with a Sony Walkman clamped to her ears, and watching 'Coronation Street' and 'Dallas' on television.

Lady Diana was losing weight at a dramatic rate, and also getting fit by having ballet and tap-dancing lessons at the Palace, tripping about to Fred Astaire's 'Top Hat, White Tie and Tails'. Much of her time was spent thinking dreamily about clothes, thumbing through glossy magazines like *Vogue* and *Harpers* and drawing up her 'no decanters' wedding list. She was having fun, going into Janet Reger's shop in Knightsbridge, famous for its silky, subtly sexy lingerie. One visit prompted her to say saucily to a photographer waiting outside, 'Do you want to know the colour of my bloomers?'

Her beloved car, a German VW runabout which had reliably taken her to trysts with the Prince, would be driven away from the block of flats. In future she would drive only British cars. In the Palace Mews there was a new red Mini Metro, a present for her from Prince Charles. Everywhere she went she was shadowed by a six-foot-tall bodyguard, Chief Detective Paul Officer, ex-public schoolboy, forty years old and specially valued by Prince Charles because he saved his life when a rating went berserk on a Royal Navy training course at Poole in Dorset and tried to smash a chair over the Prince's head.

'It's all right, I can manage,' Lady Diana said, looking aghast as she was about to pop out to Knightsbridge and Officer had climbed into the passenger seat. Firmly he explained, 'I'm afraid we are part of your life now.'

'It's lovely, isn't it?' the Queen Mother told a crowd of East-enders on the day of the engagement. Easing the horrors of royal life and the task of 'delicate grooming' of her beloved grandson's future wife was the Queen Mother's job; there could be no one better.

Nothing interferes with royal schedules. The Queen left for a world tour knowing she would never see her father King George VI again when he was dying of cancer – and she carried a Letter of Accession in her luggage. By the banks of the Sagana River in Kenya in February 1952, Prince Philip would break the news to the twenty-five-year-old Princess that she was now Queen. He had been told first of the King's death. His equerry Michael Parker would never forget the moment. 'I never felt so sorry for anyone in my life. He looked as if you'd dropped half the world on him.'

For Lady Diana Spencer, her first hurdle was saying goodbye to Prince Charles as he set off on a five-week tour to Australia, New Zealand and America. She would break a royal rule by showing emotion in public. She burst into tears, prompting a member of the royal entourage accompanying the Prince to sniff, 'It really was most touching – but she must learn to keep a stiff upper lip.'

During one of their many long telephone conversations while Charles was in Australia his bride-to-be asked if he was behaving himself. 'Darling,' he replied, 'you know as well as I do if I weren't behaving myself, the whole world would know in two minutes.'

Diana laughed. 'Where there is a will there's a way. You and I managed, didn't we?'

Although she was happy and sparkling in public, the strain was beginning to show. She had to undergo a singularly embarrassing ordeal for a girl of her age and times – a virginity test. It was veiled under the guise of a general gynaecological check to ensure there would be no problems about producing the heir. The royal family had to be discreetly reassured.

Another hazard of the engagement was more than 10,000 thank-you letters to be written. The most elaborate gifts were in the Throne Room at St James's Palace; they included a grand piano, a four-poster bed from Canada, and a couple of Welsh wooden love spoons. A Cupid, sugar tongs and a bon-bon dish from Prince Charles's old nanny, Miss Helen Lightbody, appealed to them especially. The youngest bridesmaid, Clementine Hambro, gave them two white towelling bath robes with their names embroidered on the pockets. Other favourites included two large beehive honey pots, a chicken fryer, a croquet set, a pair of Crown Staffordshire white cockatoos and twenty-four champagne glasses.

A lot of the presents were stored in the cinema at Buckingham Palace where the couple would tiptoe in, hand-in-hand. They appreciated a Raoul Dufy painting from President Mitterrand of France. Diana was less excited by the watercolour, from Lady Tryon, of Vopnafjordur, the fishing lodge in Iceland where the Prince had spent so many happy times with 'Kanga'. Their known presents to each other included for him a diamond-studded photograph frame which he put on his desk with a photograph in it of Diana wearing a green bikini. For the Princess there was handsome jewellery, but specially treasured was a silver frog mascot for her car.

On her first daytime public engagement at Dean Close School in Cheltenham, Nicholas Harvey, a precocious eighteen-year-old, offered her a daffodil and, as he bent low over Lady Diana's hand, asked, 'May I kiss the hand of my future queen?' Lady Diana gave him a warm smile. 'Yes you may,' she said, extending the hand. The other schoolboys laughed and the Queen-to-be giggled. 'You will never live this down.'

Prince Charles was not far away, hovering protectively in his helicopter. He was in Cheltenham too, visiting the local police headquarters, and now joined his fiancée. 'Come on,' he said to her, taking her away from the crowd, 'we are going to talk to the police dogs now.' But already she had given a good performance on this first royal engagement. Soon he would be saying just a little ruefully, 'Stop stealing the show,' but with a smile.

Lady Diana had a beguiling shy charm but when she turned up for her first evening engagement she wore a low-cut decidedly sexy strapless black silk taffeta dress, showing off more than pretty shoulders. Prudence Glynn, fashion editor of *The Times* thought it 'a frightful gaffe'. Admitting, 'I like to shock sometimes,' Lady Diana's cleavage cheered up a chilled crowd on a drizzly evening outside the Goldsmiths' Hall in London where they were attending a special performance in aid of the Royal Opera House. In an unusually chappish aside, Prince Charles had quipped, 'Wait till you get an eyeful of this' to the photographers.

This was no shy simpering kindergarten teacher, but a girl already with the panache and flair of a star in the ascendant. It earned gasps from the crowd and a rocket for Prince Charles from his adoring grandmother who was shocked by the impropriety. 'Wasn't that a mighty feast to set before a king,' remarked the eighty-eight-year-old Lady Diana Cooper. Young admirers used to say that sometimes Diana could have a 'wild country look'. This had hardly been a rustic milkmaid image but one of controlled and sensuous flamboyance. It took a lot of confidence; the occasion revealed much about the future Princess of Wales.

Almost on the eve of the Royal Wedding, she charmed some 2,000 disabled and handicapped guests at a Buckingham Palace garden party where the rain was torrential and heels were sinking into the manicured lawns.

'Yuk,' said the Princess-to-be as she rolled her eyes to the heavens. 'There will be no rain left at this rate. If it is like this in Gibraltar I shall sit down and sulk.' Gibraltar was the first stop on the honeymoon. And to someone else she confided, 'The weather can do what it likes today, but please, please let it be nice on Wednesday,' her wedding day.

Several people gave her single red roses and men their buttonhole carnation. One of the garden party guests was a blind old lady. Diana touched her hand gently, saying, 'Do you want to feel my engagement ring? I'd better not lose it before Wednesday or they won't know who I am.' When asked how many diamonds in the ring, she replied 'thousands'. 'I can't even scratch my nose because it is so big – the ring I mean,' she told admiring crowds. Not a great wearer of jewellery, if you have a ring like that, the giant sapphire surrounded by fourteen diamonds, it would be foolish to clutter up fingers with distractions which could never compete, and to this day, she wears it always and usually alone except for her wedding ring.

Prince Charles followed behind, sucking a cough sweet. Diana glanced back at his pale face. 'Ask him why he is looking so pale,' she joked conspiratorially. It was the afternoon following his stag night, held at White's. Being Prince Charles it had been a quiet, mature affair – dinner for twenty of his closest friends.

Asked if she was nervous about the ceremony, Diana replied, 'I am going to videotape it, then I will be able to run back over the best bits and rub out the part where I say "I will."'

'We had a wedding rehearsal yesterday; everybody was fighting,' she told someone at the garden party. 'I got my heel stuck in a grating in the cathedral and everyone was saying, "Hurry up, Diana!" I said, "I can't . . . I'm stuck".'

When a couple told her they would watch the wedding all day, she warned them with a touch of housewifely cosiness, 'You will get a huge electricity bill.' To someone else, 'Are you a "Crossroads" addict?' and added confidentially, 'I am – sometimes.' She was doing well by just being herself.

But the strain did tell. Five days before the wedding, Lady Diana had burst into tears publicly at a polo match at Tidworth where she was watching Prince Charles. She jumped up suddenly, went bright red and, as Lady Romsey put her arms around her, cried even more. Prince Charles rushed to comfort her, gave her a hug and gently steered her to the car to be taken home. In the excitement of a royal wedding it had been easy to forget the pressure on this young girl constantly in the public eye.

She had just celebrated her twentieth birthday and was bravely facing a fairly daunting future. 'I will just take it as it comes,' she said.

The night before the wedding there was a huge fireworks

display in London's Hyde Park, the biggest since that ordered by George II in 1749 when Handel wrote his 'Music for the Royal Fireworks'. Prince Charles lit the first of 102 bonfires, then 12,000 rockets, mortars and fiery fountains went crescenting over the park. The Prince and royal family were joined by some 500,000 wellwishers.

Diana was spending the evening quietly in Clarence House, and joked, 'We're not allowed to see each other the night before – we might quarrel.' She had hoped desperately to have a giggly hen party with her flatmates, but this special request was turned down; the feeling was that she needed all her rest. Nor was she allowed to have a flatmate as a bridesmaid, though she had begged for this. Palace protocol made it plain that it was too great an honour to be given lightly to these young women. Nevertheless the bride would ensure that her good friends should have the best possible seats in St Paul's.

Prince Charles had said, 'I could not marry anyone the British people wouldn't have liked.' As it happens he could not have married anyone the British people liked more; with the possible exception of the Queen Mother.

CHAPTER 14

The Horses Stepped Bravely

The wedding morning, 29 July 1981. Diana had been up since 6.30 A.M., enjoyed 'an enormous breakfast' instead of her normal tea and sliver of toast, admitting cheerfully, 'It's to stop my tummy rumbling in St Paul's.' Peeking out from a window in Clarence House, she laughed at the huge cheerful crowd carrying on with their all-night party in the Mall, merry with hanging baskets of purple, pink and white petunias, scented with verbena.

Looking bright-eyed, Diana agreed it had been 'a bit difficult' to get much sleep as the crowd kept up their spirits with flasks of coffee, singsongs and dancing the conga all through the night; while some Cambridge undergraduates sat down to a stylish candlelight supper of poached salmon and champagne. Now bright and excited as the bride herself, others put on red, white and blue helmets and punks with shaved heads had painted 'Best wishes Di and Charles' on the back.

'Oh look at that!' The more enterprising were on stilts hoping to get a better view; good-humoured policemen danced and took souvenir photographs of families who had slept the night in the Mall. They now held up posters outside Clarence House saying,

'What a Guy, Di' and made her laugh. Her calm, her gaiety were quite infectious that morning. Not a hint of nervousness.

First to arrive was Kevin Shanley, her hairdresser, who worked intently dressed in T-shirt and jeans, with his wife Claire as his assistant. Diana chivvied him, 'You'll need a tie today, Kevin.' The simplicity of her hairstyle was appealing, but it was too fly-away under the delicate Spencer family tiara.

Her refusal to have a lacquered, elaborate hairstyle was an early show of spirit. Not for her a royal Princess Anne hairdo off the face. Instead she kept her beloved fringe – something to hide behind when the eyes of 750 million television viewers round the world were on her. But today a confident Princess wears her much blonder hair layered short and sophisticated.

She grew heartily sick of that simple bob and fringe.

Barbara Daly, one of *Vogue*'s favourite beauticians, made her way past the Victoria Memorial, a riot of colour with 14,000 geraniums, and moved through the crowd clustered optimistically outside the black wrought-iron gates at Clarence House. Inside on the second floor of the Queen Mother's house she found a chirpy, relaxed bride-to-be. Weeks before the wedding Diana had asked specifically for a natural make-up close to her own complexion. Now dipping into her black Asprey holdall of natural powder, eyeshadows and creams to tone down a flush, Barbara Daly, a gentle and soothing presence, worked expertly creating a masterpiece in forty-five minutes.

As coffee was brought in for the team, Lady Diana took a telephone call. Laughing and blushing, everyone quickly knew it was 'Mr Renfrew'. As Diana talked, she abstractedly began to take her hair rollers out one by one, giving Shanley 'fifty fits'. The secret was to leave the heated rollers in until cool; then he would remove them and brush the hair into shape. Perhaps this explains why at the end of the day her style was a bit too natural – as if the bride had spent the day on a grouse moor, prompting Dame Rebecca West to remark that she looked 'like a thatched cottage'.

Outside the excitement was building up as the highspirited crowd tried to reach the banners fluttering from the lampposts with their decorative Prince of Wales gold feathers; others waved thousands of Union flags like wands as though by magic they might make the bride appear. Lady Diana suddenly became rather quiet. The time had come to put on the wedding dress; her hair and make-up were done except for the lip gloss.

Mrs Nina Missetzis, the fifty-eight-year-old Greek seamstress who had single-handedly cut out and stitched the famous wedding dress, will always remember the moment when it went on for the last time. 'Lady Diana cried . . . and shivered . . . and there were tears in her eyes.'

'Oh thank you, Nina, thank you.' She gave the delighted needlewoman, whose right thumb and forefinger are permanently bent from holding a needle, an appreciative kiss on the cheek.

The dress had worried Mrs Missetzis, keeping her awake at night because Diana kept losing weight; at the final fitting, the waistline had to be taken in a quarter of an inch on either side. Now her best thank you was a seat in St Paul's; she had never expected to be invited to the wedding. It was more difficult to thank the silk worms at Lullingstone Silk Farm, the only one of its kind in the country. Fed from a vintage harvest of Dorset and Somerset mulberry leaves, they had contributed the raw silk from English-reared cocoons.

Embroidered with tiny pearls and sequins, the dress had the sweetness of a Gainsborough painting. The wide frilled and scooped neckline and flouncy lace-trimmed sleeves with taffeta bows had an engaging simplicity. Each sleeve had a lace-edged heart and a diamond pattern stitched in sequins. 'Something blue' was a small blue bow in the waistband: something borrowed, her mother's diamond and pearl drop earrings and, for good luck, a tiny gold horseshoe studded with diamonds.

There were those who hated the dress with its twenty-five-foot-long matching train edged with sparkling lace, the longest in royal wedding history. It would span out over the 697 feet of red carpet in St Paul's, and her veil of ivory tulle would be as long as the train. It was not traditional white but Lady Diana had deliberately chosen ivory silk paper taffeta and old creamy lace which had belonged to Queen Mary. She thought their subtle colour would be more flattering against her skin which tended to go slightly pink with any excitement.

The designers Elizabeth and David Emmanuel, who have since broken up, were criticised for creating such an unwieldy vast crinoline skirt, its layers of ivory tulle billowing out from the bride's tiny waist making the least of a new spectacularly thin figure. By contrast, when the Duchess of York married in 1986, the bride, despite her problem figure, looked ravishingly slim in a white dress made in a far more classical style. Perhaps the Emmanuels tried too hard.

'My dear, you look simply enchanting.' The Queen Mother suddenly appeared. She had been relishing all the pre-wedding excitement and was one of the privileged few to have a first glimpse of the bride. Now the Glass Coach was waiting: footmen in ER crested jackets with gold pompom buttons and lace jabots were brushing imaginary specks of fluff from their immaculate uniforms as they waited for the bride to appear.

The postilions' silver breastplates had been polished so the sun glinted and danced on this royal livery buffed through the centuries with loving care.

That morning, before dawn, royal coachman Richard Boland was in the Royal Mews grooming the two bays, Lady Penelope and Kestrel, who would pull the Glass Coach which had carried the Queen to her own wedding. Making sure that the horses stepped bravely and together at the regulation eight miles an hour would need all his concentration during the two-mile procession to St Paul's. The four Oldenberg Greys which would pull the Edward VII State Postilion Landau on the return journey to the Palace had been given their final music lessons. Arthur Showell, Head Royal Coachman, said, 'The great thing is getting them to stand still when the Household Cavalry goes galloping by . . . Any fool can make the horses go forward.'

The wedding ceremonial was masterminded by the Lord Chamberlain the late Lord Maclean, 'Just call me oyster eyes', a great favourite with the royal family. Asked what plans had been made in case of rain on the day of the wedding, he replied briskly, 'If it rains, our plan is to get wet.' But the bride had a nineteenth-century parasol shaped like a pagoda which had been found in an old trunk in Bideford in Devon and it was covered in lace and silk to match her dress.

Meticulous about Court behaviour, after the Duke of Windsor's funeral in 1972, Lord Maclean was most correct and did not bow to the Duchess of Windsor who flew back to Paris feeling even huffier. He had organised Princess Anne's wedding and was an hilarious stand-in for the Queen during rehearsals. As titular head of the Queen's Household, this distinguished courtier had always been a familiar figure in his Thistle Robes, bearing his white rod of office on ceremonial occasions. This wand is ritually broken over the grave of the sovereign it has served. Other duties of the Lord Chamberlain include the care of the Queen's swans. Everything in royal ceremonial is planned. Even the colours of the flowers on the royal wedding route were to be blue, pink and mauve with silver-leaf; no red to clash with the uniforms.

The maroon and scarlet gold-trimmed door of the Glass Coach was shut very gently by smiling white-gloved footmen. The steps were taken away. The gates of Clarence House swung back. Inside the Glass Coach, the bride in a cocoon of ivory silk sang 'Just One Cornetto' to amuse her father and keep herself calm as they cantered to St Paul's on scarlet and gold wheels.

CHAPTER 15

'You Go First, Johnny'

At St Paul's, her veil flew over her head as a mischievous gust of summer wind whipped up the spangled tulle dotted with ten thousand tiny hand-embroidered mother-of-pearl sequins. She had climbed the twenty-four steps to the West Door followed by two of her bridesmaids anxiously shepherding her huge unwieldy train. Quietly she asked the designers David and Elizabeth Emmanuel, 'Am I ready?' as they fussed with the dress in full view of the camera. Perhaps they realised that this silk had not been such a good idea. Already it was beginning to look like crumpled tissue paper.

'Is he here yet?' Diana asked her little bridesmaids as she hovered by the West Door, and they were not sure whether she meant Prince Charles or Earl Spencer.

Lady Sarah Armstrong-Jones, seventeen, hair drawn back like a ballerina, poised, graceful, was keeping an eye on Clementine Hambro, the youngest bridesmaid and a great-granddaughter of Sir Winston Churchill. This four-year-old had been a pet of Diana's at the Pimlico kindergarten. As the day wore on her headdress of fresh pink roses and yellow freesias twined with ivy fronds would go awry on slippery fresh-washed hair.

The other bridesmaids included two of the Prince's goddaughters, Catherine Cameron, six, and thirteen-year-old India Hicks, a granddaughter of Lord Mountbatten; ten-year-old Sarah-Jane Gaselee was his trainer's daughter. They all wore ballerina-length Victorian-style dresses with old gold silk taffeta sashes and a lace flounce at the elbow. They were based closely on the wedding dress. Even the shoes were of old gold twill to match their sashes.

The pages, Edward Van Cutsem and Lord Nicholas Windsor, seemed grown up with their short gold-hilted dirks hung from their belts. Their indigo blue cloth tailcoats with white cord on the collar were copies of 1863 full dress Royal Naval Cadets' uniforms with cap badges in gold wire. They looked uncannily like children in sepia photographs of Alexis the Tsarevich, son of the last Tsar.

Prince Charles had arrived to a trumpet fanfare by Purcell. Even though in full naval dress uniform, he looked boyishly pink as if he had been up since dawn and had taken at least two showers. Seeing the Archbishop of Canterbury waiting to greet him, his face lit up and he made one of his little jokes. 'I like you in silver,' he told Dr Runcie, admiring the prelate's festive robes. Then to his supporters, his two brothers Prince Andrew and Prince Edward, 'You both ready? Right, come on then.'

When they reached the altar, he winked at Marina Ogilvy his fourteen-year-old wayward second cousin and made her giggle. As he waited at the altar, he turned and gave his parents a rather wan smile. He had once said that the Queen and Prince Philip were 'very wise and incredibly sensible parents . . . They have been so happy. I only hope I will be as lucky.' There was the slightest tic at the corner of his mouth.

The cathedral was a sea of pretty hats and there was an air of hushed expectancy. Most of the 2,500 wedding guests had been in their seats since 9.30 A.M., the women enjoying the clothes and whispered gossip, envying Mediterranean guests who had brought fans to keep cool in the scented heat. The flowers had been arranged by Diana's godmother, Lady Mary Colman.

'Oh, isn't that Prince Claus of the Netherlands?' The German husband of Queen Beatrix, known as 'Trix', was looking undoubtedly handsome but rather withdrawn; then the grandly swaying Queen Margrethe of Denmark in purple; she loves outrageously high heels though rather tall. She was followed by the late King Olav of Norway, looking every inch a king with his white hair and courtly ways – a loud whisper 'always think he and the Queen Mother should have married' – then more crowned heads: the King of Sweden; King Baudouin of Belgium and his Queen Fabiola serene in gold and cream, 'such a pity they never had children'. The former headmaster of Cheam who had once whacked Prince Charles was there, and Spike Milligan of the Goons in quite ordinary morning dress.

There was a lot of blue around that day. The bride's mother the Hon. Mrs Frances Shand Kydd was lightly elegant in hyacinth blue. In the royal carriage on the way from the wedding she and Prince Philip laughed and joked; they looked a rather perfect couple themselves. 'I can't believe the weather,' he said happily.

The Queen was in a floating, crêpe-de-Chine pleated aquamarine dress. Princess Anne always has a talent to surprise and was in a white silk wrapover dress sprigged with yellow flowers, her hat a delicious confection, though the French suggested she looked like an 'omelette norvégienne': a sweet omelette topped with a scoop of ice-cream.

The bride's sisters did her credit. Lady Jane Fellowes was in a poppy red silk crêpe-de-Chine sailor suit and the red-headed sister Sarah, now Mrs Neil McCorquodale, chose minty green cool chiffon.

Among the crowned heads of Europe, world statesmen and aristocratic guests, some two hundred royal retainers took their places: gardeners and gamekeepers, ladies' maids and butlers, grooms and cooks, many with years of devoted service, watched in fascination the African leaders in splendid off-the-shoulder striped robes. Nancy Reagan the American President's wife wore a white stetson. Actress Susan George, invited because of her discretion, wore a curious heavily sequinned dress and vast picture hat.

Princess Grace of Monaco was in ivory with a cocoa straw hat. This would be the last time she would be seen by the couple who were fond of this former American film star who had shown warmth and understanding behind a façade of cool beauty. Morning dress or something more formal was favoured by most visiting heads of State but President Mitterrand of France struck a democratic note in a lounge suit. The King of Tonga had a special chair to take his bulk.

The wait for the bride seemed interminable. The Queen Mother in flowered apple green georgette, occasionally dabbed her cheeks with a lace handkerchief and remarked to Prince Andrew, 'So you are looking after me today?' as if the standard could not be expected to match that set by her favourite grandson Charles.

Prince Philip often gives the impression of being slightly jumpy when one of his sons is appearing in public as if half-expecting them to do some 'damn silly thing'. Now he seemed stretched and strained. But the Queen Mother leaning towards him whispered, 'I remember your wedding.' He gave a rueful grin.

The music was wonderful and this sustained Prince Charles who had enjoyed being impresario at his own wedding. He had planned the ceremony with the same love for detail, Germanic precision and intensity as his great-great-great-grandfather Prince Albert. St Paul's was chosen, he explained, because 'musically speaking, it is such a magnificent setting and the whole acoustics are so spectacular with a ten- or eleven-second after-note.' He hoped to have a lump in his throat, especially when one of his favourite hymns, 'Christ the Sure Foundation' was sung by the Bach Choir. Diana had asked if they could be dressed in soft frilly white blouses for the day. Besides, Prince Charles has always loved Christopher Wren's cathedral with its Grinling Gibbons interior; and if any further reason was needed for his preference, it could hold 2,500 wedding guests, five hundred more than could be squeezed into Westminster Abbey, the conventional choice for royal and society weddings.

Everybody from the Queen – who had said, 'Please do take your time, Johnny' – to his chauffeur, had worried about the strain of the wedding on fifty-seven-year-old Earl Spencer. But he is a great one for last moments with his daughters before giving them away and insisted on being at St Paul's. Now he was delivering his daughter to the royal family as promised. When told that Prince Charles had proposed, he had cautioned Diana, 'You must only marry the man you love.' She replied speedily,

'That is what I am doing.' He had been full of foreboding before the wedding, saying miserably, 'I'm afraid I'll never see my daughter again you know. No, I don't think I'll see her again.' But he underestimated her spirit. If anything father and daughter became closer after the marriage.

He stepped gingerly from the Glass Coach and, leaning heavily on the arm of an usher, haltingly began the long tortuous climb up the granite steps, their sternness masked that day by red carpet. Since the cerebral haemorrhage three years earlier, he suffered from a slight limp and this had worried him: 'Just pray I get up the aisle without spoiling her day.' Now he was near the West Door, a welcome sight, with banks of pink and purple flowers where his daughter waited.

Gently she asked him, 'Do you want to hold my arm as well for a moment?' He replied breathily, 'I'm all right, really I am,' but she slipped her arm into his, holding her bouquet in her other hand, a creamy cascade of yellow roses, freesias, lily of the valley with a sprig of myrtle for luck grown from a cutting from Queen Victoria's wedding bouquet.

The clock struck eleven and from the Whispering Gallery massed trumpets played Jeremiah Clarke's Trumpet Voluntary joined by 7,080 pipes of the cathedral organ. Earl Spencer gave the word, 'Walk now, shall we? Here we go, go slowly.' It was heroic tingling music cleverly chosen by Prince Charles, who had joked with Diana at a rehearsal, 'You have to have something stirring, dramatic and noisy because if you have something quiet you start hearing your ankles cricking, you know what I mean.'

'Here we go.' Lord Spencer's brave words have become immortal on Britain's football fields, but now they were being whispered to a young daughter with an aura of pre-Raphaelite enchantment. At the sound of the swish of her silk dress he pleaded 'Go slowly.' It was a peerless performance, though afterwards Diana confessed, 'I was so nervous I hardly knew what I was doing.' She wore ivory silk wedding slippers with tiny fluted Louis heels so she would not tower over her husband; the soles, edged in gold, were made of suede so she would not slip. The femininity of the tight-bodiced dress, the huge puffed sleeves and her stillness gave her the air of a Tudor princess. Beneath the veil was still the distinctive blonde head with the short modern bob and girlish fringe giving shelter at times to those large expressive blue eyes and that shy contained smile which touched hearts with its vulnerability.

It was still a three-and-a-half-minute walk away. 'Tell me when to turn,' murmured Charles to youngest brother Edward, who half turned to the aisle, keeping an eye out for the bride. 'She's nearly here,' replied Edward on cue – he would be good in the theatre – and then whispered urgently to the bridegroom, 'She's here.' The Queen smiled at her eldest son and was so enjoying herself she quite forgot to wear her 'Miss Piggy' face.

Prince Charles turned round and when he saw the bride gave her a look of such pride and that almost rueful half smile which makes him so like his father. He waited while she and her father parted at the altar steps, Diana just stopping herself from giving him a kiss on the cheek.

Earl Spencer turned away to find his seat alone. It was a moving moment as he searched for his wife, Raine, trying to catch her eye but first meeting those of his ex-wife with her chic confidence. Then he spotted Countess Spencer, in a less good seat further back. She beamed back congratulations and suddenly his face lit up. His struggle to stay strong had been there for all to see. Now he would take his place in a seat of honour with Mrs Shand Kydd opposite the Queen and Prince Philip.

Prince Charles, with a look of delight, said softly to Diana, 'Hold my hand.' Then as they stood together they leaned slightly towards each other and could have been quite alone in all St Paul's. They looked at each other constantly and touched fingers. Her voice had all the lightness of a twenty-year-old as she said, 'I will,' following the Prince's deeper and more certain affirmation. After the vows, suddenly, from outside the cathedral, there was wild applause sounding like a rhythmic wave, for a huge crowd of 600,000 people had invited themselves to the wedding and many were listening to the service on the relay system.

In the reverent silence in the cathedral both families had to be content with just a little clearing of the throat and warm looks. A Coldstream Guardsman fainted, still to attention.

Endearingly both made mistakes during the vows. The bride got the names just slightly wrong: 'I, Diana Frances, take thee Philip Charles . . .' a quicksilver smile spread along the Spencer family row. The loyal flatmates in saucy pillboxes and smart frocks looked down. Lady Diana had almost married herself to Prince Philip by getting her husband's names in the wrong order.

But now Prince Charles was saying those beautiful words: 'With this ring I thee wed; with my body I thee honour, and all my . . .' – here there was a little dithering about his worldly goods, and he, too, was hesitant. He had generously agreed to share Diana's own goods with her, but not his own. Princess Anne joked later that he meant it – it was not a mistake at all. A wry look from the Queen at her son: his annual income was £538,000 at the time, and one day he will be one of the world's richest men.

The kindly Archbishop later consolingly suggested that Prince Charles's hesitation evened the score: 'I make that fifteen all.'

The bride refused to obey. Nothing could persuade her to change her mind even though there was some pleasant academic argument about the word 'obey' merely replacing the medieval bride's promise to be 'bonny and buxom at bed and board'. Nothing would make her budge, and later in the marriage when she seemed self-willed, the wise remembered this moment on the wedding day.

Prince Charles then slipped the ring on her finger, a slim band from a buttery nugget of exceptionally rich Welsh gold. Mined in Clogau, Gwynedd, North Wales in 1923, it has been used for the Queen's, Queen Mother's, Princess Margaret's and Princess Anne's wedding rings.

'Well done,' Prince Charles whispered. 'We are married at last.' The newlyweds sat as close together as possible on the red velvet stools placed on the dais. They listened as the Welsh Speaker of the House, the Right Honourable George Thomas, read: 'Though I speak with the tongues of men and angels' – the Lesson from 1 Corinthians, chapter 13 – 'The greatest of these is charity.' The couple smiled indulgently. Thomas looked splendid in black velvet breeches and a jacket studded with silver buttons. He peered over his spectacles, and his musical voice lent a magic as he lingered over the words 'cymbal' and 'body'.

A lyrical speaker himself, the Archbishop of Canterbury began: 'Here is the stuff of which fairy-tales are made,' but went on to define a good marriage in the poet Edwin Muir's words: 'Each asks from each other what each most wants to give and each awakes in each what else would never be.'

However, he warned them that '. . . no matter how lovely and euphoric those days of marriage,' there was a huge danger of it going sour if 'the bride and groom simply gaze obsessively at one another.' Prince Charles looked solemn, but it was clear that at that particular moment, while having the greatest respect for the Archbishop, he doubted if he would ever tire of looking at the Princess.

Prince Philip looked as if he thought a great deal of 'obsessive gazing' would go on for years. But the Archbishop was right. After ten years, when the Prince is no longer seen putting an arm round his wife's waist or kissing her hand, there has been the known difficulty of finding a mental bond as the chemistry lost its intensity.

At the end of the ceremony, the couple followed by both sets of parents disappeared into the vestry to sign the Register. The bride signed herself 'Diana Spencer, Spinster,' and her husband 'Charles Princeps'.

In a dress of rainbow colours the opera singer Kiri Te Kanawa, New Zealand's most famous export, sang the aria from Handel's *Samson*, 'Let the Bright Seraphim'. Her voice soaring to the mosaic Dome, glittering with amethyst and lapis lazuli, she seemed to set the emerald-winged angels dancing.

As they came out, Earl Spencer had for a second blocked Ruth Lady Fermoy's way, but she smiled gently; she had always liked this son-in-law.

Now the famous St Paul's Cathedral Choir, with eighteen men and thirty boys looking all crisp and groomed in sparkling white-starched ruffs and black surplices, hair cut by Vidal Sassoon, sang the Parry anthem 'I Was Glad'. And then everyone except the Queen herself sang the National Anthem with gusto and descants.

The Princess, the first English bride of the heir to the throne for more than three hundred years – the last was Lady Anne Hyde, wife of King James II – now lifted her veil off her face and looked cool in the intense heat. Barbara Daly had been in an ante-chamber with her box of goodies and cooling eau-de-cologne pads to retouch the bridal make-up.

The Princess of Wales at 21 by Snowdon.

Above left: The famous wedding kiss, the first ever on Buckingham Palace balcony.

Far left: Part of the honeymoon was spent at Balmoral, August 1981.

Left: Dancing at the Southern Cross Hotel in Australia, October 1985.

Above: Taking Prince William home from hospital, June 1982.

Right: At a polo match at Werribee Park, Australia, October 1985. The Prince has always liked dangerous sports.

Above: An informal photo call with Prince William in New Zealand.
Below left: With Prince William and Prince Harry at Highgrove, 1988.
Below right: The Princess takes the young princes to a carol concert, December 1989.

Above: The competitive Princess winning the mothers' race at Prince William's school sports day.

Below left: The Princess met this rabbit during a day-long visit to Portsmouth in October 1990.

Below right: Cartier Polo Match, 1989.

Above left: Lady Tryon with Prince Charles. An old friend, she asked him to be godfather to her son, Charles.

Above: The Princess and her brother, Viscount Althorp, leave San Lorenzo, a favourite Knightsbridge restaurant.

Left: Pushing a trolley round Tesco in Southport, the Princess, as patron of Birthright, launched a booklet on healthy eating for pregnant women.

Right: On tour in Nigeria, 1990.

Above left: At Princess Eugènie's christening with Prince William, December 1990.

Above right: At the America's Cup Ball, September 1986.

Below: A family holiday in the Virgin Islands, April 1990.

The royal couple paused; the Prince gravely bowed to his mother, the new Princess curtsied with grace, bringing a look of tenderness to a smiling Queen. The Princess was now the third most important royal woman in the land, curtsying only to the Queen and the Queen Mother.

'Well, I'm glad that bit's over,' Diana gave a sigh of relief. But Prince Charles, with his royal training, had enjoyed every minute of the ceremonial and, seeing it all in quite a different light, replied, 'Yes, it's a marvellous sensation, isn't it.'

Slowly the newlyweds began the long walk down the aisle to the West Door as a fanfare sounded and the orchestra played Elgar's 'Pomp and Circumstance March' and then Walton's 'Crown Imperial'. As they moved closely together, Prince Charles pointed to friends on either side, whispering, 'Isn't it lovely?' – to which she replied, 'Oh, everything is lovely.' But he wanted more reassurance, asking 'Are you enjoying it? What do you make of your big day?' But she just smiled.

In the coach on the way to the Palace, the bride's drop earrings bobbing as she looked up at people leaning precariously from office windows, Prince Charles suddenly remembered something vital. 'Did I tell you, you look wonderful?' and she blushed: 'Wonderful for you.'

'A simple, natural girl with the large and tender heart of a woman' – this had been a description of a Princess of Wales in 1862, later Queen Alexandra. The two brides would share a natural beauty and easy charm but this Princess of Wales would surprise.

Leaving St Paul's, the Queen turned solicitously to Lord Spencer and smiled at her former equerry: 'You go first, Johnny.'

A thousand doves fluttered up to a blue sky as the newlyweds travelled from St Paul's down Fleet Street and along the Strand in their open coach. In amongst the postilions wearing Ascot Livery, the scarlet, purple and gold of the Queen's racing colours, an armed policeman lurked. He looked like any other policeman except that he was wearing pink silk stockings, gold-buckled shoes, scarlet plush knee breeches, a wig and tricorne hat with an ostrich feather. He would ride protectively behind the newlyweds in the State Landau which was also surrounded by the Household

Cavalry. Tucked somewhere in his scarlet and gold frock-coat, with its lace jabot, was a .36 Smith & Wesson revolver.

Soon after one o'clock, the lace-curtained doors on the balcony at Buckingham Palace opened and the crowd went wild. 'Princess Di, Princess Di,' they shouted and 'We want Charlie.' They had obviously missed the Court Circular which stressed that the bride should be known only as the Princess of Wales. She was a bit diffident, a bit overwhelmed, but Prince Charles took her by the hand and urged her to 'Go ahead and wave.' Inside, close friends and family drank vintage Krug champagne.

Emotional and incredibly happy, Prince Charles said afterwards, 'Neither of us will ever forget the atmosphere, it was electric, almost unbelievable. It was something quite extraordinary . . . It made me proud to be British.'

The second time the couple appeared, the crowd shouted for the Queen to join them, and then for the best-loved person in Britain: 'We want the Queen Mum.' Out she came to another roar of approval. There had been a worry that she would not be at the wedding because of a leg ulcer and high temperature, but with a softly spoken, 'I wouldn't miss this for anything' she had made her intentions clear.

Then for the newlyweds the most enthusiastic call of all: 'Kiss her, kiss her, kiss her' – something that would seem so natural in an ordinary family. So in his old-fashioned courtly way, the gentle Prince Charles kissed her hand, just as he might the Queen's at polo. But this was not what this cheery highspirited crowd had in mind and on the fourth appearance on the balcony they shouted their instructions again: 'Kiss her properly.'

Prince Andrew, abandoning with relief his serious role as Principal Supporter, whispered in the bridegroom's ear, but got a sharp, 'I am not going to do that caper' reply. Instead Prince Charles turned to his wife. 'They are trying to get us to kiss.' The Princess raised her hand in the air, 'Why ever not?' Prince Charles flashed a quick look at the Queen who was diplomatically busy with a grandchild.

He leant forward and kissed his bride lovingly on the lips, the first-ever public kiss on the Buckingham Palace balcony. Little Clementine Hambro was heartily bored when the 'soppy kissing' began. The Churchillian spirit deserting her completely, she rested her head on her arm but clung on with the other hand to the bride.

The crowd could not ask for more so the royal couple went inside. Lord Lichfield was the photographer, and by now the Princess was beginning to wilt, a little tired. Prince Charles pulled funny faces at her from behind Lichfield's back to make her laugh, something Prince Philip did many years before when he felt that the Queen was looking far too serious in public. In contrast to the usual wedding photographs in which the newlyweds so often look stilted and solemn, there is one delicious picture of the Princess and her bridesmaids collapsing in laughter which captures the gaiety she would bring to monarchy. Prince Charles and his brothers are grinning and it is like a modern Fragonard painting with tumbling bridesmaids like playful cherubs in satin and silk dotted amongst baskets of wedding flowers.

The royal wedding breakfast was a classic of its kind. There were a dozen round tables laid with white tablecloths and gold plate, and decorated with white orchids from Singapore. The one hundred and eighteen guests ate brill quenelles with lobster sauce, then a Suprême de Volaille, which was chicken breast stuffed and covered in brioche crumbs, sautéed in butter and sprinkled with samphire, the Norfolk coastal herb which is only in season for a very few months in the summer. The royal family never like sitting for long over meals and even on this special day they were at the pudding stage, strawberries and Cornish cream, in ninety minutes flat.

The initials C and D had been carved in old script on the royal wedding cake with a miniature bridal bouquet of white flowers, grapes symbolising prosperity and doves for peace and happiness. They cut this five-tiered confection with the Prince's dress sword. A delicate masterpiece, this was not the creation of a young cordon bleu chef but of burly Naval ratings. It took four men four hours to weigh and mix the cake, and the baking an afternoon and a night – all of it masterminded by Chief Petty Officer David Avery, thirty-eight, a master baker at Chatham Dockyard. It had a layer of fifty pounds of marzipan, forty-nine pounds of white icing, royal of course, and a quarter-pint of dark naval rum. Every single glacé cherry had been checked individually.

Those not invited to the royal family party made their own

arrangements. Lady Tryon took sixty-five friends to the San Lorenzo Restaurant in Knightsbridge. When asked why she had not been invited to the Palace, she replied, 'I do not feel offended . . . I know Mrs Parker-Bowles wasn't invited either; she is holding a party for friends.'

The bride's three flatmates, sad that the days of their special closeness had come to an end, held a small party. They knew now that the flat they had all shared was to be sold.

CHAPTER 16

'This Will Cool You Down'

———————————◆———————————

The royal family stood in the courtyard, ready to pelt the bride and groom with fresh rose petals and pearly grains of rice as they left for Waterloo Station. The Princess's going away outfit was a rather fussy dress and bolero jacket by Belville Sassoon in coral, with a frilly white organdie collar and cuffs and a side slit in the skirt – not an outfit she would choose today. It was all complemented by a funny little slightly Edwardian hat trimmed with a flighty feather, and in an unusual sharing sisterly moment the Princess had removed her sister Sarah's three-strand Spencer teardrop pendant pearl choker at the end of the wedding breakfast and put it round her own neck.

Attached to the stately carriage were twenty silver heart-shaped balloons, shiny in the fading sunshine. A 'Just Married' sign daubed in red lipstick and decorated with C and D initials and hearts and arrows had been tied to the back, the work of the Princes Andrew and Edward. The Queen looked at it with an expression of 'Well I never!'

Prince Charles held his wife's hand tightly, proprietorially resting it on her knee. Her wave had been rather tentative at first, but then as they pulled out of the courtyard, she began to gain confidence; she lifted her chin and started giving Prince Charles a few shy humorous glances.

About to board the train standing at Platform 12, the Princess impulsively kissed Lord Maclean – 'A lovely surprise,' he was later to remark – as she thanked him for creating her perfect day. The train called 'Broadlands' left ten minutes late. 'Mind the step, Diana,' Prince Charles whispered to his wife, who still had rose petals clinging to the back of her skirt.

The carriage was filled with red and white carnations, and patriotic blue cornflowers. In the royal sitting room with its scarlet upholstery there was a wireless, fruit and champagne, but all the royal couple asked the steward for was a pot of tea for two. Six silver teapots were in waiting.

The first three nights of their honeymoon were spent at Broadlands in Romsey, Hampshire, ninety miles from London, where the Queen had spent her wedding night thirty-three years before. Bells were pealing a welcome from the Abbey and the churches in the old market town as the couple drove half a mile to the eighteenth-century moated country house. Broadlands had been the home of the late Lord Mountbatten. Adored by Prince Charles, there could be no more perfect place for his married life to begin. A staff of six chosen for their discretion and experience looked after them. During the day, Charles and Diana swam and walked or watched videos of their wedding, blushing and laughing at their mistakes.

From their bedroom, the chintzy pink-and-blue Portico Room with its four-poster bed, the couple had a view of the River Test meandering through watercress meadows. It is one of Hampshire's finest for salmon. The curtains, the chaise-longue, the comfortable wickerwork chairs in the window and the squashy armchair were all in historic chintz with the finely outlined profiles of a young Queen Victoria and her beloved Albert. The material had been ordered for the old Royal Yacht in 1854.

Prince Charles took his young wife round this light airy house he knew so well, with its elegant oval Adam ceilings, collection of Van Dycks in the dining room, alcoves of porcelain appreciated by the Princess, the Wedgwood room with its classic friezes and Empire-style furniture, and the Lely portraits of court beauties staring back at a Princess of Wales soon to be the most photo-graphed and fashionable woman in the western world.

They walked hand-in-hand by the river. Intuitive and tactful, the Princess appreciated on the second day that her husband wanted to fish alone and enjoy perhaps a little pleasant melancholy thinking of his beloved mentor. She stayed in bed while the Prince, after a breakfast of eggs, bacon, sausages, kedgeree and kidneys took himself off to tickle a few trout. She occasionally would go to the saloon, its delicate gilt classic decoration reflecting her own light touch, and play some Grieg on the piano.

On the night of the wedding, the royal family had fun at an informal party organised by the Queen's cousin, Lady Elizabeth 'effervescent' Anson. The Queen could hardly bear to be dragged away to have scrambled eggs and bacon she was so enjoying a television re-run of the wedding. She stayed until 1 A.M., un-usually late for her, did a little jig on her own and was obviously reluctant to leave. Prince Philip wore a boater with 'Charles and Diana' written across the hatband.

There were ten thousand street parties in Britain on the night of the wedding and beacons lit up the night sky from Northumber-land to Cornwall. Moved by this young girl's grace, touched by her confusion over the vows, people who did not talk to each other normally found themselves saying to strangers on trains and at bus stops: 'rather good' . . . 'makes you proud'. No other country has a better way of doing things.

When asked afterwards at what stage did the Prince and Princess of Wales get the idea that the wedding ceremony was a huge success, rivalled only by the Coronation and Queen Victoria's Diamond Jubilee, and actually begin to enjoy it for themselves, the question prompted a really honest outburst from the Princess: 'Enjoy something like that? It was terrifying. Such a long walk up that aisle for a start.'

But Prince Charles, with all his royal training, moved smoothly in with emollient phrases. 'I did enjoy it enormously,' he said. 'I was carried along on this wave of enormous friendliness and enthusiasm' – tactfully paying tribute to the crowds. 'I'd really like to do it all again.' 'My father says that the whole time,' his wife added with a smile.

On the evening of the wedding the beautician Barbara Daly

was at home when the telephone rang. It was the Princess. 'I just wanted to thank you, Barbara,' she said. It was, recalled this usually phlegmatic girl, 'the most wonderful staggering thing at the end of a day like that. Getting married is stressful for most people, but to remember on that first evening of her honeymoon to telephone . . . amazing, she is an absolute honey.'

On the third day Prince Charles took the controls of a fairly ancient propeller-driven RAF Andover of the Queen's Flight and piloted his wife from Eastleigh Airport to Gibraltar. The Spanish in Madrid had been annoyed about the royal couple beginning their honeymoon in Gibraltar, where they would board the Royal Yacht *Britannia* for a sybaritic Mediterranean cruise. The King of Spain, Juan Carlos, though a good friend had not been at their wedding because of Spanish resentment that the British still own this rock just off the Spanish mainland which they seized in 1704. However, the people of Gibraltar did not share this grumpy peevishness and loved seeing the royal couple whizzing round the Rock for a day in a sporty brown Triumph Stag.

Guests were invited on board *Britannia* for drinks before she sailed that evening and found a young couple 'who stood hand-in-hand . . . and kept looking into each other's eyes' while they chatted in the English chintzy country house atmosphere. The Princess kept peering out of the porthole, 'very moved by the welcome,' Lady Hassan, wife of the Governor of Gibraltar, re-called. 'She was quite overwhelmed by it all . . . and tears welled in her eyes.'

The Princess sipped a Pimms. Though not fond of alcohol, she admitted later that she liked this fruity cocktail and 'got particu-larly addicted to them on my honeymoon . . . But that is the only thing I got addicted to.' She is not averse to the little *double entendre*, public school asides, teasing remarks which usually end with chasing round the room hurling cushions and bread rolls.

As the sun went down, a romantic flotilla of four hundred small boats escorted *Britannia* out to sea and the real honeymoon. By candlelight the newlyweds had a delicious supper of lobster and fresh fruit at a table covered with old Irish linen which had once belonged to the *Victoria and Albert*.

For much of the time, they lazed together on the verandah deck, hand-in-hand, sunbathing. But the Princess, naturally exuberant, often dashed about in a skimpy bikini thinking of pranks or pouring ice-cubes on the Prince's suntanned stomach, saying, 'This will cool you down.' At night they were informal, Diana wearing a simple long cotton dress and some of her new jewellery, while he wore tropical mess kit.

Sleepy and companionable they might watch a film. The Queen had instructed her equerry, Squadron Leader Adam Wise, to arrange nine up-to-date films which included the latest James Bond, *For Your Eyes Only*, and the award-winning *Chariots of Fire*. On board there was also a Rolls-Royce.

The Prince went on with his bachelor routine, a nap in the afternoon and exercises last thing at night. The Princess would be a tactful wife and go off to prowl the deck, saying to anyone who passed, 'He's doing his exercises, I must leave him alone.'

'It's him – he's asleep again,' the Princess would laugh on the way to the fridge to get some ice-cream and point to the royal bedroom on board the Royal Yacht. The couple had had a queen-sized double bed installed having been warned by Princess Anne who, on her honeymoon with Captain Mark Phillips, had to inventively tie two single beds together.

There was a certain innocent sauciness about the Princess which enchanted most of the men aboard. Still not yet too aware of royal protocol, she thought nothing of wandering about on deck in a diaphanous peach negligée. She laughed once when, walking into the messroom, she found some of the crew sitting with towels round their middles having just had a shower. 'It's all right,' the Princess laughed, 'I'm a married woman, aren't I?' a provocative mixture of *ingénue* and flirt.

It was a heady experience and great fun to be the centre of attraction to so many men, 276 altogether, officers and crew. The 'shy Di' of a few days ago was starting to disappear. Already she was more confident, sexually aware, newly slim, a glamorous young woman and loving every minute of the attention. There was not much female competition on board, except for Evelyn Dagley her dresser.

By day the honeymooners explored coves and ate elegant picnics from old-fashioned wickerwork hampers. The Prince never swam in the sea, although his wife did; it was all a fairly elaborate performance because the yacht would have to heave to, the anchor would drop and detectives and frogmen would ensure that the water was safe. Diana and Evelyn, her maid, would swim at the back of the ship while the crew snorkelled and scuba-dived up front.

After luscious days around Greek islands visiting Santorini and cruising off the coast of Crete, the Prince kept a couple of engagements ashore. One evening when he returned to the Royal Yacht and was taking the ceremonial salute from officers at the head of the gangway, a bucket of water was emptied over his head. His blonde wife appeared above the parapet giggling: 'You're late.' He chased her along the deck, thankful that the Queen was deep in her red boxes at Balmoral.

The only hint of formality was when they entertained the Egyptian President Anwar Sadat and his wife Jihan. The four got on well. An already sophisticated Princess was at ease, and particularly liked the caring Mrs Sadat. The talk was easy round the Chippendale table in the dining room with its mementos of royal tours through the years – spears, carved masks and an enormous gold camel given to the Queen on her tour of the Gulf in 1977.

Guests always keep *Britannia*'s gilt-edged menus, with a picture of the yacht surging ahead on a green sea and the EIIR emblem in gold on the left. The menu is in French and for the Sadats the port, Alexandria, was in the right-hand corner. Food was English: Darne de Saumon Glamis, then duck, chicken or lamb to follow – inoffensive dishes whatever the religious persuasion of the guests.

As the Sadats were walking down the gangplank, Diana, with her refreshing spontaneity, blew kisses and waved until they were out of sight. It was one of her first public engagements and it had been handled in a graceful, warm way which would become the Princess's trademark, whether meeting the Pope, the blind, the old or tongue-tied children. It had seemed almost effortless; the Sadats were particularly charming. When the President was assassinated a few months later, the Princess took it very badly, and would learn quickly the need for a little detachment in public life, otherwise there is too much distress.

After all that sunshine and adoration by the crew of the Royal Yacht, it was time for Scotland. The Prince like a Walter Scott hero would bear his young wife home to Balmoral, to enjoy the abrasiveness of the Grampians, to fish the River Dee and stalk some of the 24,000 heathery acres of the royal estate.

'We look like a couple of Black and White Minstrels,' the bride joked on 15 August as they landed at RAF Lossiemouth after a six-hour flight from Egypt. Her hair bleached by the Mediterranean sun, the Princess wore an off-white knitted cashmere coat over a peach dress and carried a favourite quilted shoulder bag embroidered with red, white and blue flowers. The couple laughed and smiled as they did an impromptu walkabout. Then Prince Charles took the wheel of a midnight blue Granada estate car, its bonnet topped by a mascot of a polo player in action, to drive eighty miles along winding roads to Balmoral.

Queen Victoria, who bought Balmoral when the owner had choked to death on a fishbone, always called it her 'little paradise'. Her great-great-granddaughter the Queen shares her view, although bones from River Dee salmon have twice nearly choked the Queen Mother. London courtiers find Balmoral altogether too rugged and tartan, with its stone-floored entrance and country house clutter of green wellies, fishing rods, dogs and Barbours.

Prince Charles had never known such happiness; he was able to stalk, fish and walk and was madly in love with his young wife. Everything seemed quite perfect. It never occurred to him that she would hate Balmoral. After all, she'd seemed happy enough in Scotland before they married. But he would learn that the way a couple behaves before the wedding can be drastically different once married. Apart from a few walks through the tall forests, stopping by little pools of sparkling brown water and watching out for early juniper and blaeberries as the bracken turned gold and red, the Princess was soon extremely bored. She was seeing very little of her husband, just a lot of tartan.

She was restless, put on her headset, bopped a bit and had a quick look at the Landseer paintings of wounded stags and Highland cattle which made her even more depressed. Then the Queen, astutely spotting this restlessness, encouraged her to invite a few BFs, best friends, to stay at the 'picturesque little Castle'. There had been whispered telephone calls to London: 'I am so bored, yuk.' She asked two of her former flatmates, Carolyn Pride and Virginia Pitman, to come and keep her company. Lady Sarah

Armstrong-Jones also came and they all had fun looking at the wedding photographs.

Also there was the comforting presence of her grandmother; she had always confided in Ruth Lady Fermoy who was not far away at the Queen Mother's friendly house Birkhall, once used by Queen Victoria for her poor relations. This tall Queen Anne house has none of the gauntness of Balmoral. Outside there are sweeping borders of purple and white heather, purple daisies and Himalayan lilies. You are pressed to a second helping of black bun, a heavy fruit cake, as you sit by a huge log fire and tea is poured from a silver pot. There were many romantic memories, for the Princess had stayed at Birkhall during the courtship, when she had been happy and contained doing her needlework and wandering in the garden with the Queen Mother whose eyes are the same cornflower blue. 'Aren't these delicious?' she would ask, taking Lady Diana round the beds of Michaelmas daisies and larkspur she had planted herself.

Prince Charles, wearing a Royal Hunting Stuart kilt which had belonged to George VI, took the Princess who often wore a specially designed easy soft tweed checked jacket and skirt honey-moon suit, strolling near Lochnagar, Scotland's third highest mountain. The Prince has always loved its misty pointy peaks and they inspired him to write a bestselling book for his brothers called *The Old Man of Lochnagar*. They posed for photographs as the Princess bubbled enthusiastically about how 'fabulous' the honeymoon had been and that marriage was simply 'marvellous'.

Although 'cherished to pieces' and adored by everybody, the Princess got a sharp rebuke from her mother-in-law, and it really was not her fault. The newlyweds went to the Braemar Highland Games, and Prince Charles kept teasing and tickling the Princess's soft spots. He found her outfit endearing, a tartan suit and tam o' shanter. During the playing of the National Anthem Prince Charles, in the way of young men in love, kept nudging her and putting his hands round her neck, and told her, 'They're playing our song.' Immediately she had a fit of the giggles; the Queen turned round and gave them one of her looks which make strong men quake.

From this point on the Princess would be careful to maintain a respectful distance between herself and the Queen. Her sister-in-law, the Duchess of York, would bounce alongside the Queen on horseback, often cheerfully unaware of, and therefore blithely unaffected by, any *faux pas*.

This casual fleeting moment marked the start of the Princess's ordeal of learning to be royal. At the time of the engagement her sister, Lady Jane Fellowes, remarked in an uncharacteristically indiscreet way, 'She doesn't know what she is letting herself in for.' But Prince Charles knew and in the early years he was tender and protective. Immediately he got back from an engagement he would ask, 'Where's the Princess? . . . Is she all right?'

CHAPTER 17

So Proud of You

———◆———

'It will,' said Prince Philip, 'take her a few years to learn the ropes.' It was a nice understatement for the rigorous life facing his first daughter-in-law whose proper title was now Her Royal Highness, The Princess of Wales. To the romantic British public she would always be 'Lady Di'.

For a nursery school teacher who had never faced anything more daunting than shepherding a crocodile of small children over a zebra crossing, the newlywed Princess now had to get used to friends calling her 'Ma'am' and curtsying. Even in this blush of early marriage, she rarely saw her husband for breakfast. Nothing has changed; she still sips her morning cup of Earl Grey alone.

For the first ten months of their marriage they had an apartment in Buckingham Palace, and her friends feared she might be lost forever in this open prison. Her father, Earl Spencer, had misgivings. 'I know the royals can seem to swallow people up when others marry in and the smaller family always looks as if it has been pushed out.' But beneath the fringe, the soulful look and the tremulous hesitancy, his daughter would show in the nicest possible way that she was no compliant royal wife.

In the meantime she was expected to take formal banquets in her stride. At least the Princess experienced none of the bone-wearying royal ceremonial of the court in Queen Mary's day. One lady-in-waiting had complained after hours of standing of 'rather a perpendicular evening'.

There was nobody to teach her royal protocol; the best person was the Queen but she did not have the time. Besides, it has never been a relationship where the Princess could casually pop in; nobody does that except the corgis. The Princess would sometimes dart down to the Palace kitchens and chat to the young men-servants, but with the snobbery of 'below stairs' this was frowned upon by the butler and housekeeper, who sniffed, 'We do not approve of these Scandinavian practices,' despising the relaxed atmosphere in the Danish court, where the cigarette smoking Queen Margrethe is gloriously approachable. The Swedish king married a commoner, and the Dutch royal family thinks nothing of cycling round The Hague.

However, helped by the confidence of youth and goodwill, the Princess plunged in with naïve enthusiasm. Aware of this inexperience, she joked when she was placed next to the Liberal party leader David Steel at a dinner party, 'They must have put me beside you because I am so young.' Absentmindedly picking up a cigar, he suddenly remembered the Princess was pregnant and hated smoking anyway. Gallantly he dashed it down as 'if it was a red hot poker,' but the Princess picked up the cigar and popped it in the astonished politician's mouth, saying, 'Don't worry at all.'

A great giggler, one of the first hurdles she had to overcome was learning how to stifle laughter. This she did by biting her lip especially when men flustered by her prettiness curtsied instead of bowed. Arrivals and leavetakings were easy and graceful. She never looked ungainly, taught early on by her grandmother, Ruth Lady Fermoy, the delicate art of getting in and out of motor cars. 'Keep your knees together, dear; swivel them round before putting your feet on the ground.'

On those early engagements she was sunny and impulsive. Well meaning, she told seventy-six-year-old Miss Alice Hubbard in Lambeth, who was worried about the cost of meat, 'Try buying fish; it's a lot cheaper . . . we don't buy much meat ourselves.' Later the Princess would realise that buying fish was not so easy either for a pensioner.

But she began to relish her royal role. Seeing an old soldier wearing a string of medals she complimented him, saying, 'What nice shiny medals.' Then the practical Diana asked his wife, 'Did you polish them for him?' When a little boy whispered shyly, 'My Dad said give us a kiss,' the Princess dipped down. 'Well then, you'd better have one,' and smilingly gave him a peck.

'Where is Diana? We want Diana.' Everyone wanted to see her. 'Over here, darling,' the Prince would call out, and laugh. 'I haven't got enough wives, I've only one.' It was not just her beauty; she was a life enhancer.

Prince Charles, at first protective and proud of his young wife, would encourage her by giving small presents after an engagement: a small gold heart for her charm bracelet, a crunchy peanut bar or a billet doux under her pillow . . . 'so proud of you today'. It was not long before a cousin of Prince Charles arriving at a party 'looked across the room and said, "Where's Diana?" "Across there," Charles said, and there was this polished young woman I did not recognise.'

In Wales on a joint royal visit in 1981 much of her appeal was captured by an air of vulnerability and the way she said 'thank you very much' in Welsh: *'diolch yn fawr'*, not bad going for a first visit to a potentially sensitive region. But, a relation of the royal family says sadly, 'The trouble in that marriage dates back partly to their first visit to Wales. He is not a petty man, but her sudden success shook his equilibrium.' Prince Charles had made her famous; without him, the grooming and the glamour meant nothing. But surprisingly his confidence took a downturn.

'Diana fell in love quite quickly with the idea of being Princess of Wales,' a courtier observed. Behind her apparent demureness there was already a capacity to dazzle; she knew exactly what she wanted to achieve. Later the Princess commented in a no-nonsense way, 'There is far too much about me in the papers.' But she liked attention, knew she was getting the full glare of the telephoto lens and was at home with the gulping crescendos of cameras sounding like mad crickets.

Unwittingly, the Princess did not help matters by a little subconscious scene stealing on 4 November 1981 at her first State Opening of Parliament, one of the grandest days in the Queen's Calendar. Wearing her hair tucked up under a tiara, a white chiffon dress with a satin bodice and a four-strand pearl choker on loan from the Queen, 'She absolutely lit up the old place,' one MP goggled. 'Shimmering from head to toe,' the Princess was, he said, 'a glamorous concoction almost beyond description.' The House was more used to sturdy ladies in pleated skirts and cream blouses at the despatch box, and a dim view was taken by older members of the royal family. 'She has made a fool of you,' Princess Margaret grumbled. The only person not displeased with the day was the Queen. As photographers clustered round the Princess in the Albert Hall later that month, the Queen merely smiled indulgently and said, 'I think I'll be going on,' as she continued upstairs to the royal box.

When they got engaged Prince Charles thought she was 'a real outdoor loving sort of person'. He really believed this. He knew she had lost her nerve about horses but, with the confidence of the newlywed, said, 'We'll soon fix that.' He was wrong and she persuaded him to give up steeplechasing; it was too dangerous.

In the physical glow of being in love, the Princess supportively prowled the banks of the River Tay while her husband stood thigh-deep in the freezing water hoping to land a salmon. She was openly affectionate, hugging, kissing and staying close to him in public. Early in the marriage, it was not important that they had little in common mentally. 'We both love music and dancing,' the Princess said happily.

She liked to tap dance; the Prince went stalking. She listened to Abba and Dire Straits, he preferred Schoenberg and Elgar. Addicted to 'Dynasty' and 'Dallas' on television, she thoughtfully taped them each week, sparing her husband these improbable soap operas. These days the Princess listens less to Sugar Plum Fairy ballet music and genuinely loves opera.

In those early loving days they had trips together, stayed with King Hussein of Jordan at Aqaba, skied together every winter and worried about each other. He fretted when she went on engagements in the winter. In her enthusiasm she got wet, her hands got cold as her rings were admired. Knowing about the need to be sensible, keeping warm and dry, he protectively put an arm round her: 'Darling, don't walk about in the rain.'

She thought he needed fattening up. 'My wife thinks I'm too thin,' he told a polo-playing friend. Both were extremely health conscious and they have become virtually vegetarian. Ascetic, fine-boned and lean, they eat sparingly, sharing a positive distaste for excess.

The Prince liked her innocence, easy charm and lack of guile, her gift of merriment and the warmth of 'a great giver'. He was amazed how in love he was. 'Darling, I'm sorry, I've done all the talking, is there something you wanted to say?' Blossoming and boosted by this gentle and supportive beginning, she became a star in her own right, but the momentum astonished them both.

She was soon to be preoccupied with pregnancy. Charmingly, on the day when the announcement was made from the Palace, she put down the telephone, 'I've just been talking to Daddy and giving him the news about the baby,' she laughed, 'but all he wants to know is "How's the weather in London?"'

CHAPTER 18

An Extravagant Puss

The face looks out at you from glossy magazines all over the world, this extremely photogenic Princess in a Simla hill station, a waiting room in Ohio, the Ritz in Madrid, there she is; in white sunglasses on a tropical island, cuddling her children or solemn and beautiful in black with the royal family on Remembrance Day. Today it is virtually impossible to find a picture of her not looking good. Versatile, a chameleon, a whizzy fashion-conscious Princess, her style is *au courant*.

Endearingly stylishly slim, with spot-on fashion flair, she goes to lunch at Le Caprice in Mayfair in a khaki jacket and girl-scout shorts. This can hardly be the chipmunk-cheeked girl of ten years ago in a pale blue £310 Cojana engagement suit who had the skirt lengthened, making it even less flattering. The transformation has been magical. From being slightly pudgy, hanging on to the arm of her fiancé like any sweet *Country Life* shires girl with well-washed hair, a stand-up collar and Mummy's best string of pearls, she is today's glamorous Princess.

When she married ten years ago, she quickly realised that she would never be a match for her husband intellectually, would never enjoy the finer points of constitutional history or be able to contribute much on the subtleties of parapsychology. But she would make her husband proud of her in the way she knew best, by becoming one of the loveliest Princesses of Wales, rivalling that fragile, captivating beauty Princess Alexandra of Denmark.

If you want to annoy the Princess you will ask her if she is besotted by clothes. This below-the-cuticle suggestion prompts a swift, 'Fashion isn't my big thing at all.' Looking you in the eye, she adds disarmingly, 'My husband likes to see me looking smart and presentable.' Prince Charles says, 'What I always noticed about her before we got married was her very good sense of style which I appreciate.'

Aptly known as POW by a grateful British fashion industry, the Princess of Wales feels she is now entitled to issue her own Royal Warrant to favourite designers. But the Queen is still mulling over the granting of this honour to her trendy daughter-in-law.

The Princess's confident approach to clothes cannot be faulted. Typical was her choice of business-like suit for a first appearance as Patron of the National AIDS Trust in April 1991 for a moving speech she had written herself, stressing, 'HIV does not make people dangerous to know so you can shake hands and give them a hug – heaven knows they need it.' Unlike many women she did not feel the need to rush back to change but wore the same sleek, long jacketed purple suit to fly off for a six-day visit to Brazil.

There she practised what she had preached and clasped babies dying of AIDS in her arms. The Brazilians thought her stunning with her short bubbly haircut and, though it had not been a particularly sunny winter in England, her surprisingly honey tan, which enhanced her gold chains and bracelets. They voted her their 'Queen of Hearts', loving her in her witty choice of safari suit in the jungle, matching Prince Charles's except the Princess's had a divided skirt; her favourite figure-hugging flowery dress; racing swimsuit specially designed for her energetic morning plunge; and sexy one-shouldered pink brocade evening dress.

A recent survey by Margaret Holder of *Royalty* magazine, commissioned by Andrew Morton for his book *Diana's Diary*, reflects the couturiers' views about the Princess of Wales's taste and needs. It estimates that in the last ten years the Princess has spent a total of £833,750 on clothes.

The findings were based on conversations with designers and on available photographs. It is typical and appealing of our fashionable Princess of Wales that she have only 29 skirts – to her a boring necessity – but 95 evening dresses, not to mention the stylish, sexy numbers designed for private occasions by Valentino one of her favourite Italian couturiers. The list reveals the Princess's love of sensuous lingerie and negligées. Since her marriage the Princess has accumulated a fine wardrobe but in the circles in which she moves, these sums of money are not excessive.

In the days before animal liberation, the Princess acquired a fur jacket but, sensitive to the mood of the moment, is never seen in the offending fur. At first one wonders why she should have two tuxedos – the Princess likes this witty masculine dressing – when she could borrow one from her husband or brothers-in-law, but she is so slight they would give her a Chaplinesque outline.

This survey does not take into account her private fun clothes, costing £200,000 over the decade. Although the Princess is a nonpareil advertisement for British fashion, at a time of economic recession, a handful of critics may ask why the Princess needs to spend £4,000 on an evening dress, especially when she could look marvellous in a sack.

The prices may seem hardly competitive but to women who choose to wear designer clothes they are not excessive. As the milliner Philip Somerville explains, 'We don't make the price up out of the telephone book you know or go to Paris for a special feather.' But evening dresses rarely cost less than £2,000. 'What else could I do?' wailed the Princess when criticised originally. 'I couldn't go round in a leopard skin, I had to produce something that was decent.'

The honour of making clothes for royal women can sometimes be a doubtful privilege. One disgruntled couturier complained, 'Everyone thinks its megabucks time but it is not, and it also means that your regular rich customers get very peeved if you are not available for them.' The Princess, when offered a slight reduction by one designer, did not refuse.

Knowing she has been criticised for a wardrobe containing too many luscious clothes, the Princess retaliated once by appearing in a dress which had been seen umpteen times before, prompting a cheeky photographer to ask, 'Why are you wearing that boring old frock again?' 'I suppose you would like it better if I turned up naked,' was her quick rejoinder. She made her point. She can please neither by being extravagant nor by showing restraint. Prince Charles laughed when chivvied with 'Why can't you buy your wife a new frock then?' They both like Arthur Edwards, a chunky fatherly photographer with the *Sun* who can get away with teasing them as few could.

Most people love her exuberant style, her witty combination of one long black and one long red glove to go with her Murray Arbeid red and black cocktail dress, and would hate it if her clothes became too sensible or bleakly practical.

Some months before the royal wedding the change began: no more Laura Ashley separates. Donald Campbell was sitting in his Knightsbridge showroom one afternoon when Lady Jane Fellowes wandered in, saying casually, 'I wonder if you have anything which might suit my sister.' Soon afterwards a shy, unassuming Lady Diana Spencer appeared and bought a couple of things off the rail. He was impressed by her fashion sense and her choice, an easy silk tie top and skirt worn on honeymoon on the Royal Yacht.

Even at nineteen, she had a certain BCBG, *bon chic, bon genre* French preppy style. Her taste was for corduroy culottes, Fiorucci sweatshirts, strappy evening sandals, flatties, tiny pendants on gold chains, big jackets, easy skirts with a slash of scarlet flowers, shoulder bags and hoop earrings.

The Balmoral honeymoon suit was a brown tweed houndstooth check with leather buttons made by the Battersea designer Bill Pashley. Witty Peruvian sweaters decorated with clouds, falling rain and zig-zag lightning also helped to cheer the bracing Scottish air.

Her wardrobe was hopelessly inadequate. But not for her the house of Hartnell who traditionally designed elaborate sequinned evening dresses for the Queen, the Queen Mother and Princess Margaret. This old-fashioned house had no appeal for the young Princess. Instead Mrs Shand Kydd, 'a very sensible, no nonsense lady', introduced her to David Sassoon, a pleasant small dark man with a pretty boutique not far from Knightsbridge. He booked her in as 'Miss Buckingham' and made the off-the-shoulder pale blue evening dress she wore when snoozing sweetly, head on one side, during speeches at the opening of the Gonzaga exhibition in the Victoria and Albert Museum. The dress earned her the title 'fairy princess' with its pale blue ribbons and ethereal chiffon delicacy. He had also made her going-away outfit and special customers were given little snippets from the roll of cantaloup silk.

At first there was a flurry of 'Oh lawks, what shall I do?' panic before an official engagement. She had been introduced to one or two designers who had made dresses for her aunts, family and Norfolk friends, women who never wanted anything too striking and often turned down a flattering evening dress in a good colour saying, 'Oh no, that would make it look as if I had tried too hard.' It is nouveau to want to be noticed. The Princess did not take fashion advice either from her solid, affable lady-in-waiting Anne Beckwith-Smith, who sometimes approaches a size eighteen, joking 'too many banquets, I fear.'

It is hard to imagine that in those days Diana liked evening dresses which were high-necked, saying thankfully, 'This means I don't have to worry too much about jewellery.'

But Lady 'Gosh-Lawks' learnt fast. Her sister Jane had worked at *Vogue* as an editorial assistant, racing around picking up designer clothes in taxis and dashing to photographic sessions, and she introduced Diana to an informed, fun fashion team at *Vogue*: Anna Harvey, fashion editor; former model, Grace Coddington and dark-haired beauty editor, Felicity Clark, who said sympathetically, 'Like any kid, she didn't know where to go. Also she didn't have the time.'

There were many visits to *Vogue*, for lessons well learnt. The Princess dumped her car in the underground car park near Hanover Square and nipped up the Vogue House back stairs to lunch with Anna Harvey.

'So you want something for Ascot?' editor-in-chief Beatrix Miller would say crisply, and the Princess would wail, 'Yes, something for every blessed day,' as she stood in the board room in her bra and pants. It was charming the way she cleaned one of her shoes on the back of her leg. Soon she was shaking off the fussy flounces and *jeune fille* billowy fullness. Gone were the big frilly collars, though Prince Charles remained fond of one organza blouse which she wore with a grey suit in the evenings.

It is true she had the best possible advice, but she used it well, quickly finding her fashion feet, tried almost too many designers. Some went to her at Buckingham Palace and felt sorry for her having to live in 'some rather drab rooms, it was all rather like a faded grand hotel, quite shabby, and you could hear Prince Charles on the telephone next door.'

By the time she was twenty-two her look was already one of 'striking' straightforward glamour. All the tricks of the fashion trade had been absorbed: smoothing her skirts from the back, always wearing a silky petticoat, preferably matching the skirt lining.

In eighteen months the Princess managed to go from a size twelve to a ten; the incentive was that engagement day suit photograph she hated. Now she has an enviable figure, though she loves baked beans on toast with soft boiled eggs. Her favourite colours are still red, purple, blue and fuchsia pink; no time for sludgy shades and no man-made fabrics; for the winter she chooses wool jersey and wool crepe because they do not crease too badly. She prefers silk crepe in hot countries; it stays much cooler and crisper-looking than linen or cotton.

For the first big tour to Australia in 1983 she took ninety trunks with outfits by twenty-one different designers. The Princess says this was how she got the reputation for being an extravagant puss who was mad about clothes. 'I had to buy endless new things.' Some thought her style then pleasantly suburban.

It was Haachi who put her into really sexy dresses, stunning the staid in Melbourne in 1983. One was a dazzling, clinging sequinned jersey with a saucy one-shouldered effect; it highlighted the demureness of her lady-in-waiting's flowery frock.

Then Bruce Oldfield got drama into her style with a stunning blue evening dress again with one shoulder showing, much more provocative than revealing both. 'She is by far my favourite customer,' he says. 'Not only is she totally disarming but she also knows exactly what suits her.' Oldfield was asked by the television presenter Muriel Gray how he could bear to spend his days designing 'for a bunch of lassies with no O levels.' 'They have this enduring quality,' he said quietly, but the chivvying went on. 'I don't like my taxes going up so they can buy more frocks.' But all he said was, 'I am quite a royalist.'

Top of the Princess's royal fashion charts today are Victor Edelstein, who makes some of her more svelte outfits, and the French-born Catherine Walker of Chelsea Design.

It is 2 P.M. on a June day. The designers and milliners are waiting in a morning room on the first floor of Kensington Palace. Evelyn Dagley, the Princess's dresser, appears, saying, 'You can come in now.'

They leap to their feet. There is tremendous fussing as they gather up their pins, scissors, boxes, feathers, silks and fifteen hats and go towards the Princess's sitting room. But suddenly on the landing, the Princess appears bouncing towards them, 'boom'; she is so full of vitality as she leads the way. No matter how relaxed and easy her personality, seeing her again always gives the heart a flutter.

'Tea or coffee?' she asks, settling down in a squashy sofa. Immediately everyone feels comfortable. Windows open out on to the Palace gardens, filling the room with the scent of old-fashioned Albertine roses, lavender and honeysuckle on this warm afternoon. Prince William and Prince Harry are giggling and squashing themselves behind the door; the Princess pretends not to notice.

'You pour,' she says over her shoulder, and chases them out. Prince Harry in his commando outfit salutes. Prince William is reluctant to leave, so he is given a swatch of different coloured fabrics, 'Choose a colour for a hat for Mummy.' Spot on, he selects a perfect deep maroon.

The Princess comes back and pours, then it is quickly down to business. Thoroughly professional, she does not waste time. Every minute is precious. Her clothes and hats, her accessories, her image, are about to be decided for the six months ahead – for Japan and Brazil, India and Czechoslovakia, also an outfit for church on Christmas Day. 'Don't suppose I can have red again.' Decisive, there is no dithering but occasionally a little gasp of pleasure, 'Oh, this is a winner.' Her way of refusing is still charming; she puts her head on one side, 'Well, I adore red but I did wear it last year.' She stole the show at her niece Eugénie's christening at Christmas 1990 in St Mary's on the Sandringham estate, wearing a highly fashionable red and white checked jacket with a black and white skirt. Lyndsay Reed, aged nine – her father is based at RAF Coltishall, Norfolk – thought the Princess 'smelled of lovely scent' when she handed her some pink carnations. 'She gave me a nice, big warm cuddle.' 'It was,' said the Princess of Wales, 'a wonderful service. We all sang our hearts out.'

It is always 'Mr Oldfield', 'Mr Haachi', no Christian names, no personal questions, but the Princess will notice small things. 'I see you've got a Jaguar,' she remarked to one of her favourites who usually arrives in a Volvo estate. 'No Ma'am,' he replied, 'it's just my little Daimler Sovereign today.'

Unlike many women she does not pull funny unnatural faces in front of the mirror as she tries on a hat, or in a dress pose extravagantly with one foot out at an angle.

Occasionally a designer gets carried away at a fitting and will sit down, then apologise profusely. 'Oh, that's all right,' the Princess says. Another designer says, 'What is so fabulous about her, she never makes you feel like a second-class person.'

Edelstein seems to tower in the Princess's tiny sitting room. He is 6 foot 4 inches tall and resembles a daddy longlegs as with fluttering hands he holds out sketches for her approval. The grandson of a Russian tailor, he could not wait to get away from the East End, says he hated the smell 'of all the steaming cloth'.

His evening dresses costing upwards from £1,800 make women feel young and beautiful. The actress Gayle Hunnicutt explained when she wore one of his emerald green dresses, 'It was the first time ever that I didn't look at other women and think, "Grrr".' The Princess feels wonderful in his dresses too; especially when one of his young dressmakers, Nati, took a whole day to make a perfect red belt to match her red dress with its black velvet collar.

The Princess listens to him, is amused by him. Edelstein hates 'very high heels, they look common', lacy tights which make legs look 'disastrous', dyed hair and boyish cuts in women over thirty. Fortunately the Princess was able to sneak in her new gamine *comme les garçons* hairdo in the summer of 1990 before her twenty-ninth birthday. She makes up her own mind anyway.

Occasionally she got things wrong. At the wedding of her friend Carolyn Pride in 1987 she wore a low-waisted crushed raspberry silk dress and a white boater and was criticised for looking like a D'Oyly Carte sailor. 'The dress was like something worn by a Mack Sennett bathing beauty in 1910,' declared Earl

Blackwell, but nobody took much notice of this self-styled American fashion expert.

'Her main job,' says Germaine Greer, 'is to be pretty and slim and to wear a hat,' and certainly if the Princess never put another hat on her head, what she has done for the millinery world in reviving this luxury accessory can never be overestimated. At today's fitting her hair is wet. 'I've just been swimming so we won't worry about hair.' Perhaps she is wearing fewer hats lately but she remains decades away from the woman who buys one for a wedding and puts it back in its tissue paper so it can quietly go out of shape before the christening.

She likes a classic plain boater. 'It's good for church,' she says tongue in cheek, and if something flashy is produced will say, 'Oh dear, no, I don't think that is for the family,' meaning the royal family. At Ascot in June 1990 when women were wearing hats shaped like clocks or equatorial jungles on their heads, trying too hard, the Princess chose a sculpted scarlet and violet pagoda hat by Philip Somerville and a scarlet silk bolero jacket with a purple skirt.

Royal milliner John Boyd, a delightful, droll Scot with large baby-blue eyes, recalls the early days when he had to draw little arrows to show the Princess how to wear a hat. 'Often they were the wrong way round,' but rather fetching. She adored his workroom, squashing in jammed by hatboxes, boxes of pins. She'd 'sit on the stairs' and chat to the sewing ladies and the trimmers. 'If you live in a Palace surrounded by beautiful things it must be a novelty.' One day the Princess raced into the boutique wearing rust velvet corduroy rompers and was about to dash upstairs when Boyd called out, 'We don't allow wee laddies in the workroom.'

Her appreciativeness makes her special. After Ascot last summer she appeared in the milliner Philip Somerville's shop off Bond Street. He is one of the reasons she is so keen to be allowed to create her own Warrant Holders. 'Harry, give Mr Somerville the card.' Prince Harry said 'Thank you for Ascot,' and gave him a written message. Then the Princess handed the doyen of hat-makers a bottle of champagne. Taking a mischievous glance into the storeroom with its hatboxes piled high, in mock seriousness she asked, 'Where is it?' She had brought him a corgi teatowel from Scotland. Now it was in a frame and they both admired it doubled up with laughter.

Her shoes, 350 pairs altogether, are a mixture of flatties, soft shiny pumps bought from High Street stores, the soft covetable leather of Charles Jourdan or Manolo Blahnik which smell so good when they come out of the box. A fashion expert remarked sourly, 'We don't want her being like the Queen who has been wearing the same ghastly pair of Rayne shoes since before the war.'

The first Princess to appear in public brown-legged without tights, in the winter she wears Bruce Oldfield tights or fun seamed stockings with bows on the heels and puts them on carefully wearing white cotton gloves.

She buys her bras from Fenwicks at £16.95 each and matching Huit knickers; she likes sleeping in £69.75 Derek Rose pyjamas; wears slinky blue and grey underwear from Janet Reger and enjoys print shoulder bags from Souleiado in Fulham Road which exude the heat of sunny days in Provence.

Her clothes are never thrown away, but often adapted by being belted or shortened; Evelyn Dagley keeps a card index and notebook. A pale blue long-sleeved embroidered evening dress worn in 1983 was altered to a sexy strapless dress for the première of *Licence to Kill* in 1989. The Princess lends clothes to her sisters: 'Sometimes I simply can't find a dress because my sister has borrowed it,' but she still has a frock or two left in her enormous Kensington Palace walk-in wardrobes.

Royal evening dresses are sent to Tothills in London SE 17, to be dry cleaned for about £70 a time. Watermarks can be the bane of royal women's lives if they hold a bouquet of flowers too close; ideally they should be dry and never wired in case they snag soft wool. Embroidered blouses and very fine silk tops are hand washed in a special ecologically 'green' washing powder. Dresses are hung on padded hangers and evening gowns have special covers embossed with her own cypher made by the Royal Warrant holders Eximious. Black and white tissue paper, a wise old Victorian travelling habit, gives clothes a luxurious feel when they are unpacked.

So much of her time is spent being dutiful, it would be a waste if the curves were never shown. Privately she likes casual, quirky clothes. In the early days she might buy nothing more outrageous than a pair of denims from Jean Machine in the King's Road, as she did in 1981 – they made a copy of the cheque and put it in the window. Nowadays she loves sexy Patrick Kelly leopard print dresses; trying one on in Harvey Nichols she came out of the fitting room and asked her daydreaming bodyguard sitting outside, 'Do you think it too tight?' He nodded approvingly. 'Good,' said the Princess, 'then I'll buy it.' Her detective discreetly paid the bill with a Duchy of Cornwall Amex card.

Looking as polished and sveltely glowing as any international model, the Princess appeared in *Vogue* December 1990 in an off-the-shoulder evening dress leaning provocatively against a regency chair. The saucy impression is given that she is wearing nothing on top as she clutches a satin sheet to her bosom, not to reveal too much in her slinky Victor Edelstein evening dress.

What is the point of workouts, hours spent slaving in a gymnasium, swimming every morning, saying 'no' to ice-cream, if you cannot turn up at *Phantom of the Opera* in sexy red leather trousers and high heels? The Princess loves sensuous suede and has a tan cowgirl skirt which hides legs she thinks too skinny. And yet she skipped up the steps to Wetherby School with a young Prince by the hand showing them off in navy city shorts; just the thing for a confrontation with a headmistress.

Her private wardrobe includes fantasy ostrich skin jodhpurs from Hermès. She is a fan of Ellis Flyte, married to Brian, son of Jim Henson, the Muppet king, who died in 1990. She also designs for David Bowie, Emma Thompson and Terence Trent D'Arby, the pigtailed, leather-loving black singer.

On board the Spanish King's yacht *Fortuna*, there was almost a little girl look about the polka-dotted T-shirt covering her swimsuit and her hair tucked under a baseball cap. She took her favourite pair of yellow Bermudas and, like any smart blonde, knows white always looks good, so keeps a stock of Ralph Lauren white cotton shirts beautifully ironed by the devoted Evelyn Dagley. She adores her new figure-hugging black and pink neoprene and hyplon swimsuit, hoping it hides those cavalier stomach muscles which have never behaved properly since the birth of the boys.

With the delicate elegance of a feminine woman, the Princess knows she looks good in men's shirts or big jackets. She used to pinch Prince Charles's shirts, but he got rather fed up with this so now his shirtmakers Turnbull and Asser make shirts for her at £55 each. At weekends she loves to wear a baggy Don Johnson type linen jacket or jazzy waistcoat with one of her husband's cricket jumpers and old school tie.

The Princess has tried hard to change Prince Charles's fogeyish appearance though in its way it is quite fashionable amongst thoughtful youngish men. Thanks to the Princess's influence he will wear trousers with pleats at the front, but thinks this very daring. Sounding a little martyred, he quickly explains, 'I do it to please my wife.' The Princess even persuaded him to change tailors, which in a man's world is like switching religion. He now goes to Anderson and Shepherd in Savile Row for his classic double-breasted pinstriped suits with narrow lapels and trousers with turnups. He feels his slightly padded shoulders are rather continental. The Princess has bought a flamboyant collection of silk ties which, like most husbands, he puts in a drawer and goes on wearing his navy blue with red spots. As for casual sports clothes, the Princess has not been able to persuade him to wear jeans or even corduroys. He always looks immaculate; even talking to his carrots in the vegetable garden at Highgrove, the shoelaces appear ironed. The naval training dies hard. He really only feels at home in a kilt and beloved ancient tweed jacket. He says he would do anything to please his wife, but there is a limit. All the same he is constantly amused by her innovative, cheeky off-duty élan.

There is a cabaret style about her private dressing, those silk waistcoats from Hackett's the men's shop in Chelsea. 'Sometimes I enjoy being outrageous,' the Princess admits. 'It's quite nice.' It is appealing that although she outshines the most glamorous film stars in the world, inspiring uncritical adulation, her values put this admiration in perspective and she has never become vain, silly or pouty. The Princess is now totally confident about her own style, whether it is a Jasper Conran short sexy black skirt or a romantic sequinned tulle evening dress.

Steeped in fashion, she has lots of opinions on design, but was seriously dismayed some years ago by the attention paid to her and asked, 'How long can this go on?' Prince Charles told her, 'Until your daughter is as old as you are now.'

Normally she wears British, but paid a compliment to the Italian President by wearing a green Italian Moschino designer suit with brass buttons and a nipped-in waist to welcome him at Victoria Station. Next day she was in a Michael Jackson tour jacket getting a soaking on a Big Apple roller coaster with Prince William and Prince Harry.

Whatever the Princess wears today the rest of the country will be chasing tomorrow. Of course, she loves to shop and, in the words of the old song, believes, 'If you've got it, flaunt it.' 'World style' leader, 'most attractive female face', 'best dressed woman', 'best body', 'stunning Princess', she beats them all. Jerry Hall, Joan Collins beware; she is the world's cover girl.

CHAPTER 19

The Expectant Father

———————•———————

It is hard to know which of two comments made the Princess of Wales blush more when her pregnancy was first announced on 5 November 1981. The Lord Mayor of London, Colonel Sir Ronald Gardner Thorpe, said emotionally, 'Babies are bits of stardust blown from the hand of God,' while Prince Charles's statement was 'The royal breeding programme is now firmly under way,' as if referring to a new strain of Aberdeen Angus on the Duchy of Cornwall estates. The Princess's reaction was definitely, 'Yuk, how embarrassing.'

The baby would be born in the private wing of St Mary's, Paddington, a National Health hospital in London. The Queen could see nothing wrong with Buckingham Palace; after all she had three of her own four children in the Buhl Room and Princess Anne was born at Clarence House, still home. This totally revolutionary step, unheard-of in royal circles, was a brave and defiant move by the Princess. She had the Queen's gynaecologist, the respected Mr George Pinker as an ally. Her mother-in-law was slightly taken aback at first by this decision, but remembered that her forceful daughter, Princess Anne, had also to bow to Pinker and go into hospital for her first baby, Peter Phillips, born on 15 November 1977.

A firm believer in natural childbirth and mothers helping themselves, the Princess went to exercise classes, learnt about breathing correctly and hoped not to need any drugs when the baby was delivered. Betty Parsons, an up-market midwife and nurse who helped the Queen when her youngest Prince Edward was born on 10 March 1964, went regularly to Kensington Palace to teach the Princess how to relax and prepare her for each stage of labour.

From the start Prince Charles always planned to be present at the birth. 'I am after all, the father and I suppose I started this whole business so I intend to be there when everything happens,' he said.

Unlike previous royal mothers who would disappear almost into a harem-like cocoon in one of the royal palaces to await the birth of their child, the Princess defiantly went on with her life almost as normal and never thought of herself as in a 'delicate condition'. Having always enjoyed excellent health, and desperately wanting babies, she somehow thought she would sail through pregnancy and was totally unprepared for the physical misery of the early weeks. 'The trouble,' a member of the family revealed, 'was that in Diana's case . . . it was morning sickness that went on all day,' and she hated the thickening of her waistline.

Although thrilled about her first baby, the Princess was only too willing to share with every pregnant woman she met her real horror of that sickness, perhaps in the hope they might have some old remedy which would make it more bearable. Suffering from nausea and a deep body weariness right until December, she would openly complain about the shock pregnancy had been. 'Nobody told me I would feel like this,' she said to Mrs Dorothy McLeish, a bakery worker who rather unfeelingly replied, 'You'll feel much worse before it's over.' Nothing had quite prepared her for the disagreeable side of pregnancy. This fine-boned girl was appalled by the business of being physically sick.

So much frankness about a royal baby was very different from the royal reticence of the past. Even the Queen's birth by

Caesarean could not be mentioned publicly. An arch communiqué issued by the Palace referred to a 'certain line of treatment' being 'successfully adopted'. Princess Anne had typically announced her first pregnancy in trenchant flying terms: 'I'm grounded.' Even Prince Charles got a bit fed-up with being the expectant father and, when offered a Morris man's fertility symbol, replied, 'You can keep the bloody thing.'

It was at about this time that the Princess altered her lifestyle considerably and influenced Prince Charles so that they both turned much more to health foods, virtually giving up meat and eating a great deal of fibre, wholemeal bread and salads.

Flat shoes became her favourite; the Princess wore them to complement her husband's height but also because they were so good for exhausting hours on public visits. In Wales the homely women in the valleys thought the Princess looked peaky – she had lost fourteen pounds since the pregnancy. This was a visit undertaken because they had always promised that their first tour after the marriage would be to the Principality.

The Princess also kept an engagement to switch on the Regent Street Christmas lights. Teased by the singer Cilla Black, who said, 'I've brought my old man with me, where's yours?' the Princess replied, 'I've left him at home watching the telly.' She made a short speech with the aid of index cards.

'She looked absolutely sweet,' commented Mrs Elizabeth Villiers, Chairman of the Regent Street Association, whose brother-in-law is the doleful-eyed actor James Villiers. 'Although she didn't look pregnant we had to make arrangements and wondered if she was going to be sick.'

As a 'thank you', she was given an antique scent bottle by Mrs Villiers who had scoured Portobello market to find one pretty enough. It was engraved by Lady Vivian Hay and then filled with the Princess's favourite scent Diorissima.

After a fall down some stairs at Sandringham the Princess was soon her cheery, irrepressible self and saying to a woman with twins, 'I don't think I could cope with a brace,' and giving that little laugh which is often her upbeat way of ending a chat.

When she was five months' pregnant, Prince Charles took her off to the Caribbean. Under the name Mr and Mrs Hardy, they travelled by commercial flight and settled down on the island of Eleuthera to enjoy sun and peace, but were not pleased when photographs of the Princess appeared showing what Queen Victoria called 'that miserable lump' in her bikini.

In May she eased her aching back by clasping her hands under her stomach as she stood about watching Prince Charles play polo, wearing a koala bear sweater which outlined her proud eight-month bulge. When she felt particularly bad Prince Charles would kiss and cuddle her and was so supportive his old polo-playing friends were frankly surprised. In June during Royal Ascot week she had trouble doing up the seat belt of Prince Charles's roomy Aston Martin.

Pregnant during one of Britain's sultry heat waves, the Princess refused to cut down on engagements and was busy at Highgrove. She often drove herself to Gloucestershire, her car seat pushed back as far as possible, nipping down to oversee the work on the old Georgian house. She was creating the blue and gold nursery on the floor above their bedroom with its charming hand-painted furniture. For the baby there was a woolly, fluffy frog, always a romantic joke between the Prince and Princess, a musical box which played the 'Love Bugs' and a wickerwork white basket trimmed with blue ribbon. And the Princess found time to do some tapestry, a small cushion which is at Highgrove today and reads, 'There's no place like Home'.

In London she trudged up and down stairs at Kensington Palace, working on the decoration of the wing which had been bombed in the war. They say next to death and divorce, moving house comes third on the list of stressful events in everyone's life. It was not until five weeks before the birth that the Prince and Princess were able to move into their new London home.

The Palace announced that the Princess would take no further public engagements, but two weeks before the birth she defied them all and danced at Broadlands where Prince Charles had organised a fund-raising ball for the United World Colleges.

The dancing went on till two in the morning, the Prince stretching his arms around her trying to steer her sedately. But she would have none of it and preferred to jig around at arm's length when the music got lively, perhaps bringing on her labour ten days earlier than expected. Only the day before the birth the

Princess had felt well enough to pick up Prince Charles in her black Ford Escort. He had been to a Parachute Regiment memorial service in France and had a meeting with President Mitterrand. Back at Kensington Palace he was not duped by his wife's apparent perkiness and cancelled a polo match at Smith's Lawn, Windsor; the ultimate sacrifice for him.

The baby had been due, the Princess thought, on her twenty-first birthday, 1 July, but late on Sunday evening, 20 June, she telephoned Miss Parsons: 'My contractions have begun.' Around 4.30 A.M. they became more acute and Prince Charles became Action Man, switching with military precision into the routine rehearsed for months. The Princess got into her green maternity smock and Prince Charles made 'hotline' calls, first to his personal detective, Superintendent John McLean, then to Mr Pinker at home at Kingston upon Thames; at that hour the journey to London would be easy.

He helped the Princess into the back seat of a royal blue police Rover which had been on constant alert for six weeks. The Prince sat with her and held her hand during the ten-minute drive to St Mary's, an old Victorian red brick hospital near the canal and Paddington railway sidings. Arriving at 5.10 A.M., the Princess was taken to the private Lindo Wing.

Her bedroom on the twelfth floor was plain and functional but had been freshly painted; the only frivolous touch was a rose-patterned wall behind the typical hospital steel-framed bed and jaded fringed curtains. The Princess padded over an elderly brown carpet to the bathroom across the corridor. Usually shared, she now had the use of two lavatories and two baths, her privacy on the short journey ensured by a screen.

For once the Princess had few clothes with her, just a maternity dress to go in the small brown wardrobe. Her silver-backed hairbrushes were placed on a dressing table and there were two bedside lockers, one with a telephone, the other with a television. All babies there are delivered in the mother's own room, in her own bed and mothers wear their own nightdresses.

Everything is conducive to an air of relaxation; lights are lowered, mothers-to-be can put their mattresses on the floor if they are happier with that position; they are encouraged to bring their own photographs and mementos and even their own music.

Doctors and midwives tap gently on the door so the couple's closeness and privacy is always respected.

Under Pinker the hospital had a fine reputation. It was not in the business of making an impression on Arab patients and their huge families by trying to pretend it was an hotel. The cost was £126.90 a day and the view from her window was of Paddington's rather murky Wharf Street.

CHAPTER 20

Both in Such Fine Condition

'I think it is a very good thing for fathers to be present at the birth,' the Prince told Mrs Shirley Bowen when he visited patients in the Llwynpia hospital in the Welsh Rhondda. This was something fairly revolutionary in royal circles. When the Queen was born on 21 April 1926, apart from the medical team, the only other man present was the Home Secretary. The Duke of York was furious, and by the time their next child, Princess Margaret, was born in 1930 he had abolished this intrusive custom; the relieved Cabinet Minister could stay at his desk and get on with sorting out rural problems.

The Queen Mother may be amused now to recall the Home Secretary's presence, 'Ah yes, that was when we were York' – her pleasant way of referring to those sunny days before the Abdication. But with her passion for privacy especially in matters of health, the barbaric custom dating back to the seventeenth century, when a substitute baby was believed to have been put in James II's wife's warming pan, would have been totally abhorrent. Especially in the twenties when pregnancy and anything to do with women's bodies was treated with furtive coyness.

Through the long day of 21 June 1982 the Princess had a difficult sixteen-hour labour. Mr Pinker, almost tailormade as a royal medical adviser, the classic silver-haired gynaecologist with his musical voice, soothed the anxious father, talking easily about many shared interests in gardening, music, skiing and fell-walking. It was pretty traumatic for the Prince, who tried to help as much as he could while keeping out of everyone's way. Sister Delphine Stevens several times disappeared outside for a quick cigarette.

Betty Parsons was with the Princess during the contractions shouting encouragement. At her classes Diana had been taught to 'huff and puff' and how really to relax and prepare herself for each stage of labour. Now Betty's cry 'doggy, doggy' was to encourage the Princess to pant, then to make her exhale as if blowing out a flame, she would cry, 'candle, candle'.

Finally the Princess had to be given a painkilling epidural, an anaesthetic which numbs the body from the waist down but leaves the mother conscious to enjoy the baby's arrival. Prince William was born at 9.03 P.M. on 21 June, a Cancerian who 'cried lustily', weighing in at 7 pounds 1½ ounces and was tagged 'Baby Wales'. The Princess took off her huge sapphire engagement ring for the first time since the wedding so that the baby was in no danger of being scratched by diamonds.

Prince Charles had been with his wife throughout the labour in the tiny twelve-foot-square room and, fortunately, with the grit expected of the heir to the throne, did not faint. If he had busy maternity staff would have done the usual thing with fathers who are overcome and unceremoniously bundled him under the delivery bed.

In the House of Commons MPs used to using their lungs to discredit their opponents, cheered when the birth was announced by the Speaker, Mr George Thomas: 'We rejoice with the couple.' How different, and in retrospect ominous, were the Labour MP Keir Hardie's words to the House on 23 June 1894. He predicted that the newly arrived royal baby, the future Edward VIII, would be 'surrounded by sycophants and flatterers. He would be made to believe himself a superior creation.' The Commons shouted him down yet this baby would abdicate in 1936 and shake both monarchy and people.

In the rain outside St Mary's Hospital, champagne corks popped, cans of beer were drained and the crowds danced, many sated with strawberries and cream sold all day for seventy-five pence a plate. 'Lady Di is the best of the lot,' Mary Finn told a group of nurses. 'She likes to meet working-class people.' This got a unanimous shout of approval.

Inside, the medical staff, led by the urbane and kindly Mr Pinker, who really always favoured fairly conventional confinements, tiptoed out after congratulatory handshakes, sensitively leaving the Prince and Princess alone for half an hour with their son 'to savour the first precious moments.'

As muddled as most new fathers, Prince Charles said, 'I can't say who he looks like,' but added 'he is blond, sort of fairish, with blue eyes.' Later the Princess would make it clear that the Prince was definitely fair and not a redhead as Princess Michael had told guests at a lunch in London. On a visit to Wales that November the Princess took the opportunity to say four times, 'He hasn't got red hair, he's fair . . . he's got masses of beautiful blond hair.'

The news was flashed to Prince Andrew who was in the Falklands with the South Atlantic Task Force. The Queen Mother was at London Airport about to fly off on an engagement and, on hearing the news, thought, 'It's always nice to have a new one, isn't it?' as if he were a flowery new hat.

In New Mexico, where Princess Anne was on an official visit, when asked what she thought about the new arrival, the infant Highness's aunt retorted bluntly that 'too much fuss' was being made about him.

As he emerged from the hospital at 11 P.M., slightly stunned, Prince Charles admitted, 'I'm overwhelmed by it all. It was a very grown-up experience.' Pleased with himself but fiddling nervously with his tie in classic Prince Charles style, he spoke of feeling 'immensely relieved when it was all over. Yes, the Princess was well . . . it's marvellous . . . The Princess had a natural birth, well, very nearly.' It was a typically reticent comment and not one endorsed by Earl Spencer, as always engagingly honest. 'It has been most harrowing . . . it was a particularly slow birth . . . a very worrying day.'

The Prince was a bit dazed when asked if his son was the

prettiest baby in the world and replied, 'Well, he's not bad.' Other fathers who had brought their wives to the hospital blinked in the TV spotlights when they saw a strip of cardboard which had been stuck on the railings saying, 'It's a boy.'

Prince Charles pleaded with the good-humoured, highly excited crowd with that appealing earnestness and smiling grimace. 'Do me a favour, could you quieten down. My wife is trying to get some rest; sleep is badly needed.' But this was the signal for a bucolic suggestion. 'Give us another one,' to which the Prince replied, 'Bloody hell, give us a chance.'

It did not matter about the noise outside Buckingham Palace where another huge crowd delighted in the official announcement saying, 'Her Royal Highness the Princess of Wales was today safely delivered of a son at 9.03 P.M. Her Royal Highness and her son are both doing well.' It was signed by Dr John Batten, head of the Queen's Medical Household, anaesthetist Dr Clive Roberts, Dr David Harvey, paediatrician and of course Mr Pinker, Surgeon Gynaecologist to the Queen.

'It's a boy, it's a boy,' shouted the cheering crowd. 'We want the Queen!' The Queen had been 'absolutely delighted' with the news and was 'smiling at everyone' when she was told about her latest grandchild at Buckingham Palace, but she did not appear. Instead she ordered a forty-one-gun salute in Hyde Park fired by the King's Troop of Royal Horse Artillery and another at the Tower of London.

She would visit her new grandson the next day but thoughtfully not before his maternal grandmother Mrs Shand Kydd. Meticulous about protocol, Mrs Shand Kydd, who always referred to her daughter as 'the Princess', raced in to see her at 9.22 A.M., arriving with her daughter, Lady Jane Fellowes. Afterwards Mrs Shand Kydd said, 'There is a great deal of happiness in there . . . It is a lovely baby and the Princess is looking absolutely radiant.'

Flying home to Scotland Mrs Shand Kydd organised a less grand impromptu celebration. 'It would be nice if we could all toast the royal birth as we fly over the border,' she suggested to Miss Mary Brown, a stewardess on the BA Trident. When she offered to pay, the airline gallantly refused.

At 10.52 A.M. the Queen arrived in her much-loved ancient green Rover with its K registration. Wearing a cheery pink dress

with white spotted lapels she was kissed on the cheek by Prince
Charles waiting on the doorstep. He had been at the hospital
since 8.42 'to be with the Princess'. He had filled the simple white
room with roses, around her bed, on the television, beside the
windows, his special romantic 'thank you'.

Earl Spencer, predictably, was astonished by the comeliness of
his royal grandson, whose face, he marvelled, 'wasn't puckered
at all.' Then he clambered into a waiting Rolls-Royce and announced he was off to have a beer.

In the old days royal mothers could take up to three weeks to
recover, in and out of bed, resting on chaise-longues or day beds,
just being languid. But for the Princess, a girl of our time, twenty
hours and fifty-seven minutes after the birth was enough time
in hospital. She was going home with her baby and no one could
stop her.

Prince Charles was slightly bemused though he agreed that
the baby was 'looking much more human already: absolutely
amazing'. He had been expecting to pop in on a pleasant routine
visit to his wife in hospital, but suddenly had to prepare for
her homecoming. This was an early example of this girl's independent spirit. Already there were those in Palace circles who
thought her 'a strong woman, decisive and likely to have her
own way'.

'I want to come home,' she had telephoned Prince Charles
earlier. 'I am ready.' The Prince mumbled something emollient
and decided on a word with Mr Pinker, who surely would not be
persuaded by even the Princess into supporting any rash decision.
But the sage of gynaecology sided with his young wife, 'Mother
and baby were both in such fine condition' that he saw no problem
in their leaving. The usual stay in hospital is a minimum of
forty-eight hours and can be up to ten days.

It was 6.01 P.M. when Prince William Arthur Philip Louis set
out *en route* for his own nursery and the world got its first glimpse
of a future king. The arrival of Prince William put Prince Andrew
down a notch. After Prince Charles, the royal baby became second
in line to the throne, with Prince Andrew third, then Prince
Edward and Princess Anne.

Apart from a few blond wisps, all that could be seen was a little
bald head and crumpled face which one day, when he is King, will

appear on bank notes, stamps and coins. He could just be glimpsed peeking out from a large white shawl. The Princess, wearing a turquoise polka-dotted folksy maternity dress and pop socks, smiled indulgently as she handed the baby over to Prince Charles with cautious tenderness. As they drove away in a police-escorted cavalcade the tiny prince heard for the first time the strains of the National Anthem and the sounds of 'Land of Hope and Glory' switched on by a royal enthusiast in the crowd.

'The Princess is a very young person and she is going to exceptional circumstances with exceptional back-up,' Mr Robert Atlay of the Royal College of Obstetricians and Gynaecologists explained. But there was a note of caution for other recent mothers who might want to race back to their home environment. 'If the Princess of Wales can do it so can Mrs Thing – except that Mrs Thing is not going back to the same circumstances at all as the Princess.'

Far from it, at Kensington Palace there would be a well-equipped nursery but at Highgrove there was the luxury of day and night nurseries, a playroom and a bed-sitting room. To begin with the baby would have the attention of a temporary day nurse and a night nurse. In the day nursery at Highgrove he would wake to a mural of humorous tigers, small Bugs Bunny rabbits and foolish flop-eared dogs, all chosen by the Princess to amuse and stimulate her firstborn. In Kensington Palace glass-fronted cupboards were filled with toys, some of them old from the Prince and Princess's own childhood, and pretty painted furniture from a shop called Dragon.

And of course, the Princess had secured an excellent nanny. Once enlisted herself with Kensington Nannies, she would make her own selection, determined to get away from the dyed in the wool, starched apron, 'no uncooked joints on the table, Master William' brigade. Anyway, it was hard to find one these days like the Queen Mother's treasure, who had to ensure the starching and perfection of Princess Elizabeth's hundred bonnets.

Surprisingly it was Princess Margaret, long past the need for nannies herself, who came up with an inspired choice. On several occasions in London, Scotland and Mustique she had been impressed by the independent nanny of great friends Lady Anne and her husband Colin Tennant. After fifteen happy years the informal thirty-nine-year-old Barbara Barnes felt it was time for a move. With a tendency to check shirtwaister dresses, she would not wear a uniform even for the Princess of Wales and liked to be known by her Christian name, not 'Barnes' in the usual public school and army style. This daughter of a forestry estate worker who now owns a share in a London children's clothes shop would be a refreshing change from the old-fashioned 'nanny says' variety.

Barbara Barnes was exactly in tune with the Princess and would push the old-fashioned heavy black pram used to wheel the heir to the throne amongst his subjects near the Peter Pan statue in what Disraeli once described as the 'sublime sylvan solitude' of Kensington Gardens. Nowadays the royal babies are more likely to think they are in Morocco, Saudi Arabia or on the banks of the Nile as exotic turbanned figures and small black-veiled women pad round the Serpentine. Their children tire of their expensive little mechanised boats and leave them on the striped deckchairs or in the water; a replacement will be there next day, Harrods is only minutes away. For the chauffeur it is easy, he knows Knightsbridge as well as the route to the gold mosque in Regent's Park.

The Princess was home for her twenty-first birthday and after so much excitement was happy to have a quiet dinner party with close friends. Everyone expected her to be besotted by her firstborn, but Prince Charles was more than sharing his wife's enthusiasm, proudly announcing on the polo field how William was proving to be a 'very noisy baby'.

A summer baby was ideal. They could get away to Highgrove when the meadows were in full bloom. At thirteen days old, the infant prince was 'totally dominating' the lives of the couple. Close friends were almost shocked by the Prince's preoccupation with his son. The man they had considered a slightly remote aesthete was now found crouched over the baby bath or head down consulting baby books instead of reading Nietzsche or Jung. The Princess was breastfeeding and at eight in the evenings the baby was given a supplementary bottle.

Prince William made his first real public appearance at twenty-nine days old, looking rather confident, lying back on a cream lace cushion in his mother's arms, hands clasped, already kingly some thought in an excessive outburst of loyalty. 'My wife,' the Prince would say proudly, 'deserves a medal for the first one.' Prince Charles thanked her in his quiet way with a luscious diamond necklace with a heart set in the centre which she would wear at the christening and, as a little extra, a bright green Metro with a sunshine roof.

The Princess had been married when she was barely twenty, she had produced her first child before her twenty-first birthday, the wedding and birth all in twelve months giving the monarchy a glamorous refreshing renewal. As a courtier said later, 'She did well producing a boy first time . . .' For in a way that was what the marriage was all about, to secure the throne. It had been a lot to achieve.

CHAPTER 21

Sprinkled with Jordan Water

'Is he all right, Baba?' the Princess would ask Barbara Barnes a hundred times a day. 'Is he breathing properly?' The Princess, exceptionally devoted, could hardly believe her eyes every time she looked in the frilly cradle to admire her first baby. 'I find,' the Princess confided, 'that I can't stop playing with him.' He would be more than all right by the time he was one, slightly overweight at thirty pounds but very keen on learning to walk.

A doting mother, the Princess said, 'I always find time each day for William; he comes first . . . always.' Fiercely protective, she broke with royal tradition by rejecting any suggestion that he should be circumcised. When she bathed him she listened to Capital Radio between 4 and 7 P.M. Prince Charles preferred classical music.

The Princess disappeared from public life for some months after his birth and resentment built up that she should be out of the greedy public eye. Rumours began to fly. 'The Princess was depressed,' 'the marriage was unhappy,' and she was 'anorexic'.

It is true that she did have some delayed reaction to the birth. Everything had been almost too effortless as she came swinging home from the Lindo Wing. Now she was nervy and a bit weepy, often too anxious about the baby and her own weight. The Prince worried about her and made sure she had a medical check-up. However she would be cheerfully reassuring on public engagements. 'Married life is wonderful' was the chirpy, unsolicited testimony when the Princess opened a new extension for the Royal School for the Blind.

Everyone loves a new baby and Prince William's birth came at a time when the country needed a boost; too many young men had been killed in the Falklands War. Potentially one of the richest people in Britain, almost in the world, this baby will succeed his father as one of Britain's biggest landowners and become the 25th Duke of Cornwall. He will be entitled to some 128,047 fine acres scattered over Gloucestershire, in Cornwall, parts of London and the Scilly Isles. He will also have the use of a couple of castles and palaces, 171 farms and rents totalling over £2 million at the time he was born on 21 June 1982.

The Queen would always treat William differently and her word would be vital in the upbringing of this most important child. From the moment he was born Prince William was under the unofficial guidance of a loving, but in the end professionally dedicated, royal 'Think Tank'. But to begin with, his grandmother liked the thrifty notion of digging out old toys like 'Jumbo' the woolly blue elephant from the nursery store at Buckingham Palace. On wheels, Jumbo had already been the walking frame for Princess Anne's children, the boisterous Peter Phillips and irrepressible Zara. It made the Queen rather nostalgic for the days when her own firstborn Prince Charles was toddling about dreaming of being an engine driver and wondering how long his 2s 6d weekly pocket money could last.

The Princess of Wales gave a brunch, champagne and scrambled eggs, to celebrate the birth. Princess Michael of Kent was there, Lady Sarah Armstrong-Jones, lots of royal wellwishers, everyone sadly except the father. Prince Charles had to be away on a private engagement, already a sign of the demands which would keep them apart. The baby was officially called Prince William but his parents affectionately abbreviated this to 'Wills', just like any other jokey, up-market couple. His other names were Arthur, his father's third name, Philip after his grandfather and Louis for

Earl Mountbatten. If you wanted to be struck off the parents' list, no longer invited to supper to enjoy fresh vegetables from the garden, then you would call the baby prince 'Bill'.

Prince William's birth had to be officially registered, but with one big difference. The registrar, Joan Webb, went to the parents at Kensington Palace. The Prince became entry number 115 in the Westminster Register of births. Mrs Webb is a veteran with royal babies, having recorded the births of Princess Anne's children, Prince Michael of Kent's and the Duke of Gloucester's.

Mrs Webb had tried once before to register the birth but when she went to the Palace was told Prince Charles was out. This was not rudeness. The Palace was in a state of shock because an intruder, Mr Michael Fagan, had broken into the Queen's bedroom and the staff misunderstood the reason for Mrs Webb's visit. After her second more successful attempt the parents were handed a shortened birth certificate and a pink NHS card. In the register Prince Charles listed his occupation as Prince of the United Kingdom. The baby was twenty-three days old.

Prince William, who comes of age in the year 2000, will probably travel in space and will certainly have to be more European than his immediate forebears. In the meantime, his parents' choice of name, Guillaume, Willem or Wilhelm, strikes a happy chord in places as far apart as Derry in Northern Ireland, Holland and Germany although nobody was quite sure why William was chosen.

The most famous William was the Conqueror, who left his comfortable duchy of Normandy, crossing the Channel in 1066 and, after a good battle at Hastings, conquered England. His third son, the hapless William II, who had a predeliction for homosexuals and an antipathy towards the church, was killed by an arrow out hunting in the New Forest on 2 August 1100 after thirteen years on the throne. In those days coronations were not planned steadily for a date six months ahead. There was a certain indecent haste about the speed with which his younger brother rode to Winchester to seize the royal treasure, and three days later became Henry I.

The next William, in the seventeenth century, has always been revered by Ulster Protestants. In trying times in the beleaguered province, the choice of name by the Prince and Princess was seen as a special message of support to resolute Orangemen. It is never forgotten.that it was one of Prince William's predecessors, the Protestant Dutch King William of Orange, who defeated the Irish Catholic army under James II at the Battle of the Boyne in 1690. Riding his white horse, giving orders in halting English, he became a legend in Northern Ireland. 'King Billy' as they affectionately shorten his name in those parts, can never be praised enough and has almost been deified. His victory is celebrated with passionate intensity as a glorious example of Protestantism triumphant every 12 July. The Orangemen march through Derry with drums, pipes and banners, King Billy's flag as prominent as the bowler hats of the Apprentice Boys.

King James II fled the battlefield. Arriving in Dublin he complained to his Irish hostess Lady Tyrconnel, as he mulled over the day, that his Irish soldiers had left him. 'Your countrymen, Madam, can run well,' he said bitterly. 'But not so well, Your Majesty,' his hostess retorted swiftly, 'for I see you have won the race.' While James II settled down into exile in sybaritic comfort at the French court, William and his wife Mary had responded to an invitation to become King and Queen of England.

William III was a lacklustre fellow. He kept a mistress, Barbara Villiers, but tended to be rather introverted. Apparently indifferent to his childless wife until she died in 1694 of smallpox at the age of thirty-three, he found himself inconsolable and survived her by only eight years.

King William IV, the son of George III, although enlightened in many ways was not an example of sound behaviour; with his passion for his mistress Mrs Jordan, he had ten known illegitimate children. When he heard about his brother's death in 1830 he asked with mischievous glee, 'Who is Silly Billy now?' Scarcely able to contain his excitement, he rode recklessly through the London streets in an open carriage alternately spitting, offering lifts and being kissed by stallholders. But modern for his day, he refused an expensive coronation. He loathed the Duchess of Kent, the mother of his successor Queen Victoria, who was just eighteen when he died in June 1837. The most recent William in the royal family was the Duke of Gloucester's eldest son who was killed in an air crash in August 1972.

Royal babies are still christened in a robe of flowery Honiton lace, originally white but now the colour of country cream, which was worn first for the christenings of Victoria and Albert's children who all slept in a Saxon cradle. Occasionally the lace which has wrapped at least fifty royal babies is sent to the couture house of Hartnell for a few stitches. After each christening the robe is washed in sterilised water and folded away in tissue paper at the Palace. All royal babies are baptised with water from the River Jordan, a charming custom dating back to the Crusades.

Queen Victoria had an intense distaste of childbirth when 'our poor nature becomes so animal and unecstatic'. In her opinion, until they were about four months old babies were 'frightful when undressed: in short, for as long as they have their big body and little limbs and that terrible, frog-like action.' She never overcame her dislike for tiny babies and one of the reasons the Prince Consort felt so responsible for the christenings was this antipathy. At the baptism of one of her children, she was so terrified she might drop the creature that she insisted a servant should hide beneath her bombazine prepared to catch it. Prince Albert had composed a christening anthem for the occasion but it was ruined on the day because the Duke of Wellington's late arrival prompted the choir to break off and burst into an emotional rendering of 'See the Conquering Hero Comes' from *Judas Maccabaeus* to honour the victor of Waterloo.

The Prince and Princess deliberately chose the Queen Mother's eighty-second birthday for the christening of the forty-four-day-old person they loved most in the world. On 4 August 1982, a warm sunny Wednesday, to the chords of Handel's 'Water Music' on the grand piano, the Queen, Prince Philip and the Prince and Princess of Wales arrived for the ceremony in the Music Room of Buckingham Palace.

The sun danced on the ornate gold mirrors and the gold Lily Font which is made of silver gilt. Now it had been decorated with white freesias and roses from Windsor. In seats of honour were Mr Pinker and four Lindo nurses. The scarlet-cassocked choirs of the Chapels Royal sang 'Oh Jesus, I have Promised to Serve Thee to the End' and 'Guide Me, Oh Thou Great Redeemer'.

The principal arrived in his nanny's arms at 11.59 A.M. He remained calm in his beautifully starched frills until sprinkled with Jordan water by the Archbishop of Canterbury, Dr Robert

Runcie, when he let out three small cries. Real howls were saved for later, and not even the old ivory rattle held by the Queen at her own christening could soothe. 'He gets noisier and angrier by the day,' his father explained proudly to the Queen Mother, who thought William certainly had 'a good set of lungs'. 'He'll be a great speechmaker,' the Queen drily observed.

His mother, quite unflustered by the racket, deftly stopped the noise with her little finger, only hers would do, and in an instant he was tranquil. Perhaps at close range he was overcome by her new hat. She had bought it the day before when she shot out to Knightsbridge and came back with the look of a woman who had found just what she wanted. Pink and striking with a wide brim, it matched her pink, blue and white flowery silk dress.

For the photographs, Prince Charles produced a handkerchief from the top of a dark striped suit and wiped away an unseemly dribble from the baby's chin. Then he sat down with his wife on a chaise-longue and asked in his best Goonish voice, 'Hello, who are you?' to relax her for the historic photocall. The Queen Mother put down a gin and tonic and, looking slightly like *Alice in Wonderland*'s Duchess, picked up the baby who looked completely comfortable in that ample lap as they posed for a classic four generations picture.

The six godparents were Prince Philip's cousin 'Tino', ex-King Constantine of the Hellenes, aged forty-one; Lady Susan Hussey; Lord Romsey, the thirty-three-year-old grandson of Lord Mountbatten and a close friend of Prince Charles; the Duchess of Westminster; Princess Alexandra, aged forty-five, always valued in the royal family for her stateliness and the seventy-five-year-old South African-born sage Sir Laurens van der Post who has given Prince Charles such insight into 'spiritual imponderables'.

'One of the reasons I asked him to be godfather to my son was because he is one of the best story-tellers I have ever come across,' said the Prince who has always lamented the decline in the ancient art of story-telling, passed on from generation to generation. He has blamed television for the disappearance of 'the mystery and excitement, romance and imaginativeness . . .'

Only 'Tally', for Natalia, the stunning 6-foot twenty-two-year-old Duchess of Westminster, was really the Princess's personal choice. A daughter of Colonel Harold Phillips and his wife Georgina, who are great friends of the Queen's, she is not unlike the Princess. Shy originally, when she married Gerald Grosvenor, one of the wealthiest men in Britain, when she too was only nineteen. She has blossomed and, the Princess teasingly says, 'She is too grand for us now.' But as a new wife the Duchess said demurely, 'I'd much rather start young. Then I can be taught the proper way to do things' with the servility affected by these aristocratic girls, adding that she loved cleaning baby's puddles from the nursery carpet.

These two great friends had endless giggly chats about babies, the Princess gleefully confiding that Prince William was 'extremely heavy and he keeps widdling all over me.' Five months earlier, the Princess had become godmother to the Westminsters' second baby, Lady Edwina Grosvenor.

Apart from the predictable gifts of silver rattle and spoon, there were also about two thousand others: toys, mainly fluffy, silver napkin rings and photograph frames. The more imaginative included a case of claret, a gift from a French diplomat to be enjoyed when the Prince is eighteen and, from the American President's wife, Mrs Nancy Reagan, a charming Chippendale child's chair.

The taste in royal christening cakes was at its most baroque when Queen Victoria's first child was baptised on her wedding anniversary, 10 February 1841. Prince Albert himself designed a confection for Princess Victoria. It is hard to imagine Prince Philip and Prince Charles laboriously working at the icing, creating symbols like royal yachts and polo sticks. Prince William's cake was cut up and sent to the 182 men of the Welsh Guards and the Parachute Regiment wounded in the Falklands war.

The ceremony lasted twenty-five minutes and exactly fifteen minutes after the champagne was poured into long-stemmed crystal glasses the baby was taken away so that he could have his own midday sustenance. On the way back to the Kensington Palace nursery, the Princess asked if her car could slow down by the Palace gates and lifted Prince William up for the crowd. It had been an incredibly hot day, and now, as everyone began to drift away, there was a violent thunderstorm. Against all good advice, people scattered to shelter under the trees in St James's Park where seventeen, six of them children, were struck by lightning and taken to hospital semi-conscious with burns and shock.

In August, the public had a slight frisson when Prince Charles flew his successor to Scotland with the Princess and Prince Philip on board as well. Monarchy is a hard-won art with a long apprenticeship. For safety reasons the Queen never travels with Prince Charles, the loss of such inherited knowledge would be irreplaceable. Prince Charles needed to be reminded and warned; baby books had not mentioned rules for 'Heirs in the Air' but it was folly for the first and second in succession to travel together. This public concern would remind the Prince and Princess of the task ahead of them, how this first child should be brought up always aware that one day he would wear the crown, yet hopefully enjoying an ordinary rumbustious life as a schoolboy.

The Prince and Princess would rely less on textbooks before the birth of their second child. Their friends knew they were longing to have another but the Princess found it less easy to conceive second time round and used the 'temperature test' which helps to indicate when a woman is at her most fertile.

The first telltale sign that she was pregnant again was the sight of Prince Charles barely able to conceal his good humour, teasing his wife, nudging her, whispering and affectionately putting his hand round the back of her neck in mock strangulation. You never see them clowning like this in public any more. The news of the expected second baby was announced on St Valentine's Day, 14 February 1984. When Prince Charles visited a Jaguar car factory – the Princess drives a green XJS – he remarked to one of the men on the assembly line, 'Your production is going well.' To this there was only one reply, 'Your production is going well, too, Sir.' But the Princess was overheard saying dubiously on another occasion, 'I don't think I'm made for the production line, but it's all worth it in the end.'

So it was once more into the Lindo Wing of St Mary's Paddington. The 'absolutely adorable Harry' was born on 15 September 1984 at 4.20 P.M. and was described by his father in clubland language as 'a thoroughly splendid chap'. The labour pains had begun at 7.30 A.M. that morning; the couple were at Windsor and were whisked along the M4 with a police escort. As often with second babies, the delivery was much quicker. Another change was the cost of the room in the Lindo Wing, which had now gone up to £140 a day. Prince Charles was again in attendance for the birth, soothing his wife and passing her lumps of ice to suck, giving her cream to stop her lips chapping.

The unflappable Mr Pinker was also present; this was the ninth royal baby he had welcomed into the world. He had saved the Duchess of Gloucester's first baby, the Earl of Ulster, who was born two months early, in a Caesarean operation lasting four hours. He also helped a grieving Duchess of Kent to cope with the loss of her fourth and last baby and is truly a royal favourite.

After the birth, Prince Charles telephoned the Queen and Prince Philip who were on holiday in Balmoral; next in order of precedence was Earl Spencer, who immediately flew the family flag at Althorp, and finally mother-in-law Mrs Shand Kydd in Scotland.

'We've almost got a polo team,' the happy father said, but he looked tired as he told the enthusiastic crowd of fifteen hundred, 'I'm going home for a stiff drink'. The next day, Prince William, in a beautifully laundered smocked top, was taken by the Prince of Wales to see his baby brother.

Looking decidedly more fashionable than she had done after Prince William's birth, the Princess, in a red dress and shoes with red bows, her hair blonder, fluffy and glamorous, once again left hospital early, after a twenty-two-hour-and-twelve-minute stay. The Prince drove his wife and new baby home to Kensington Palace in a blue Daimler, made sure they were comfortable, and then raced off in his Aston Martin to play polo at Windsor. Polo has always been a priority with the Prince. There was an impromptu party for him as his chums drank champagne from paper cups in the back of a Land Rover at Smith's Lawn.

Prince 'Wills' had adapted to his newly arrived sibling but got very bored at the christening with all that Honiton lace and Jordan water. He amused himself in the Music Room at Buckingham Palace by clambering round the Archbishop of Canterbury's gaiters pretending to be a snappy corgi. Baptised Henry Charles Albert David, sadly Prince Harry would not be known as 'Prince Hal' which has a nice ring to it. In Shakespeare's *Henry V* there is 'a little touch of Harry in the night'. This Harry did cry in the night but only once at the font on the day of his christening.

For this christening the Princess, who is herself godmother to twenty-eight children, was able to choose more personal friends as godparents. Brian Organ, the artist who did a striking and simple portrait of the Princess in the early days, dressed in black jeans and a waistcoat and looking out with a calm eye; one of her flatmates, Carolyn Pride, and Lord Vestey's wife Cece. The Vesteys are enormously rich landowners in Gloucestershire, almost on a par with the Grosvenors.

This second child has been less trouble than Prince William or perhaps his parents were more confident. An 'extraordinarily good baby, he sleeps marvellously, eats very well and doesn't wake us up too much in the middle of the night,' his mother said proudly. The Queen and the Queen Mother with their strong sense of history needed no reminding of the curious streak of fate which has meant the last two kings, George V and George VI, have been second sons.

CHAPTER 22

Some Charming Rustic Plan

Kensington Palace is like a royal village. Home for fourteen members of the Queen's family, it was just a bit overpowering for the Princess in the beginning.

Three centuries old, part of a design by Sir Christopher Wren, it is where Queen Victoria was born and was also home to King William and Queen Mary, who wanted a modest, homely little palace quite the opposite of his enemy Louis XIV's gold ostentation at Versailles. Today it still has a sweet, relaxed quality, unlike Buckingham Palace where guests feel a little daunted immediately they set foot on the red-carpeted steps as the door is opened instantly by a liveried manservant. The Princess has tried very hard to create a gentle atmosphere, but leaves a surprising amount of the domestic arrangements to her husband who likes to keep an eye on the day-to-day running of his homes. She enjoys organising food and flowers and wishes she did not need a large staff. 'Diana would prefer it if nobody but her own private secretary needed to be in the house,' an aide who had been made to feel intrusive complained.

Nicknamed 'KP', Kensington Palace has an old-fashioned charm and is off Millionaires' Row, that leafy wide street of embassies. The red mellow-stoned building has a cobbled courtyard and a chiming clock. In spring the Dutch Garden is a riot of tulips. At dusk the gas street lamps give the romantic atmosphere of a stageset.

Callers may find the Princess in the yard saying goodbye to friends, perched exuberantly on the bonnet of their car. Rows of gleaming black official cars purr in readiness and you could do your make-up by the shine on Prince Charles's Aston Martin. 'Get off the bonnet before you dent it,' he has been known to say crossly to the Princess.

'KP' is very handy for Knightsbridge, which made it attractive for the Princess, who, in the lightest disguise, big sunglasses, occasionally a headscarf, used to skip out to Harvey Nichols and Harrods. Nowadays she feels even less likely to be noticed in her jeans and fun T-shirt with a moon and stars glittery design.

The Prince and Princess have two apartments, Eight and Nine, linked in an L shape. The atmosphere is 'homely', but even so on each landing there are portraits of grand royal ancestors to remind them of their destiny. One is of George II who designed the 275 acres of Kensington Gardens, now home of the famous Peter Pan statue and the Victoria and Albert Memorial. One of the first signatures you see in the Prince and Princess's guest book is 'Spencer' with 'Daddy' in brackets.

It is not all that big. The Princess has a large eau-de-nil dressing room – she is quite keen on green – and insisted on a mirrored bathroom. The Prince has a study on the first floor where papers fly when he does his Canadian Air Force exercises. He had his 7-foot-6-inch four-poster bed transferred from Buckingham Palace to Kensington Palace for his wife. They sleep separately. As a friend of the Princess's explained, 'I don't think it hugely worries her . . . Diana has been brought up with this kind of arrangement, her father Earl Spencer sleeps separately from her stepmother,' a typical aristocratic arrangement. Prince Charles explains why it is eminently sensible, a decision 'one arrived at for purely practical reasons. Diana and I each have such busy schedules that if we shared a room we would only get under each other's feet.' It can also be an elegant way of sustaining interest.

Staff find the Princess is a good employer, fun, human but a stickler with high standards exactly like the Queen Mother.

Servants sleep at the top of the Palace in small rooms with dormer windows in the roof. It sounds charming but can get fearfully hot in summer. They are up at six in the morning to prepare a light breakfast for the Princess who likes to be called at 7 A.M., when she reads the *Daily Mail* over orange juice and toast. The Prince tends to read *The Times* and sometimes the other 'heavies'.

The light lemon and peachy colours all reflect the Princess's taste. You will find no mannish tobacco-coloured walls at either Kensington Palace or Highgrove. The yellow drawing room is where you first meet the couple if you are invited to dinner: 'Come around eight.' There you are given a glass of vintage champagne by a footman before going in to a light supper which may be watercress soup, gravadlax, fromage frais and champagne sorbet, all the Princess's favourite foods. Sturdier male guests have been known to go on to a hearty late supper of pâté and steak while their figure-conscious wives have been delighted by the delicacy of the Princess's hospitality. Both are passionately opposed to chips, which predictably enough their sons adore. Naturally fond of food, the Princess shows great restraint, but still loves babyish things like Chocolate Bath Olivers.

Nowadays, after an engagement, the Princess races up the two stone steps and the wide Georgian staircase to see Prince Harry, and often Prince Charles is racing down the same steps to the helicopter pad. In the past, it was for a few chukkas, but recently for more contemplative hours at his easel as his arm healed from the fall he had playing polo.

Close by, in Number Ten, are Prince and Princess Michael of Kent; the Gloucesters have thirty-five rooms, partly because Princess Alice, who is ninety, lives with them and their three children; Princess Margaret is in 1A Clock Tower. Nearby and lending family support to the Princess are her sister Lady Jane Fellowes and her husband Robert, the Queen's Private Secretary, who have a house called 'The Old Barracks' at the Palace.

Prince Charles is very much the boss. He infuriated Princess Michael of Kent by sending her one of his memos. 'Why doesn't he pick up the telephone and complain to me if I have done something to upset him?' she asked crossly. Marie-Christine, as she is known to all the family, was aggrieved, feeling she was being treated like a faceless tenant.

The Prince was annoyed because his queenly neighbour told his butler Alan Fisher off for using foul language in front of her two children Ella and Freddy. The offending flunky had shouted 'Go and fetch the bloody salt' when setting up lunch in the garden for the Princess of Wales. Like all little family squabbles, it was a bit silly and comical, and the butler has since left. But the Prince made it clear he wanted to know about everything going on in his Palace. 'Why doesn't she complain to me?' he asked but, to give Princess Michael her due, she thought it all too trivial.

Whatever she does it seems Princess Michael, like the Duchess of York, tends to cause irritation. Envious of the Prince and Princess's roof garden, with sun terrace for topless tanning and barbecue where the Prince cooks salmon steaks for his wife and jacket potatoes for the children, she persuaded the Minister of the Environment, Michael Heseltine, to allow her one too. Even better, she got the Ministry to pay for it. Like most men, the wavy-haired Minister was susceptible to the Princess's charm.

The Princess of Wales was rattled because the Kents' terrace overlooked her bedroom, but got her own back by smartly pinching nanny Ruth Wallace from under Princess Michael's nose. Prince Harry and William had met Miss Wallace when she was out in Kensington Park walking round the sunken gardens and lily pond with the Kent children and kept telling their mother about the wonderful 'Roof'.

Noisy plumbing has always driven Prince Charles mad, as have rooms that are overheated, sending him straight to a window, where he curses if it does not open easily. Men in the royal family have been dogged by porphyria which makes skin sensitive to heat and sun.

The Princess is a stickler for orderliness. The boys must stack all their toys away in red toy racks and keep the nursery neat with its wickerwork chair, decorative rocking horse, cream sofa and table with American cloth which can be sponged down. Her touch is everywhere; her sitting room is soft with pale blue trellis wallpaper, pink squashy sofas and pictures hung with velvet bows and ornate gilt oval mirrors.

'It's rather garish, isn't it?' Bob Geldof, the Irish pop singer who did so much for Ethiopia, for once kept his language in check as he glanced at the green carpet with the Prince of Wales feather motif and thought it not to his taste. The Prince shrugged and smiled.

The Princess is not an animal person, so her pets are in porcelain – usually birds, rabbits and particularly frogs. You never find her with a cat or a dog and she keeps her distance from Prince Charles's labrador Harvey, now banished to Highgrove because he was not house-trained. Prince Charles has the sensible sportsman's attitude to animals but he cannot abide cats and it is not unusual for callers to get a mouthful of fur as the Prince hurls out some unfortunate stray moggy.

On Fridays, like other Londoners, the Prince and Princess love to get to the country. The cook, a butler and dresser and valet will drive down earlier, and in the evening, the Prince and Princess of Wales follow with their detectives to Highgrove. As the car carrying the princes leaves the old Roman road between Bath and Cirencester, the boys become very excited as they look out for the 'two toads totally tried to trot to Tetbury' tongue twister in a tea shop window in this seventeenth-century market town where their mother buys fudge and Strawberry Chew.

Highgrove is very dear to Prince Charles, 'a self-confessed countryman' who has long been in love with its centuries-old stone walls and rambling garden. It is set in some of Gloucestershire's best farmland; late lambs are up to their hocks in meadows of buttercups, cow parsley and bluebells. The graceful nine-bedroomed Georgian house is protected by glossy horse chestnuts, good posts and railings. Sadly, many of the charming old stone cottages once lived in by estate workers now have to be police listening posts.

From the Prince's point of view it is perfect, only eight miles from Cirencester where he can play polo; eight miles from Gatcombe Park, Princess Anne's house and no distance from Camilla Parker-Bowles' home – three good reasons why his wife was not at first enthusiastic. With his architectural instincts the Prince has restored the house to its eighteenth-century elegance, giving it back its dignity by creating Ionic columns at the front and a decorative balustrade at the top.

Originally the Queen had misgivings and, in Oscar Wilde style, sniffed, 'Highgrove sounds like something in Wimbledon.' But once she set foot in the terracotta hall with its highly polished floor, she recognised a classic country house decorated in soft warm pinks and yellows, with flowery Kelim rugs.

As soon as you arrive you notice the air of calm and restfulness. It is a peaceful house with its mahogany furniture, ticking grandfather clocks, piano and cello, parquet floors and gentle watercolours. Everywhere there are bowls of freesias, jasmine and lilies, and decorative porcelain boxes which simply say 'I Love You'.

In the German kitchen at the end of a long polished wooden corridor the Princess finds it fun to wash up, putting on a pair of pink rubber gloves, or makes herself a bowl of custard before going to bed. The couple are completely relaxed at Highgrove except that Prince Charles gets cross if the boys are too boisterous and the Princess hates it if they bring mud into the house. She is perhaps just a bit too tidy: her neatness makes you hesitate about leaving a magazine in the wrong place. Yet the Prince's office is a dreadful clutter of papers and blue boxes of state documents. He is particularly proud of his collection of Victorian lavatory seats and cartoons done by his tormentors in the newspapers and keeps these in much tidier order.

The Prince, like his grandfather, adores gardening and finds it a way of getting peace, a perfect excuse for not having to indulge in idle chatter with his wife's friends at weekends. Imaginatively he has planted wildflower walks and a rosemary hedge near the swimming pool where the Princess enjoys her early morning skinny dip. Silver-leafed herbs soften the stone urns of geraniums and fuchsias and there are intriguing apple tunnels loved by the boys.

On a summer's day butterflies hover on the espaliered pear trees. In the kitchen garden there are quinces. The Prince is such a purist that his marmalade comes from this fruit as originally made in Henry VIII's time when it was a delicacy enjoyed at the end of a royal banquet. All the soft fruit, plums, apricots, nectarines and peaches, are bottled, made into jams or preserved.

In the afternoon, if the weather is hot, the Prince goes into his walled garden past the box hedge with its romantic intertwined C and D. The Princess telephones her friends or sits in a cool arbour of white trellis with classic English roses. Sometimes the local fox calls and leaves paw marks on the pink gate.

They rarely have breakfast together, even in the country. Usually up first around 6.30, Prince Charles listens keenly to the farming programme on Radio 4, then walks, runs or swims and has a poached egg, his idea of something solid before a day's hunting. The Princess is up half an hour later for a light breakfast of pink grapefruit with a healthy spoonful of wheatgerm and maybe some live yoghurt with a cup of tea. She never allows herself more than two slices of wholemeal toast. They are both terribly health conscious, ordering all the staff to have flu jabs because he was so worried about any infection when his smashed arm took so long to heal.

The Prince goes off to the farm to talk about the number of organic loaves sent to London supermarkets with the Highgrove stamp. Or else when he has looked at his papers he will do some weeding, which he finds 'very therapeutic . . . and it is marvellous if you can do enough to see the effect.' He may gather some nettles which he brings back to the kitchen to be made into a nourishing favourite soup. He relies heavily on his handyman Paddy Whitehead, an old retainer who came with the house when the Prince bought it in 1980 for nearly a million pounds. It had belonged to a former Prime Minister's son, Maurice Macmillan. This craggy-featured old retainer was the only one kept on at Highgrove when Charles took over the house, and on Paddy's word a whole team of builders could be virtually dismissed. Paddy could be seen sitting in the back of the Prince's Aston Martin to watch him playing polo. His wife Nesta, a birdlike woman, is the housekeeper. The Prince is a son to this childless pair and he relishes old Paddy's outspokenness.

The couple meet again for lunch. They hardly ever eat meat and enjoy delicious egg dishes or homemade soup, salads and ice-cream made from Highgrove eggs. All butter, milk and vegetables come from the farm. The cook is free to serve what she likes so long as fish is meticulously filleted, there are no seeds in the tomatoes and definitely no garlic. Both like boned chicken and the Princess is extremely fond of a soup of boiled cabbage and potatoes mushed up together and seasoned with horseradish and paprika.

The Princess, who says she is 'an average cook', believes you are what you eat. In her case it may be a delicious diet of avocado and kiwi fruit with fresh orange. On Saturday lunch might be carrot soup, scallops or spinach soufflé. They are very proud of their homegrown white and purple carrots and the Highgrove version of shepherd's pie is called 'mince 'n' mash mush'. The Princess has no time for bubbly designer waters, preferring the tranquillity of Malvern.

The children love Highgrove and in the royal horsey tradition already look forward to hunting. In their pristine hacking jackets and jodhpurs, Prince William on Trigger and Prince Harry, already a promising horseman, on Smokey are seen at local gymkhanas. Their mother will abandon them for a while, leaving them to girl groom Marion Cox while she goes for a brisk walk over the network of footpaths round Highgrove. Or she may drive into Cirencester and have a joke in a local music store, asking the owner, 'Got any Val Doonican records?' when everyone knows she is a Phil Collins, Billy Joel girl. Sometimes she steals into a tree museum about four miles away and is easily spotted in a white jogging outfit in the green shadows before the crowds come to admire the conservation.

At the end of a day picking flowers and fruit, cycling, walking, gardening, the couple fall into bed, usually by ten o'clock. Sometimes, however, the Prince stays up long after his wife has retired. He loves these quiet night hours when the telephone never rings. The Princess worries about the time Prince Charles spends on official papers. She may pad into his study wrapped in her red cotton dressing gown to plead with her husband to get some rest. If it is Highgrove, she often finds him not sitting crouched over some abstruse papers, but a picture of contentment in his beloved patched dressing gown with his personal emblem on the pocket, listening to opera at top volume.

The Princess has a pretty pink bedroom with trellis wallpaper and on her bed lacy cushions, and one in silk which has a charming motif: 'You have to kiss a lot of frogs to find a prince'. Before putting the light out she reads a few pages of a Danielle Steele novel or, as she is in Gloucestershire, Jilly Cooper on errant husbands and polo.

Surprisingly it is the Prince of Wales and not the Princess who is deeply devoted to soft toys. Prince Charles dotes on his battered and much travelled teddy, which has accompanied him on trips abroad and occupies a special place in the Prince's affections. It too is royally treated, being put to bed in fine linen and snuggled down carefully. So worn is the teddy that the Queen Mother volunteered to provide him with a new set of pads. The teddy has yet to make an official appearance, or perch on the podium as his master makes a challenging speech.

Sundays are lazy mornings at Highgrove. They love the privacy of their weekends, only disturbed by the ritual of polo. It is curious that the royal family do not seem to care for ball games such as cricket or golf, but Prince Charles has built a £10,000 tennis court at Highgrove for his wife. From a window of the house, the Prince and Princess can see the tall spire of Tetbury's church of the Virgin Mary, one of the prettiest in Gloucestershire and just a few minutes away. They can hear the church bells, too, as the good burghers of the market town go to Sunday Communion at ten. Some of the children and little old ladies can barely see above the oak pews. But two little heads which are never seen are those of the Princes Harry and William; the Princess has not attended the church once since her marriage.

A parishioner shook his head as he folded away the vicar's white wool creamy High Church alb and said sadly, 'We could do with his support.' He looked up at the scaffolding, 'Half a million we'll be needing in the New Year.' John Hawthorne, a late vocation vicar, says the Prince very occasionally slips in to Morning Eucharist. He called at Highgrove in July 1990 and was given three-quarters of an hour by the Prince before he went on holiday to stay with King Juan Carlos. Hawthorne needed all his television marketing expertise to appeal to his royal parishioner, coming away with only a guarded assurance of some blessing for the restoration work.

The Princess, for all her goodness and gaiety, is not a church-goer; she does not care for the long readings, the formality and the hour and a half it takes for an average service. Prince Charles as future Head of the Church has an obligation, but as one of his advisers says, 'The trouble is he sees everyone's point of view . . .'

It is more likely that the Prince is taken up with some charming rustic plan on a Sunday morning than deliberately ignoring church. He tried to get all the cattle at Highgrove to wear antique bells around their necks after he had found the music they made charming in Tuscany. But they were terrified so he had to make do with fastening bells round the necks of a few docile sheep too daft to resist.

CHAPTER 23

Fighting Talk

Nowadays as the Princess begins a foreign tour, glossy, confident with hand outstretched, there is nostalgia for Australia in 1983. People remember a girl taking her first tentative steps on the red earth of Ayers Rock, the mystical aboriginal place, in a pale blue shirtwaister and inadequate, ballet-thin flatties. The old people of the Pitjanjatjara and Yangunkuntjatjara tribes came to honour her with a glimpse of a Thorny Devil lizard, ruining her chance of a photograph of the sunset. So instead the Princess listened with her head on one side and became intrigued by their aboriginal 'dreamtime' legends.

An experienced member of the Queen's Household in his dark suit and highly polished black shoes watched her in the searing heat and rocked back on his heels. 'It will,' he said with quiet authority, 'take about ten years,' and turned away to talk to a Canberra diplomat about aboriginal rights.

But he was wrong. She learnt to be royal on that visit. They say it was Australia with its buoyant 'We take you as you are' attitude and the gentleness of New Zealand which gave her confidence, helping any diffidence and shy awkwardness to disappear. The transition has been so complete, it is hard to recall a Princess who wept often and before the visit complained, 'I am finding it very difficult to cope with the pressures of being Princess of Wales.'

She did things never known before on royal tours: she went hatless; her hair was often 'messy and limp' in the humidity, you would never see it looking so natural again; she got suntanned, her nose sweetly pink; she went sunbathing at 'Snob Hill'. At Tennant Creek, in 92-degree heat, she whisked off her tights and became the first royal woman to appear publicly with bare legs; she shook hands with a freshness and touching vulnerability, a willingness to go forward which can never be recaptured.

Initially the Australians had not been excited about this royal visit. There had been mutterings about the £1,500,000 cost of the tour. A recent election had brought in the outspoken Robert 'Bob' Hawke leading a Labour Party which firmly believed that monarchy was outdated. Fighting talk. But in no time they were calling her 'Dinki Di', which is much more of a compliment than it seems. Dinki is an abbreviation of dinkum and to be 'fair dinkum' in Australia is about as high as you can get in plaudits. 'You're so beautiful,' dustcaked outback stockmen shouted, and the Princess laughed. 'Thank you. I shall blush now.' Soon Hawke was slavishly admitting, 'The Princess is a lovely lady.'

She shook so many hands that there was an SOS to Kensington Palace saying, 'Please send more white gloves.' She made so many appearances, wearing a different outfit nearly every day, and used fifty of the two hundred outfits she had taken with her for the forty-two day trip. Looking back, it was too much, a wild and wonderful collection from several designers. Today she believes in 'Less is best.'

A nine-month-old baby was unheard of on a royal tour but for the Princess it had been unthinkable to spend a month in the Antipodes without her son. Royal mandarins were shocked by the steely resolve of this young girl who had until recently been fairly malleable. But she was determined. It was quite simple, either Prince William went to Australia with them or Prince Charles could go on his own. She held the trump card. So Prince William jetted to the antipodes with his assertive, independent mother. A Harley Street psychiatrist, herself a mother of six, applauded this 'just and courageous decision'. It had taken a lot of spunk.

'We are bringing him up on grass and beer,' the Prince said

when the baby was on show in New Zealand where the Maoris had welcomed the Queen as the 'Rare White Heron of Singular Flight'. Her daughter-in-law now rubbed noses with them and the baby stuck his tongue out which was applauded as a true Maori greeting. Taking Prince William Down Under was a brain-wave. They loved his mother's spirit. 'Ah, his first Australian fly,' the Prince joked as one landed on the baby's cheek when the family arrived at dawn after their twenty-four-hour flight from London. Several flies gathered on the back of the Princess's dress. 'Perhaps,' a wag suggested, 'they don't know who she is,' as Prince William was handed over to his nanny Barbara Barnes.

He was being taken off to Woomargama, a pleasant 4,000-acre sheep station in New South Wales, but the crowd wailed, 'Aaw, Billy the Kid's feet haven't touched Australian soil.' The Princess laughed. 'Goodness, he isn't the Pope you know.' A quick bright reply is just what the Australians love to hear. Even the start of the tour was quirky. Delayed by floods, the royal couple had to spend their first night in a motel room near Alice Springs. They had a cold supper in bed and watched a video about the outback.

The Princess would cope with the media, cheerfully calling them 'the wolf pack'. In a radio station, separated from them by a glass viewing panel, she pretended to be a caged animal, baring her teeth and clawing the glass. You would never find her doing that today though she may now feel even more imprisoned.

But they could hurt her, too. When she was still inexperienced she pointed to her heart and said, 'When they write something horrible I get a terrible feeling right here and I don't want to go outside.' She thought it might take her five or even ten years to get used to the media but that estimate was wrong, too. Today there is goodwill on both sides.

The Prince and Princess found that Prince William's arrival was a talking point and valuable on walkabouts. Instead of, 'How long have you been standing here?' there was baby banter: 'Thank you, he's fine . . . he's got six teeth.' Mrs Jill Shoebridge, a housewife among the crowd of 7,000 who had turned out to see the royal couple in Canberra, remarked wistfully to the Princess, 'I wish I had a nanny like you sometimes' as her fifteen-month-old son Simon vigorously tore up a bouquet of flowers. The Princess replied quickly, 'I would swap with you any time. I wish I didn't have to leave William with a nanny. I would rather do what you are doing.' William was being looked after by two nannies but even they could not stop him putting his toy koala bear down a lavatory.

Like summer bees busily circling, the Prince and Princess would buzz back to see their baby every so often. While they relaxed in the cool scented rose garden near the swimming pool, Prince William would have his first dip wearing tiny royal blue trunks and be quickly nicknamed 'Prince of Waves'.

Prince Charles watched his wife blossoming in Australia. During one engagement, when asked, 'Where's Lady Diana?' he grinned and replied, 'I'm sorry, you'll just have to put up with me. It's not fair, is it? You'd better ask for your money back.' He added ruefully that 'perhaps it might have been better to have had two wives.'

At night the Princess appeared in apricot taffeta, grey silk dotted with butterflies or shimmering blue and, on her shoulder, the Queen's seal of approval – a delicate hand-painted picture of the Sovereign on a pretty enamel brooch. The Queen's Family Order is presented only to women in the royal family and it is a sure sign of acceptance; yet not every young wife wants to go about with her mother-in-law pinned to her dress.

At a gala ball in Sydney the Prince proudly told his audience after lobster, beef fillet and strawberries that the last time he had been in Australia, he had been engaged 'to a lovely lady . . . and now he had been lucky enough to marry her.' The Princess, who had been looking fixedly at the honorary koala bear carved in ice and large flamingos made of lard, pulled a funny face behind his back and giggled. The Prince turned round. 'It's amazing,' he said with a half-smile, 'what ladies will do when your back is turned.'

They were a couple clearly in love. There had been many a tender touch as Prince Charles put his hand gently on his wife's wrist, or an arm around her waist just to let her know he was near. The Prince later whirled her round the dance floor, taking her breath away. 'Slower, slower,' she pleaded in her shimmering blue 'Gonzaga' dress. His style was so racy some Australian matrons were 'quite surprised' by his high spirits. But the Prince, who is an exceptionally good dancer, only went faster as the orchestra played 'The More I See You'. Nowadays, they no longer seem to have that sort of fun.

CHAPTER 24

A Pleasant Away Day

A typical working day for the Princess was in Brighton on Thursday, 12 July 1990. The sun was beaming on the shimmering Sussex Downs, the sea was inviting like smoky glass and on the Promenade striped deckchairs were fluttering their canvas seats in the breeze.

It is the morning of the International Congress for the Family in Brighton; a nun from Ripon shakes her head and wonders what has happened to the West Pier, sliced in half and never repaired, and goes inside to wait for the royal visitor and hear lectures about the importance of having children.

Polka dots, a white jacket and dotted black skirt are just right, but when the Princess draws up in this crisp outfit, one delegate snorts, 'What a short skirt.' In general it was a day for women with long straight hair and Provençal smocks, creators of bean stews and ragouts with fennel, pamphlet enthusiasts; others in navy suits carry briefcases; a small Indian woman called Emily asks, 'Oh, is lunch included?' and was pleased. Large German ladies with short silver cropped hair got down to serious business.

Roman Catholic clergy were having a pleasant away day from the parish and mixing with young Moslems.

Inside the modern Conference Hall, the Princess opens the conference with an address to the 3,000 delegates on what she believes in passionately, the family. Next she will visit an AIDS centre, gladly backing a cause she cares about deeply and finally make a lot of old people very happy opening new premises for the Brighton Society for the Blind.

The Princess speaks to this 16th Congress. Her delivery is speedy, staccato with appealing little intakes of breath at the end of a sentence. Her speeches have marks in felt-tip pen: 'Lift your head here . . . smile at this point . . . pause . . . smile again . . .': part of Sir Richard Attenborough's coaching. With each paragraph she is a little more confident. 'The family,' she says, 'is after all the most human and hence the most imperfect of institutions.'

Relieved it is over, the Princess grinned as she put away her notes in a smart little cream clutch bag, hinting that this item was all it carried. Complimented afterwards about her speech, she is diffident. 'My family are my worst critics,' she says and laughs. 'Rude royal relatives knock my speeches.'

It was a thoughtful speech which took into account single parent and broken families and she recognised the possibility of families with homosexual parents. This was a major departure from the highly conventional view in her brief from the organisers, which she was expected to endorse. It displeased the predominantly Roman Catholic audience.

During the other speeches, the Princess sat quite still and listened with an intensity which borders on meditation: eyes down, almost closed, but not dreaming; fully aware, they flash open at any instant. Mother Teresa had been expected, but she was too frail after a heart attack to travel. This was a relief for the Princess who was going to be told by the seventy-nine-year-old nun from Calcutta that she should be having more babies.

In April 1987, the Princess had visited a purpose-built ward for AIDS sufferers at the Middlesex Hospital in London. She met nine men dying of AIDS, shook their hands, sat on their beds, talked about their problems and almost apologised for the hysteria surrounding the disease. Professor Stephen Semple, a senior physician, found her visit 'very moving'. Her gesture was better than any Government education programme. But today, her second appointment, visiting an AIDS centre in Brighton, is a private occasion.

Then on to the third engagement, with no sign of flagging. 'We wanted the Princess Royal first,' said Gloria Wright, Director of the Brighton Society for the Blind. Princess Anne was sorry, the society was told, but she could not come. A few weeks later, there was a call from Kensington Palace. 'Yes,' the Princess of Wales would be delighted to take up the invitation.

The Society took over a church hall six months earlier to make a haven for people suddenly disabled by blindness and to make sure they are not in isolation. Thanks to the efforts of a team headed by a former Mayor of Brighton, Mrs Jackie Lythell, and Mrs Wright who has a gentle sweetness with a festive bow in her hair, it has become a home for some one thousand people. One of the top twenty places in the country caring for the partially sighted, it offers counselling, advocacy, home visiting, love and comfort.

'I'll kneel down.' The Princess, deft and agile, moved delicately amongst the old ladies, some swerving about with excitement. 'You've done exactly as my husband has done,' she said to Margot Turner who had her arm in a sling. 'Well yes, but his was off a horse and mine was off a chair,' and the seventy-seven-year-old great-grandmother explained how she had been nursing a baby when it dropped a toy. 'I bent down to pick it up when the chair went and we all went over.' 'Oh dear,' said the concerned Princess, biting her lower lip, but the old lady, not one for self-pity, was much more interested in telling her about the art classes where she helps to teach the partially sighted to paint.

'Sometimes we pop in a quick seagull for them,' she explained to the Princess, who was fascinated by the watercolours done by the nearly blind and was touched by the clarity of scenes of children walking along Lakeland paths, the spring landscapes and green valleys, memories of days when the artists could see.

The partially sighted old ladies quickly got down to celebrating her visit over tea and huge wedges of thick, homemade chocolate cake, telling each other what the Princess had said to them and talking about her touch because blind people know about these things. They remembered how once a blind pensioner had said to the Princess, 'Oh, if only I could see you,' and she had replied, 'But you can,' and took her hand and gently ran it across her face. 'Does it feel craggy?' she had asked and both laughed at the very idea.

Someone started to play the piano. 'Is that the tango?' asked Mrs Lily Gregory. In an instant she was on her feet surprising those who had known her for ten years or more. It had been that sort of euphoric afternoon; everyone was in incredibly high spirits.

The Princess spent half an hour longer than she should have done. Her equerry tried to hurry her along but she would have none of it. She touches everyone with a brightness of spirit which stays long after the anonymous black car has whisked her back to Kensington Palace, her gloveless right hand enjoying a well-earned rest.

The Court Circular recorded that the Princess had opened new premises for the Blind and been received by Admiral Sir Lindsay Bryson, Her Majesty's Lord-Lieutenant for East Sussex, the laconic prose conveying none of the elation of a day when she lightened the spirits of the disabled and the dying.

That night the Princess went to the ballet in a shimmering, slinky blue catsuit, for the first night of the English National Ballet's fortieth anniversary summer season at the Coliseum. It was a classic day in the life of the Princess of Wales.

CHAPTER 25

The Wind is My Enemy

Royal tours may look glamorous on our television screens on a windy January night but the Princess will tell you they are a minefield, full of proverbial banana skins. Prince Philip found this out when he told Western students, 'If you stay here too long, you'll develop slitty eyes' on a visit to China with the Queen in 1986. His self-taught daughter-in-law, on the other hand, has become our best ambassador abroad. No Palace expert could have taught the Princess, who has shaken a million hands since joining the royal family, the art of remembering each name in a line-up, the bright funny word for each person that will make them feel they are the only one that matters.

Her approach is professional and watchful and she takes advice. A team from the Prince and Princess's Office at St James's goes on a recce beforehand: an equerry, a detective and a press secretary all with exquisitely good manners, and cheerful even though they are dropping with the humidity of Pakistan or have a stomach upset. Beneath this patina of courtly behaviour they are razor sharp and check every hazard – except in the case of Pakistan in September 1990 when there was a coup. Benazir Bhutto, the

Prime Minister, someone the Princess admires, was overthrown by the army. The visit was cancelled, leaving the Princess with spaces in her autumn diary.

She has to know about local customs, the food and the weather. High temperatures worry her: 'I don't look good in the heat.' Like many blondes she feels better in crisper weather. 'I'll be perspiring madly and there'll be all those telephoto lenses trained on me. Then a fly will land on my nose and I'll look a fool trying to swat it away.'

'The wind is my enemy,' the Princess says. 'Wherever we go there is a gale blowing.' So her milliners make a couple of matching hat-pins, always cleverly hidden in each hat.

Unlike the Duchess of York, who does have terrific legs but can look like a bandy-legged dowager when her skirt rides up getting out of a car, the Princess never wears skirts that are too short. She is far too smart for that sort of revelation. 'If my skirt is too short, when I bend over there are six children looking up it . . .' she says, and laughs. 'You'd be amazed at what one has to worry about.' And so weights are put in her hems. Sleeves must be worried about too, as she explains. 'You've got to put your arm up to take hold of those flowers so you can't have on anything too revealing.'

Whether it is cutting a ribbon, signing a visitors' book, opening buildings, planting trees, unveiling plaques, making a speech, putting a child at ease, glittering at a banquet where the Prime Minister speaks only Serbo-Croat, there is never a bad-tempered aside or sulky look. Her appeal is international and she can pluck success from nowhere. Even the strain, mental and physical, of a royal tour is not allowed to show; she simply faints.

The Princess has always had an affection for the Canadians because they smoothed those early years for her when she was a willowy newlywed prone to passing out. She would faint again in Canada in 1986. It was thought she must be pregnant. But the simple answer was that she was exhausted and very thin. But like the late Duchess of Windsor, the Princess believes a woman can never be too skinny.

After that first tour in 1983, Canadians, who hate to display emotion, were unashamedly waving and cheering, and holding up painted placards which read: 'We love you Chuck and Di.'

One of Earl Spencer's favourite photographs, which he shows off at Althorp, is of the Princess dressed up as Klondyke Kate in a tight-waisted dress with a bustle. It was taken on that first tour of Canada, when the royal couple ate red-eye steaks and beans and travelled in horse-drawn carriages. Celebrating Canada's 116th birthday, the Prince told his Canadian host, 'We are having a wonderful time.'

'They are always having fun,' said Brian Peckford, Premier of Newfoundland, who thought the royal couple very romantic.

The skill of the Prince and Princess is that they can dress up for a happy, folksy occasion like the Klondyke Celebrations, take part, and yet keep that certain distance. They listened to mining songs and celebrated the good fortune of those early gold diggers. The Princess tapped her feet to the music, waved her scarf in the air and laughed at scantily dressed Klondykettes as she tried unsuccessfully to get Prince Charles to join in the singing.

Dressed like his great-great-grandfather Edward VII when he visited Canada in 1860, Prince Charles in cravat and carrying a cane was behaving with much more propriety than 'Good old Teddy', the playful king.

When it was all over the Princess breathed a sigh of relief as she changed back into 'an ordinary dress' instead of the traditional tightwaisted long white dress which, she confessed, had been 'whalebone from throat to waist'. A shapely blonde, Katie Wiegert, a Royal Mounted Policewoman who was the Princess's constant shadow, was also in a bustle and long flouncy dress; ideal, she laughed, for chasing away terrorists.

What the Palace planners had not allowed for in the recce of this Canadian royal tour was an embarrassingly gushing speech by Richard Hatfield, Premier of New Brunswick, who raised a glass in an emotional 'toast to love'. The Princess was vexed. 'It sent shivers running down my spine . . . I've never been so embarrassed in my life. I have no objection to things being informal, but that man went right over the top. Poor Prince Charles didn't know where to look!' But the Prince quite understood the impact his wife was having on this Newfoundland politician and was quietly amused. Hatfield apologised later: 'I was totally drunk on her charm.'

At St John's, Newfoundland, a sleepy little town of wooden houses on the edge of the Atlantic, they still talk about 'Chuckle heads', a term passed on from Cornish and Irish settlers who arrived four hundred years ago, that means 'thoughtless'. But that was the last word they would apply to the Princess.

'Over here, over here,' a little boy with huge dark glasses and a bow tie had called out and given the Princess flowers. 'Thank you for the beautiful flowers; you should not have spent your money on me,' she often tells children.

Only later, she heard that four-year-old Edward Barnes had been blind from birth. Somebody should have tipped her off. Being the Princess she immediately set about putting things right. Although her programme was packed with engagements, she made time for him after an official lunch and together they held hands. The small boy tugged at her skirt and when some gooey onlooker asked if he wanted to kiss the Princess, replied 'No' with the good manners and restraint of a child. The Princess laughingly agreed, saying Edward was right. He was too young to be kissing girls. With her charmingly relaxed way of easing things, the Princess left Mrs Mary Barnes and her son on a high graceful note.

Flying home at the end of the trip, the royal household helped celebrate the Princess's twenty-second birthday. Everyone sang 'Happy Birthday, Dear Princess' at 30,000 feet over the North Pole. The royal party sipped champagne. The Prince gave her a gold wombat charm, their joke name for Prince William, which he had had made in England and brought with him when they left for the tour three weeks earlier. The cake had the words 'I love you darling' scrolled on the icing. It was quite all right to nibble at a homebaked cake ordered by her husband, but usually the host country is warned that the Princess does not like rich sweets, garlic, red meat, long lunches or a buffet. 'I find it impossible to talk and eat at the same time,' she will explain. 'So I end up chasing a bit of chicken round the plate.' But the poorer the country, the more the hosts try to lay on gargantuan meals to show the warmth of their feelings towards this young couple. Fortunately, they have not yet had to face a huge cold roast sucking pig with the Union flag stuck in its snout and a lobster the size of a dolphin, the fate of the Queen at a welcome lunch in Tonga during her 1977 Silver Jubilee tour. Looking her most inscrutable on a cushion, she focused on a distant palm.

Not to enjoy a 'mutton grab' is seen as an insult in the Gulf. In 1986 the Prince and Princess were on tour to encourage investment in British expertise. All visits have a special purpose. Not a big eater, the Princess in delicate gossamer sat cross-legged with practised ease at banquets by desert oases, inwardly appalled by the greasy lamb and rice put before her on golden dishes while flies hovered in swarms both in and outside the tents. On these occasions she manages to toy with her food while hardly eating at all.

Far from being offended, as a token of his admiration, Sheikh Jaber al-Ahmed al-Sabah, Emir of Kuwait, gave the Princess a diamond choker as wide as a polo neck worth £500,000. No other Arab leader has been so generous, but in March 1989, the Prince was given exotic desert robes, a silver falcon inlaid with gold and diamonds and, to complete a romantic nomadic image, a solid silver coffee set for recitals of Bedouin poetry in the desert.

In contrast, the Prince and Princess of Wales give very modest mementos. However, back in the Prince of Wales's office at St James's Palace, an equerry will tell you with prim certainty that there can be 'no more appropriate gift than a signed photograph of the Prince and Princess of Wales'.

There are fewer official visits to Europe these days, except for Hungary, as the Prince and Princess concentrate more on long-haul trips. In November 1989 the newly serious Princess had been shaking hands with a hundred lepers in Jakarta in temperatures soaring above 94°F and meeting drug addicts in Hong Kong. So it was galling for her to find that the world's attention was captured by pictures of the 'Princess of Wows' doing the backstroke in a jazzy halter-necked swimsuit. The picture was very fuzzy. You could really only see a lot of foamy water but the incident created great excitement. The Princess loves her daily swim but was mortified by the photographs.

But they adored her even more for it in Hong Kong, shouting, 'Over here, your Loyal Highness,' though not feeling warmly pro-British. It was a sensitive time as five million people worried about their future. They were unhappy that the Queen, who is acknowledged as 'The Landlady', seemed unable to help when the colony is to be handed over to the People's Republic of China in 1997, but there was no hint of anti-royal feeling.

These normally very reserved people thought of her affectionately as 'Di on na wong fei', royal concubine. Her clothes were streamlined, unfussy, a touch of power dressing which was appreciated by the business community for which Hong Kong is famous. The tai-tais, the wives of Chinese businessmen, adored her Catherine Walker pinks and purples.

The Princess stunned the world-weary lawyers and politicians on the Hill in Washington when she and the Prince of Wales were on a mission to promote 'British' goods. By day, the caring Princess visited a drug addicts centre with the President's wife Mrs Nancy Reagan, then later went with Mrs Barbara Bush to a British-sponsored Home for the Incurables in Washington and much enjoyed the future First Lady's wit and refreshing directness. But by night she was the starry Princess dancing with the President, with Clint Eastwood and John Travolta at a White House party. 'The lady has style,' Travolta remarked later.

It was typical of the Princess to spot the distress of a local war widow who collapsed during a Remembrance Day ceremony in Japan in November 1990, when she and Prince Charles were attending the enthronement of Emperor Akihito. Without hesitating she left Prince Charles's side and immediately went over to the woman to be with her. The cost of the visit brought criticism, and questions were asked by a Labour MP, Mr Bob Cryer, why the royal couple had to charter a 360-seat jumbo jet for themselves and a staff of fifteen for the twelve-hour flight to Tokyo instead of travelling on the usual and more reliable RAF VC10.

Even though the British couple were not high in the order of precedence, surrounded as they were by so many heads of state and crowned heads, the Princess received almost more attention than the Emperor taking his Chrysanthemum Throne. Her clothes were fashionable, a natty tartan suit, a solemn black Chanel suit for a Remembrance Day service and best of all the white band with a net designed by Philip Somerville, who also designed the red and white rising sun hat which she wore with a long embossed blue silk dress for the ceremony. Prince Charles seemed full of pale strained tension and slow to smile, while in contrast the Princess was cheekily glowing almost behind his back in her

Queen Mary tiara and fuchsia off-the-shoulder dress – smiling, flirting lightly with Albert of Monaco, Willem Alexander of Orange and Spain's dashing Crown Prince Felipe, all young European princes.

After much speculation about the state of the royal marriage – the Prince and Princess were said to be hurt by the insinuations that theirs was a loveless relationship – they refused to appear romantically together for the cameras and instead concentrated intently on the ritual of the Emperor's 'heavenly feather' which is believed to see him on his way from this world to the next.

By day she was full of ebullient high spirits. Visiting the Honda factory near Tokyo she was very taken with Ayrton Senna's 212-mph Formula One racing car. One of the media band shouted, 'They would never catch you on the M4 in that, Ma'am,' recalling how recently she had been told off by the police for speeding, and received a 'I'll make the jokes, thank you,' as a swift reply. She was in such good spirits it was like old times when she responded gaily to teasing by photographers after a visit to the Gulf; 'Why d'you let those greasy Arabs run their hands all over you then?' To which the Princess replied, 'Oh, I just let it all wash over me.' And she found time to visit Japan's only National Children's Hospital at Setayay.

In Delhi, at the Presidential Palace, the Prince and Princess will have been offered the Victorian four-poster double bed slept in by the Queen and Prince Philip during their visit to India. In classic ingenious Indian style, and as masters of improvisation, the bed was speedily lengthened to accommodate the Duke's long legs. Next time, it is the Princess who will be glad of the leg room rather than Prince Charles, who is a few inches shorter than his wife.

It is easy to accept flowers serenely and be charming in a glossy Western environment. The real test is a royal visit to a fairly run-down Third World country where the simplest facilities are primitive. The tour of Nigeria in March 1990 saw a Princess even more mature and confident. Princess Anne does not have sole prerogative on tough assignments. This visit by the Prince and Princess of Wales was the first by British royalty in thirty years. The country was on the brink of a revolution which was followed by a coup. Everyone was struck down by tummy bugs including the Princess, who dashed out of a mud hut she was visiting. 'Quick, where's the loo,' she laughed, running past the dignitaries with their fly whisks. She has the ability to be utterly natural. There is no embarrassment for herself or her hosts.

It is hard to imagine many other members of the royal family being quite so willing to run any risk of looking foolish as she did in Port Harcourt where a woman was weaving a loin cloth. Urged by village elders to have a go, the Princess went down on her knees and immediately got spinning, quite unselfconscious.

The visit had its moments. Standing in front of the fishtank belonging to Colonel Rasaki, the Governor of Lagos, Prince Charles nudged his wife. Romantics were pleased to see any little gesture. 'Look at the frog,' he said, pointing to a plastic toy in the water. For them the frog has always been a private joke. It became public on another tour, when the Princess saw one and laughed. 'I kissed one once,' she said, 'and look what I got.'

CHAPTER 26

Carlo e Diana

Take the Queen's two daughters-in-law, a princess and a duchess. Before they married, one was travelled and worldly, the other, shy and inexperienced, had hardly been abroad at all. However, as in good fairy stories, diffidence triumphed and today it is the Princess of Wales who is the sophisticated traveller famous for looking cool in the heat and keeping her luggage to a minimum, a sure sign of confidence.

From the moment any of the royal family goes abroad, the spotlight is on them even more relentlessly. The Duchess of York, scooping up Vuitton holdalls from airport carousels around the world, has earned black marks for conspicuously inelegant travel. After a short private visit to New York she arrived at London Airport with £2,116 in excess baggage charges but, because of her position, they were waived. A Customs official described 'a mountain of luggage and more than fifty parcels'. It reminded people that Edward VIII used an RAF plane to bring Mrs Simpson's shopping back from Paris without going through Customs.

Later a member of the York household admitted the Duchess is sometimes over-excited on visits abroad, and with a healthy appetite for any goodies offered. Her attitude seems to be: 'Live for now; tomorrow the monarchy may have gone and where does that leave Andy and me?'

But the Duchess should beware. The British people share with King George V a deep distrust of foreigners. 'Abroad,' he would say, 'is awful. I know because I have been there.' Every time the Duchess is seen jetting off with a baby tucked under each arm of her Chanel mini-suit, it is assumed that she is dissatisfied with the nice life provided for her in England.

Abroad, the Princess of Wales waves the flag and makes Britain the envy of the world with her glamorous clothes, flying the flag of mainly British designs. On official tours her luggage is unostentatious, though she does have those wardrobes which are trunks on wheels which most women would envy. Coming back from a visit to Hong Kong where the demands of the visit and also the climate meant the Princess needed to change at least three times a day, still her luggage was sparse.

The Princess has made far fewer private visits abroad than the Duchess but took a leaf out of her sister-in-law's book in August 1990 and went on a discreet jaunt to Italy with a little canvas holdall over her shoulder. The visit caused a flutter and mild chaos at Kensington Palace when she flew off so unexpectedly on an early-morning scheduled flight to Milan to hear Luciano Pavarotti give an open-air concert in Verona. Her plan had been to leave on the evening of the Queen Mother's birthday, but Prince Charles cajoled her into staying around for the whole of his grandmother's ninetieth birthday celebrations.

The Princess, who stayed with Count and Countess Guerriera-Rizzardi on their estate at Bardolino on Lake Garda with its organic vineyard, explained, 'I couldn't resist being here.'

It seems unfair that, just because the Princess wanted to go and hear some classical music, there was an intake of breath and disapproving clucking. Yet it is perfectly all right for Prince Charles to go to Italy whenever he likes, staying with the Frescobaldis in Florence where he paints and relaxes in their elegant Palazzo.

The Prince and Princess feel at home in Italy, admired but free to lead civilised lives whether it is wandering around art galleries or listening to Verdi's sonorous Requiem played by the Moscow

Philharmonic on a balmy summer's night. But the sad thing is that they are rarely there together. Their first visit was in May 1985, and an almost unique example of a rare royal tour *faux pas* upsetting both the host country and the Queen.

There really seemed no particular reason for this visit to Italy. 'Trading links' they muttered at the Palace. The truth is Prince Charles longed to go; he had heard so much about Italy from the Queen Mother. As a little girl she had holidayed with her maternal grandmother, Mrs Caroline Scott, at a Medici villa near Arcetri outside Florence.

Here in this tall house with its pale pink shutters, sitting on a terrace overhung with full-blossomed roses, the eleven-year-old Elizabeth Bowes-Lyon met Lady Ottoline Morrell, a niece of her grandmother's, and first heard about the 'Bloomsbury set'.

Neither the Prince nor the Princess had ever been to Italy except for the briefest stop once in Trieste. The Prince wryly recalled how as soon as he got out of the royal car an 'elderly man put both his arms around me and gave me a kiss on both cheeks.' Now the artist in the Prince made him long 'to see the light in Italy' and he also wanted to hear some music. 'I become moved very easily by the Italian operas. I am a great admirer of Italian opera singers.' The Princess is too.

The Prince had been corresponding with the Pope and had arranged to attend privately an early morning personal Mass in the Vatican with the Princess. The news leaked out. The very idea of flirting, even mildly, with Popery, sent shockwaves through little stone churches in English villages attended at summer evensong by five old ladies in straw hats and a thin organist in Sunday suit and brown shoes. Not since James II has a future king attended Mass – in public anyway.

The Queen is always mindful of her role as Defender of the Faith in England which dates back to the lascivious Henry VIII. He was married to a Catholic but broke with the Church of Rome because the Vatican refused him a divorce. She has a distaste for any hint of 'bells and smells' and any mention of incense can bring a wrinkle to the small nose. A smart reminder was sent to Prince Charles that, as future Head of the Church of England, he could not possibly be seen at a Catholic service.

The essence of the Prince's thinking has been always to question and be open-minded. He could never be called a Popish poodle, and was outspoken in his criticism of the Vatican when Princess Michael of Kent was not allowed to marry in church because she was divorced. But he was mildly intrigued by the Catholic Church as he might be about Buddhism. Not a dedicated churchgoer, he is fully aware of his forthcoming role in the Church. The Princess of Wales is no stranger to Catholicism. Her Irish roots have produced a saint but, for all his sanctity, he was disregarded and died in a ditch.

Now Prince Philip told his free-thinking son, 'Don't dabble in Roman Catholic affairs. You'll only stir up a hornet's nest. It will serve no useful purpose.' The Prince and Princess had to cancel; it was humiliating for the pair to be so openly 'rebuked'. However, most Italians were more interested anyway in the glimpse they got of the 'Bellissima Princess' and her white petticoat, when her pink twenties-style dress fluttered in a mischievous breeze.

'Young, beautiful and lucky,' a woman said, watching her in St Peter's Square in Rome. Earlier in the Baby Jesus hospital a small boy asked, 'Is it true you have a crown?' Instead of a blunt 'Yes' the Princess, famous for her feeling for children, answered softly, 'Yes, but I have left it behind today.'

In piping Sloane Italian, the Princess told the crowds outside the Town Hall in Florence: '*Mio marito ed io siamo molto felici di essere qui*' . . . 'my husband and I', that classic phrase of the Queen's, 'are very happy to be here.' That brought another torrent of 'Oh, you are beautiful . . . oh *bella, bella . . . carissima.*'

Prince Charles then had a chance to speak to the Florentines and afterwards got an encouraging, 'Well done, darling' from his wife. His openness and enthusiasm made the Italians a tinge regretful they no longer had a monarchy. The Prince could never be called a Philistine but he did disappoint by appearing less interested in the time spent by the poet Byron in La Spezia than in the engine room of an Italian Navy battleship.

'A modern Primavera' was the designer Emilio Pucci's description of the Princess. It was charming later to see her sitting on a leather seat in the Uffizi Gallery in Florence in a small reverie as she studied the delicacy of the Botticelli painting. Talking to

Pucci, the Princess told him she loved his clothes but explained regretfully that, since her marriage, and gave that mischievous laugh, 'I have to wear the flag,' and that meant 'British clothes only, in public.'

Of that famous low-cut black dress she wore on a first public evening engagement which revealed more about the Princess than the Palace might have wished, she simply said she felt that it might be too much for Italy, 'Because people don't know where to put their hands when they are guiding you and find it rather embarrassing when they touch bare flesh.' The Queen Mother and the Queen loathe anyone touching even their elbows and there is an instant frost for any hapless mayor who puts a guiding hand near a Windsor shoulder-blade.

The royal couple were a good combination, the Princess 'so gentle, so beautiful and so democratic' with her thoughtful, interesting husband.

The romantic Latins were convinced that Prince Charles had instructed his valet to make sure that all their beds in Italy were big and the bedrooms soundproofed. They would have been disillusioned to learn that soundproofing of the royal suite is not so much for erotic rompings but to ensure privacy for hotline calls on delicate issues and frank analysis of how a tour is going.

They went to a trattoria to eat pasta 'just like anyone else', except for the 800 security men disguised as customers and waiters. Refusing a second helping, the Princess grimaced, 'If I eat this sort of food, I'll get fat – I'll explode.' In the jokey refusal there was a hint of her obsession with being slim.

Being thin has always preoccupied the Princess and is as important to her as it is to any model. Both share the same need to look skinny in front of cameras where a trick of the lenses can add a good three inches. Besides, Prince Charles 'loves the way she looks', his taste for this slim blonde being shared by most men round the world.

A final evening of music and poetry at the British Embassy in Rome, hosted by the ambassador, Lord Bridges, and with sonnets by Michelangelo and music by Benjamin Britten, gave an air of studied calm and elegance after the hectic enthusiasm and uproar about the cancelled Mass.

Then the royal couple, referred to as 'Carlo e Diana', had a romantic break together in Venice, though normally after an official visit the Princess likes to race home. The reward for her of a tour well done is getting back to the boys. 'I always miss them so dreadfully.' It never stops being the most 'terrible wrench' leaving them for any tour no matter how short. This tug at the heartstrings may ease a little now Prince William is away at boarding school and soon Prince Harry will follow. On this occasion the reward was that the Princes were joining them in Venice and now waited on board *Britannia*.

An adoring and protective mother, the Princess is not quite like Alexandra, better known as 'Mother dear', who could never quite think of her children as grown-up. When the future King George V was twenty-five and a chunky naval officer in command of a gunboat, his mother sent him a letter ending with 'A great big kiss for your lovely little face' which fortunately he opened in the privacy of his cabin. And the man who would become a stern, outwardly grumpy future Prince of Wales wrote back signing his letters as 'Your loving little Georgy'.

A gondolier with a gold-tasselled red shawl slung over his hip took the royal couple out towards the Royal Yacht in his carved special black gondola once used by the Queen Mother. The Prince and Princess smiled happily from the black and gold seats with gold columns and cupids which the gondolier was convinced looked just like thrones.

Before disappearing on to *Britannia*, nicknamed the Love Boat by the Italians, who swore the royal bed on board was shaped like a gold embossed boat, Prince Charles was asked for his impressions of their country. He turned to his wife and rather wickedly left it to her: 'What do you think, darling?' The Princess, longing to hug her sons privately, gamely managed to blurt out a few sunny words about the 'warmth of the people' before racing on board and scooping the boys up into her arms.

Everyone expected the Italians to go wild about the Princess, but it is the same in the rest of Europe. She is exactly how a Princess should be. In Germany they adore her clothes sense and say she is the most fashionable woman in Europe. The Swedes love it when she wears a provocative dress. The Spaniards give the Princess more editorial space than their own ideal royal family headed by King Juan Carlos, and they admire the way she has kept her own bubbly personality and yet conformed to royal tradition.

In France it is quite simple. Frenchmen think of the Princess as their ideal woman and envy the British. 'Normally,' they say, 'your English princesses wear velvet uniforms and terrible Girl Guide hats.'

CHAPTER 27

Don't be so Stuffy, Charles

The lady is a flirt. Her friends are skittish, his are serious. Most men adore her, saying happily, 'One glance from those sapphire eyes and we are putty.' Her husband once belonged to this happy band of the entranced, saying to friends as he admiringly watched her go out of a room, 'a lovely view from the back'. The Princess has a blend of sex appeal, charm, funniness, is self-aware without vanity. But it has to be said that she does not enjoy very serious conversation.

'Oh, don't be so stuffy, Charles,' she will tease if things are getting too intense over the Balmoral venison at Highgrove, and not for the first time complained jokingly to a woman sitting close to her, 'He's become somewhat unworldly.' No match for his wife who delights in being worldly and knows she can manipulate people with her arsenal of charm. But an attractive, bright young woman in their set, in gold shoes and long gipsy skirt, says, 'I always have the best fun sitting next to Prince Charles at dinner. You are sure of a good, juicy conversation and he remembers what you said when you were last at KP.'

The Princess got a reputation for being ruthless when she

indulged in what is known and feared in royal circles as 'the sievage factor'. This is the pruning of hangers-on, or people who have boobed socially or been indiscreet. 'She had to shake off the riff-raff, the social climbers,' one of the inner circle explains, 'so there are a lot of pissed-off people.'

Shrewdly the Princess distinguishes between 'besties' and 'wannabees'. Besties make up her circle of friends, handpicked, upper-class girls, assured but not debby. Some new blood and money revitalises the old circle and is acceptable. These are the girls who are entitled to call her 'Duch', the affectionate nickname she earned in childhood. Very often they may call her Diana, or possibly Ma'am in front of wannabees, but never Di as she hates it. Wannabees are often the mothers of children at school with Prince William or Prince Harry who strive desperately to get into the Diana Set. Kate Menzies is a bestie, an attractive blonde and daughter of a wealthy newsagent, with a substantial house on the Scottish borders where the Princess likes to relax. Many were at West Heath with the Princess, all are public school products from schools such as Benenden, Heathfield or St Mary's Ascot. The men, friends like Major David Waterhouse, a bridge partner of the Princess's, and the Marquis of Douro, are bankers, brokers and farmers drawn from Eton, Harrow and Radley with a statutory spell at Cirencester learning how to run the family estate and to talk to the factor without appearing 'a complete clot'.

'Do you remember *Just So Stories*?' the Prince once asked at a supper party one evening at Highgrove and, to his surprise, his wife replied quickly, 'Just so what, Charles?' He shrugged and did not even attempt to explain about Rudyard Kipling.

So the Prince does not invite the eighty-four-year-old Sir Laurens van der Post or Professor Riordan, his newest 'green guru', to an evening with the Princess's friends, when conversation can be mainly about children, clothes, other people's affairs, the latest film or a television soap opera. 'I used to like "East-Enders",' the Princess will say. 'Dirty Den was a lovable rogue.'

They are good hosts. Neither drink. The Princess is so ebullient, water seems to have the same sparkle for her as champagne. Prince Charles hates red wine, but for guests there is Pimms in summer or gentle white wine. The mood is light and the atmosphere created by the Princess a conspiracy to have fun.

She never gives buffets, and the food at Highgrove is always delicious: a tomato mousse; poached egg in pastry; cold salmon; fresh apple pie; cheese but only at lunchtime. Supper may be a poached fish, perhaps brill from the chic fish shop Charlie Barnett's at Cirencester; plums, nectarines or strawberries come from the garden or the Prince's version of bread and butter pudding full of candied fruit, rum and bananas. The Princess is a picker and in public has the appetite of a sparrow.

The mood can be like an end of term party, with lots of giggling at mildly suggestive *double entendres*, none better than those made by the Duchess of York, trusted because she is liked and also family. Laughter carries out on the Kensington air as the Duchess complains about the privations of being married to a serving naval officer. Asked the blue riddle, 'Why am I like a Pakistani newsagent?' she replies, 'Both fucking 'andy on Sundays.' This goes down well on the polo field too. After dinner games include musical chairs and the hilarious 'Twister', a children's game which ends up with adults screaming with laughter in a tangled heap on the floor; lots of horseplay, no need to look up rules in Debrett's *Are You There, Moriarty?* It is no wonder Prince Charles will leave the room saying, 'I find the whole thing very immature.' The royal family prefer the more dignified charades or Scottish dancing, without the boisterousness of the Regimental Mess.

It was the high spirited Julia Dodd-Noble, whose husband deals in helicopters, who organised the famous raid on Annabel's at the Duchess of York's hen-party.

Friends of the Princess include Catherine Soames, the estranged wife of Nicholas, the Tory MP, with whom she plays tennis twice a week. When Mrs Soames eloped with three-times-married antique dealer Piers von Westenholz the Princess was totally on her side. Prince Charles, who has a strong sense of propriety, was very disapproving and icy with his wife. It was not long afterwards that he took his party out on the daredevil skiing expedition at Klosters and one of his great friends, Major Hugh Lindsay, was killed in an avalanche. He coldly rebuffed the Princess when she ran white-faced to embrace him after the accident.

Not many of the Princess's friends have gone to university; it really is not fashionable in that set to be too highly educated.

But, one of the circle caustically protests, 'Don't think we are all upper-class airheads.' They are highly social, have no feeling of guilt about their money, are not too driven by *Angst* for the homeless but are expressing more overt concern these days because it goes down well with the Princess. They pretend they are no longer 'out for husbands' or quite so keen to marry well, but it is expected one will marry a 'suitable bloke'. Highly fashionable, the girls are usually up on trends long before they have caught on, been vegetarian for 'yonks' and now everybody is 'green'.

Old friends such as Julia Samuel, Viscount Bearsted's daughter-in-law, Lord Rothschild's daughter Hannah, and 'bestie' Millie Soames, the sister of Philip Dunne, who was married in 1988 to Rupert Soames, say the Princess is still the same easy lady, despite becoming a princess. 'Diana is very English, very warm; warmth is a form of intelligence and that really draws you to her,' they declare. Many of their joint friends are young couples with children. The Palmer-Tomkinsons, the Romseys, the Douros, the Grosvenors and the Yorks.

They have friends they like to go skiing with, others for opera, some who are mad keen gardeners. A very close friendship has grown up between Patti Palmer-Tomkinson and Prince Charles since the skiing disaster in 1988 when his equerry Major Lindsay was killed. It was only the quick reaction of the Swiss guide, who shouted at the Prince: 'Go, Sir, go' which saved his life.

The Prince is attracted by high speed and dangerous sport, and has been back to face the challenge again. Mrs Palmer-Tomkinson, forty-nine, a pretty, dark-haired woman, lives near Highgrove. She visited immediately the Prince had his polo accident though in the middle of a party for her husband's fiftieth birthday. The Prince had visited her regularly when she was so ill in Davos Hospital in Switzerland after the skiing tragedy. It is the Princess who has been so supportive to Lindsay's widow Sarah who was pregnant at the time with her daughter Rose, and held her hand during the funeral.

They also have their separate friends. The Prince finds Camilla Parker-Bowles entertaining company and she was one ideal companion for him during a two-day cruise on the Turkish west coast in 1989. The Parker-Bowleses so value their friendship with the royal couple that rather than risk being posted abroad Colonel

Parker-Bowles, who has commanded the Household Cavalry, has taken a low-key job in charge of the Army's horses and sniffer dogs. The fifty-year-old army officer is now naturally known as 'chief barker'.

Mistress of the one-liner, an assured hostess, it is hard to imagine that once upon a time the Princess sat sobbing in her bedroom saying, 'I'm a failure, I'm a failure.' She puts people immediately at ease whereas Prince Charles tries. In his chappish way he thinks that by saying 'pass the bloody salt, please,' he may help some tormented architect or tense homeopathist to relax, imagining this is how ordinary people talk.

But it is a great relief at least not to find a royal corgi in either Highgrove or Kensington Palace. There is happily no equivalent of the Queen Mother's savage corgi, Ranger, who killed one of the Queen's favourite dogs. After ten sessions with a dog psychiatrist Ranger has gone back to ankles. Guests at Clarence House raise their highly polished shoes in high goosestep of exaggerated strides on the way to the 'presence' fearful of the furry creature yapping in anticipation.

As a couple the Prince and Princess are less volatile than they used to be, when they would flare up at each other but then kiss and hug. It was like a tropical storm, violent while it lasted, sunny immediately afterwards.

They really are not keen on giving many dinner parties. The Princess's idea of heaven is to be snuggled up reading *Vogue* and *Harpers*. Prince Charles pretends to conduct an orchestra as he plays classical music on their Marantz compact disc player. They are not late owls and like to be at home by ten, but they had to attend the ex-King Constantine of Greece's fiftieth birthday party. It was held in the grounds of Spencer House which overlooks Green Park and belongs to the Princess of Wales's family. Leased to Lord Rothschild, he has spent £16 million on this eighteenth-century house so that it can be used for parties. The 650 guests included Earl Spencer and the Countess who, in a black dress with red cabbage roses dotted round the neckline, was a florid contrast to the Princess in simple svelte bead-encrusted white.

A marquee draped in pink chiffon had been fitted with wooden windows: chairs and tables created to look like antiques. Crowned and uncrowned heads and European aristocrats drank champagne, ate smoked fish, poussin and British strawberries in the flattering chandeliered rainbow light.

Lady Elizabeth Anson of Party Planners, who organised the £250,000 Hellenic evening, recalls: 'The Princess was so sweet, she came up and took my hand and said, "Liza, can I do anything to help . . . ?" and I said, "Well, can you get the dancing started?" I said to her, "Who is the best dancer in the room?" and she said, "My husband . . ."'

CHAPTER 28

A Nice Little Earner

On the island of Necker in the Caribbean the Princess of Wales is buried in the sand up to the waist by her sons and nearby, looking serene and stately even on a beach, is her mother, the Hon. Mrs Frances Shand Kydd, looking out to sea. Mother and daughter share the same independent tilt of the head, determination and hint of measured raciness. A blatant family get-together, this is a rare chance for talk, laughter and complaints about the pressures on all of them since Lady Diana married Prince Charles. They really are the Princess's only true confidantes; in the end she cannot trust anyone outside.

Lady Jane Fellowes is there, steady, phlegmatic, and sister Lady Sarah McCorquodale, always amusing, and now laughing about their entertaining brother Charles. The easygoing but ambitious twenty-six-year-old Viscount Althorp has been able to hold down a job with American television as an NBC roving correspondent, not because he is the Princess of Wales's brother but because he is good on camera. 'America is the place for me . . .' he says. 'People prejudge me in Britain.' Somewhat cynically he adds, 'It must be better than just sitting back on the estate in

Northamptonshire watching all the paintings go to the National Gallery. All the same these days he is spending time at Althorp and taking over the running of the 13,000-acre estate, even firing the land agent Richard Stanley who worked for his father for fourteen years.

Instead of choosing the more usual aristocratic girl, he made a slightly unconventional marriage in September 1989. His wife, Victoria Lockwood, a twenty-five-year-old model with long straggly dark hair, is the daughter of a Civil Aviation executive and extremely skinny even by model standards. Before they married the couple could be seen round London, mooning together over raw fish in the Japanese restaurant at the Shepherd's Bush Hilton. Now they live at The Falconry which was built in 1613 and which Lady Althorp has revamped.

The Viscount's brother-in-law Prince Charles helped his sister Sarah Spencer through an anorexic phase. Now 'Charlie' Althorp has been instrumental in rescuing his wife from any slimming obsession. On Friday 28 December 1990, she gave birth to a baby girl. At 6 pounds 2 ounces, the Hon. Kitty Eleanor Spencer was born two weeks' prematurely by Caesarean at St Mary's Hospital. The Princess comforted Victoria when the Viscount admitted a kick-up in Paris with former girlfriend Sally Anne Lasson a mere six months after his marriage.

Mrs Shand Kydd and her youngest daughter have grown closer. It was not a strong relationship until the Princess first became engaged. Her mother, who lived in a penthouse in Pimlico's leafy Warwick Square, admitted then, 'I've actually been seeing far more of Diana now than I have for ages. We have had a lot of fun.' They both enjoyed visiting couturiers before the royal wedding.

Never possessive, Mrs Shand Kydd has always believed in a cool distancing once children are grown up and, with 'three daughters marrying in just over three years . . . they should be self-sufficient and take responsibility for their own lives. Whatever you taught them at a certain age, that is finished . . . however badly or well you have taught them.'

The Princess is a Daddy's girl, much more so than her two sisters. When given a present of some crystallised sugar on tour in Canada, she said, 'My father adores it. I'll save it for him.'

Perhaps there is rationing at Althorp to help pay for the step-mother's £2 million renovations which Lord Spencer's children loathe.

Until recently the Princess never quite understood her mother's unhappiness in her first marriage. Now married herself to a man who can be remote, she realises that Earl Spencer, lovable to small children, an appealing father playing bears on the nursery floor, might not have been exciting for her lively, sparky mother. Perhaps after ten years of marriage the Princess sees more of herself in her mother – both wilful, very attractive, with a core of steel hidden under the lissom blondeness. But the Princess was shattered when her mother's second marriage failed. She had liked the amiable Peter Shand Kydd, quite the opposite of her phlegmatic, orderly father.

The Princess is supportive, taking her mother on jaunts to Italy and the Caribbean. This is no self-pitying deserted wife but the epitome of cultivated aristocratic Englishwomen, who tend to still look extremely good in their forties and fifties. Mother and daughter have the same ticklish humour and more in common than they ever imagined, and Mrs Shand Kydd is discreet.

After the holiday, while her daughters returned to their young husbands, she went back to Clachan Seil, a lonely island just off the west coast of Scotland, to Ardencaple, a tall, windswept white house where she has lived alone since the breakup of her marriage to Peter Shand Kydd. They first moved there in 1972.

She never has got used to the attention her daughter's marriage to a future King of England would provoke and spends a lot of her time in Scotland unless invited to Kensington Palace, when she says discreetly, 'Well, that's me off to London for a fortnight.' Coming home the twelve miles from Oban she crosses back to her romantic Hebridean island, driving over the charming little eighteenth-century Clachan bridge, the only one to cross the Atlantic. This is Mrs Shand Kydd's flight to freedom.

The white house is high on a hill overlooking sweeping wild heathery hillsides and lochs below. Often with only sheep for company, the place tells you something about her strength. In its natural state with badgers, seals, kestrels and herons and where the people have a simple directness and exceptional integrity, it is wonderfully uncompromising.

She is admired and respected by the locals – who left her free to run her shabby little Card Shop with its blue and white painted front at Number 13 Stafford Street. As a child Diana liked to help in the shop and loved going out in boats dressed in denim, helping local fishermen look for lobsters.

Local tourists who hoped for a glimpse of the future King of England's mother-in-law were disappointed. Mrs Jessie Smith, an assistant, gave uncompromising 'ah has' to nosey inquiries then quickly took their money and wrapped up their souvenir black and white teatowels printed with a Drinker's Fault-Finding Guide.

The shop was a nice little earner but really so out of character for this aristocratic divorcee that it was not surprising when she sold it at the end of the 1990 summer season. Mrs Shand Kydd's contemporaries in Norfolk might perhaps arrange dried flowers for a mildly genteel living, but certainly did not run shops stocking satin Disney deer sitting in Babycham glasses or 'To a Wonderful Daughter' birthday cards. But Mrs Shand Kydd loved the chance it gave her to meet people on a genuine footing and she still parks her blue car outside the Highland Arts shop with its collection of stuffed eagles, reduced mini-kilts and 'lucky white heather' but no longer goes to the shop.

If in love, there could be no more romantic place than Ardencaple. The Shand Kydd sheep farm stretches over a thousand acres. In spring, when osier catkins are in bud, dotted with pollen, it is a place for scampering wood mice and everywhere there is the heady scent of wild hyacinth. In summer small tortoiseshell butterflies rest on the heather, a mute swan is at the water's edge and elegant snow buntings with orange bills hop deftly amongst the juicy seaweed. Views stretch across to Seil Sound and to the islands of Iona or Fingal's Cave made legendary by Mendelssohn's Overture.

Often in jodhpurs, boots and a bright scarf – like her youngest daughter she adores the colour red – Mrs Shand Kydd loves to walk alone, head held high, long quick strides along hazel paths where in summer bumblebees hover over tall foxgloves. By autumn the wind whips down the hillsides and blows the wool of the creamy long-haired sheep and only goats hold fast as herring gulls whirl and screech. It can be desolate in winter as dark mists cloud over and the view from her window becomes menacing. No matter how daunting, Frances Shand Kydd has chosen to stay on, loving the sight of the occasional grey seal, whiskers and eyes above the water.

The house is not flashy; her taste is very traditional. It could be a house in Hampshire with its button-back chairs, glazed pink chintz curtains with silvery red tie backs, lots of pretty enamel Halcyon Days boxes – the any-occasion good taste present. Glossy magazines are piled high and on a long sideboard there is standing room only for so many family photographs; Prince William is grinning in school uniform and Prince Harry at his christening. Near the conservatory there is a fetching line of feminine hats and a straw bonnet trimmed with flowers.

When the Princes stay with her they look for sea urchins and whelks and, followed by burly detectives, paddle in small pools and laugh at sandpipers dancing ahead. At night William and Harry lie tucked up in Granny's house and listen to the barn owl.

Running the sheep farm singlehanded, Mrs Shand Kydd is admired by the locals. If you want to understand the daughter, they say, look to the mother; here you see the resilience and the spirit which have enabled the Princess to carve out her own identity.

By the late eighties, the Shand Kydd marriage was in trouble. Increasingly he seemed to spend more time away at his farm in Perth or in London. Coming back at midnight he preferred to wake up a local guesthouse where you can get the best oysters, saying, 'Afraid I'll be locked out at Ardencaple. Can I have a bed?'

High on the wall in the room used as an office there is a black and white photograph of Diana as a little girl with her brother. In the good days, when the marriage was going well, Mrs Shand Kydd worked as a bookkeeper for her husband; they also did rather well breeding miniature Shetland ponies and cattle. She made an elegant cattle drover's wife as she whacked the beasts down a track on the Shand Kydd Australian property outside Canberra.

Rather poignant is the upturned red boat called *Laura* hauled up close to the house. In the small homely green and white painted kitchen, pink lilies sit in tubs on the windowsill alongside orange washing-up gloves. It is just off the dining room and is where Mrs Shand Kydd likes to cook a fish pie in the Neff oven for her grandchildren or the young artists at the Oban Festival invited by her to save money by staying at Ardencaple. 'We sing and play the piano; she is a lovely lady,' they say.

The breakup of her marriage saddened the small community, but only in Scotland could her privacy be so respected. She is direct. 'I have been told that I am honest to a degree which some people might say isn't good. I suppose I have to learn to become a politician.' In Scotland those qualities are valued.

Mrs Shand Kydd has also been turning towards the Catholic church. For years she worshipped at the gaunt Scottish Episcopal Church, welcomed by Provost Allan Maclean into the chilly dark stone church with its steel buttress and Leprosy Mission box.

'She is a lovely person, very kind, and does a lot of good work,' says Father Angus Galbraith, the slightly dimpled administrator of the busy Roman Catholic Cathedral in Oban. It overlooks the windy romping water and the caves which once hid the earliest remains of human occupation. Buffeted fishing boats go bravely out to sea and people wrapped tightly in waxed jackets are whisked along the seafront where there is little shelter. The town rises up, a Victorian seascape of crags and pines and tall gloomy villas.

Rightly sensitive about Mrs Shand Kydd being in his congregation – 'Being Catholic and associated with the royal family . . . well . . .' The priest shrugs, looking inscrutable over National Health spectacles and the sentence is left unfinished. The 1701 Act of Settlement prevents a British Prince from marrying a Roman Catholic and remaining in line of succession to the throne. Any dealing in Popery is naturally frowned on by the Establishment.

Whenever Mrs Shand Kydd leaves the church she is reminded of the hardline approach of the Catholic church on many issues by the leaflets, 'Abortion – Stop it' and another on marriage breakdown. Marriage is forever for Roman Catholics. This most famous parishioner is, Father Galbraith says, being 'very open, but very contained'.

Everyone was touched when they heard the Eriskay Love Lilt sung by Kenneth McKellar. It had been requested by Mrs Shand

Kydd on the Art Sutter show on Radio Scotland for 'My beloved daughter on the eve of her twenty-eighth birthday'.

Alone on Seil, Mrs Shand Kydd says, 'If circumstances are such that you can't alter them,' her voice is strong, 'it's always helpful to know there's a holiday and a little bit of privacy at the end of the tunnel.' It spoke volumes for her own marriage and for that of her daughter, the Princess.

CHAPTER 29

All-Bran and a Run in the Park

Just like any other young woman, the Princess goes to work most mornings, but in her case the office is a suite of rooms at St James's Palace and she drives in by the Stable Yard. This is the dynamic young court and the Princess likes it being separate from Buckingham Palace.

There is a distinct hierarchy. At the top the Private Secretary, the fourth since 1967, is Major-General Sir Christopher Airy KCVO, a military man aged fifty-six and Prince Charles's own choice. His deputy, Peter Westmacott, is thirty-nine years old and was formerly with the Foreign Office; Guy Salter, thirty, was brought in from the Burton group and also works mainly for the Prince, concentrating on his youth and business interests. Assistant Private Secretary is Richard Aylard, seconded from the Royal Navy. This thirty-seven-year-old who works for both Prince Charles and the Princess has done much to make her public life more interesting. With a little subtle prompting, she became more involved and would read up thoroughly before an engagement startling even the experts, surprised by her knowledge and flattered as she tells them, 'Oh, I've read your book.'

Her stamp is everywhere, although the office buzzes with efficiency. The cool rooms in what was once a hospital for women lepers now have pretty duck egg blue walls and smart sacking curtains. The furniture is country house style, and often as they sit round the large mahogany table everyone has to strain to hear the Princess's light voice above the noisy Changing of the Guard.

Her equerries and male Assistant Private Secretary are pleasant young men who all seem to have dark curly hair and perfect manners: 'Is Earl Grey all right?' They can be almost too attentively polite. Bright-eyed, watchful, the absolute cheerfulness of it all is almost a hallmark. The staff are noted for their short haircuts, gleaming shoes and the healthy pinkness of people who have had early morning showers, All-Bran and a run in the park before reaching their desks each morning eager and freshly bright.

The Navy has had a monopoly in supplying equerries, like Lieutenant-Commander Patrick Jephson who works specifically for the Princess. These young officers can be commanding frigates one minute and the next putting ideas forward for a speech which has come back from Kensington Palace daubed with blue. After a two-year royal secondment they expect to return to sea. But if they have been exceptional, they are invited to stay on, a decision which, one admitted, 'Makes one think long and hard . . . for half a second . . . and then say, "Yes, gosh, isn't it super?"' This is the satellite court.

'Suppose it was because I was the right age, didn't smoke and had a driving licence.' They tend to be drolly self-deprecating when asked why they have been chosen to serve the Princess of Wales.

The man on whom much rests is the former equerry Commander Richard Aylard, a pleasant naval man with a sense of humour and certain doggedness. Always a potential Royal Navy high flyer, he originally did well behind the scenes, presenting well-researched analysis and gently urging the Princess to become more involved in engagements. He seriously thought of a career in public relations; the money is not good working for the royals. Highly valued, he was happy to be persuaded to stay by Prince Charles.

'Patrick, does that allow enough time to see schoolchildren?' the Princess asks, looking at the engagements diary. She calls them Anne, Lavinia and Patrick and they call her Your Highness or Ma'am which rhymes with pram. A Staff of about twenty of these nice, civilised people from public school and polo ground, impeccably behaved, loyal and assured, work from 9 to 5 for peanuts. Perks include lunch in the Household dining room and a room at Buckingham Palace when late engagements make it difficult to get home. But most rely on private family money.

They are as English as the reassuring voice of Henry Blofeld at Lord's or a Pimms after tennis in a Wiltshire country house garden, where they meet, and later marry, 'super' girls in silk summer dresses. Their children go to Eton and Benenden: 'Fearfully expensive; thank goodness for Aunt Boo's money.'

Being parted from their children from the age of eight is as inevitable as grouse shooting in Scotland. They miss the little chap terribly but brighten when reminded how well he is doing in the Colts. Reliable as the seasons, the men have a tradition of royal service and are often the grandchildren of colonialists, bankers and earls. Their women, smiling, restrained whether as the colonel's wife cheering up the Regimental Wives Club or as a lady-in-waiting, are utterly dependable.

Since the marriage, at least forty people on the Princess's staff have left. Her admirers say, 'They were the stuffy old guard, people who might seem totally respectful but really not so behind her back.' A more recent departure from a potentially interesting post has been their Private Secretary, Sir John Riddell, who has become a £200,000 Deputy Chairman of Credit Suisse First Boston. He had given up a high-powered City job to survive on the £60,000 Palace salary but never had any real appetite for publicity, saying once to a television team, 'Dealing with you people is like having one's private parts slowly nibbled by rats.'

The fifty-five-year-old Old Etonian baronet and the Princess did not always see eye to eye. He became irritated when his plans for her diary were upset when she might suddenly decide to go to a friend's wedding or christening. The Prince of Wales took his side and agreed that his wife must have a more structured approach. But the Princess made it clear that she would see whom she liked when she liked. Exit Sir John.

She keeps those dates scribbled in the gold-trimmed fine pages of her personal blue leather diary. It will be kept after her death for a hundred years in the vaults at Windsor Castle, when it will be released to royal historians.

'It is all so ebullient,' said a more serious-minded former member of staff. 'It is like working for a couple of pop stars.' Everybody seems revved up, including the man at the front reception desk, in an atmosphere of 'Aren't we jolly lucky to be working for this high-profile pair?' This is quite different from the Queen's office at Buckingham Palace where boxes are done in the morning and afternoon and there is a definite chain of command within a stately aura of restrained power.

Some of the Prince and Princess's more intellectual advisers, particularly those with legal training, have often been exasperated by the Prince of Wales's attitude. His crime has been that he is too democratic and approachable. His door is always open. Ideas are constantly changing. Half an hour passes and the theme of a speech will be completely different. As one adviser recalled wearily, 'If the kennel maid is going past and has a view on inner cities, then he listens and we rewrite the speech.' This is refreshing but makes the job of his principals virtually impossible.

Capriciousness is the right of princes; one minute he makes someone feel they are important and valuable, the next they may be frozen out by a chilling silence. He can be cranky and irascible, not at all easy, 'often on a short fuse' – in this respect quite like his father. However, because the Prince does things with flair, working with him is always stimulating and unpredictable.

The Princess can be chilly too, 'a bit off' some mornings, but brightens quickly. They tell you in the Princess's office, 'There is a good interaction with other royal offices,' but not about the rivalry and jockeying for position.

'A lot of bitching' goes on, a former senior courtier revealed, but added, 'It is never boring working for the Waleses. There is plenty of laughter. Wit is expected and encouraged. At a lunch for half a dozen top City advisers, Prince Charles kept asking earnestly, 'How can I be relevant?' Over coffee one of his aides joked in conclusion, 'Well, it seems what we need at the Palace are more one-legged, one-eyed, disadvantaged blacks.'

*

Originally called the 'geese' because they quack warnings to their royal mistresses about difficulties ahead, the Princess's ladies-in-waiting generally share her background of not too strenuous academic study, have perhaps done a cookery course and had a little taste of abroad, usually Italy or France, rarely the steamy hotspots and of course Firsts in the Faultless Behaviour Tripos.

The pace is hectic, a clear day is one free to do administration at St James's. Their job nowadays is still carrying flowers and writing bread-and-butter letters. Always pleasant, helpful, neat and tidy, they are experts at bland conversation – forbidden topics have always included money, illness, religion, sex and servants. Never divorced, agreeable company, some become genuine friends of the Princess, who says, 'They have to be friendly and cheerful above everything else. It's no good if they look glum and stand around saying nothing. Luckily all mine are old friends and we share the same sense of humour.'

As a lady-in-waiting for the Princess, Anne Beckwith-Smith's credentials were peerless. The Queen knew her father Major Beckwith-Smith, a respected figure on the turf and former owner of Lingfield racecourse, long before his daughter came into the Princess of Wales's life in 1981, when the Queen Mother suggested this cheery, capable girl as ideal. In time she became so indispensable that she was promoted to Assistant Private Secretary. She had studied the classic Sloane speciality, History of Art in Florence, but did much more than look diffidently knowledgeable in a flowery skirt and ivory tights in a Mayfair art gallery, pointing out to rich Arabs nuances of the Impressionist style. After she left she became assistant to the director of Sotheby's English picture department.

'I just couldn't have done it without you,' the Princess enthused at the end of the first major tour in Australia, giving her thirty-nine-year-old lady-in-waiting an impulsive appreciative hug and a large diamond clip with a D on it and earrings to match. And for years Miss Beckwith-Smith was quite perfect: friendly, loyal, bright and nice too, though people found she could be quite sharp, 'a bit chop choppish'.

The Princess also relied on the quiet support of this senior lady-in-waiting when her marriage was in difficulties, and would pop around to see her 'for a natter, and to enjoy a snack of whatever I had going, more often than not it was scrambled egg.' The up-market snack is always an egg, never cod-in-a-bag.

For scrambled egg and a lot more, the Queen rewarded Anne Beckwith-Smith with an LVO (Lieutenant of the Royal Victorian Order) in 1989. Nevertheless, the word got out in January 1990 that Miss Beckwith-Smith had been fired, so much so that this ultra-discreet lady-in-waiting felt prompted to say, 'It's my decision alone to leave. I will still go on engagements,' and tactfully she slid gracefully off the royal ice-rink with applause still ringing to enjoy, she claimed, 'more time to myself'.

This young woman who had helped the Princess purge the office of any hint of nanny-goat, velvet-trousered, Victorian courtiers had been ousted by the male chauvinists who had bided their time but should never have been underestimated. They argued at Buckingham Palace that the increasingly important job of steering the now high-profile Princess through engagements, which were escalating rapidly in importance, should be given to a man, a former equerry Commander Jephson. Miss Beckwith-Smith now holds the less important job of senior lady-in-waiting.

The seven ladies-in-waiting are not over-glamorous but always agreeable, 'genuinely nice people; gentlefolk in the real sense'. They include Alexandra Loyd, a schoolfriend from Riddlesworth days, Laura Lonsdale who took a year's farming course at Cirencester and speaks beautiful French, and Jean Pike, the Roman Catholic daughter of General Lord Michael Fitzalan-Howard.

Viscountess Campden, like the Princess herself, is a devoted mother and does not like to be in waiting during school holidays when her only child thirteen-year-old Robert is home at the family estate in Rutland, Leicestershire, hunting country. Her husband, Lord Gainsborough's heir, forty-one-year-old Viscount Noel, also prefers to be in the country running the estate though the couple have property also in London's Earls Court. Lavinia Baring, a good friend of Anne Beckwith-Smith, is married to a Kent farmer, the Hon. Vivian Baring. About ten years older than the Princess, her husband's family is connected to the Princess through her Irish antecedents.

Hazel West is popular in her village in Gloucestershire. She and her husband, Colonel George West, the Assistant Comptroller of the Lord Chamberlain's office, found much sympathetic support when she had a miscarriage. They live in a house said to be haunted by Cavaliers, which she adores, and have a dog called Percy. If she has even an hour or so off Mrs West will race back to the country. It was in this village of Orcett, when she stayed with them for a weekend, that the Princess tentatively went, in great secrecy, for a cautious canter on a nearby estate at Etterington.

It is no secret that she does not like having too many pretty women on her staff and becomes somewhat jealous if the girls, the secretaries particularly, are having too much fun, especially on a royal tour. Mischievously, in exotic hot spots they are kept busy writing thank-you letters, often until two in the morning, and know the reason. Perhaps it was because Major Ronald Ferguson was in hot pursuit of one of the young secretaries and the Princess disapproved. She knows and likes his second wife, the former Susan Denfield, who was in the Cowes party when the romance with Charles began.

The Princess first became aware in 1985 that nobody was really noticing what she did, only what she wore. She decided to change, developed a more tailored style, appointed a young energetic team, and acquired a reputation for being ruthless. Thoroughly professional, she shook off people round her who knew all about her husband's past, nor did she want men around her who were fat. Out went Edward Adeane, forty-five, a portly bachelor lawyer and Private Secretary to the royal couple, perhaps more in tune with the *ancien régime*. He was distinctly offended to see Prince William's bootees on Prince Charles's desk. His father, Sir Michael, was private secretary to the Queen, and his great-grandfather, Lord Stamfordham, to Queen Victoria and George V, so he had stern views about what was appropriate in a royal office.

To the chagrin of the Foreign Office, Oliver Everett, a diplomat, formerly in New Delhi and later in Madrid as Head of Chancery, had been seconded to Kensington Palace. It was Everett who had rushed Prince Charles to a hospital in Florida when he collapsed playing polo. The Prince said, 'Don't leave me, Oliver, I think I'm going to die.' Thin, with a wayward lock of hair, he had a fine sense of protocol but a wry humour which took the terrors out of early official engagements for the Princess. Often complaining, 'Everyone is so old round here,' the Princess was pleased to hear Oliver had a daughter of fourteen and seemed to identify with her.

They shared many jokes but after a while the Prince found a job which would suit this clever but serious man more as Keeper of the Queen's pictures, giving him enough time to play polo and see more of his wife Theffania and four children at Kidlington in Oxfordshire.

This newly serious Princess spent hours at her desk. Speeches were tried out on Prince Charles, who encouraged her as she wailed, 'I just hate the sound of my own voice, I can't bear it.' He sympathised. 'I felt the same way. I couldn't believe that yakkety-yak voice was mine. So upper-class.'

Now as the Prince of Wales seems to be deliberately leaving 'meet the people' engagements to his wife while he concentrates on discussions and working lunches with experts at Highgrove and Kensington Palace, the Princess seems to relish a heavier work-load. There was a considerable increase in her fifty-seven engagements carried out between January and March 1990 compared with forty-two for the same period the previous year. In T. O'Donovan's *Times* league table they also compare very favourably with those of other royal women for the year.

	UK	Abroad
The Queen	476	122
Princess of Wales	234	111
Duchess of York	85	39
Queen Mother	118	6
Princess Royal	449	401
Princess Margaret	148	10
Duchess of Gloucester	119	-
Duchess of Kent	137	13
Princess Alexandra	102	83

The programme is planned with military precision as equerries, private secretaries, ladies-in-waiting and detectives sit around a table covered in green baize to plan forward engagements at six-monthly meetings in June and December. It all goes in the Seasons Calendar, the working royal diary with its Prince of Wales coat of arms embossed on the cover. As patron or president of some forty charities the Princess is besieged by invitations. Before one is accepted, a request is put on to an 'Engagement Possible' card and her lady-in-waiting asks for a draft itinerary. If approved, the engagement is entered in fountain pen, blue-black ink, of course, on a parchment ivory page, and also on a card marked 'Engagements for week ending . . .'

Informative details such as: 'the Princess does not like wired flowers,' 'the Princess never drinks alcohol' and 'she dislikes elaborate meals; hand pumping is not encouraged' are helpfully forwarded. If the Princess is likely to meet someone as publicity-conscious as the soccer star Paul Gascoigne, strict instructions will be sent from Kensington Palace warning that on no account should 'Gazza' attempt to put an arm round the Princess's waist or be photographed with her. There must be no repetition of his over-familiar arm round Mrs Thatcher, playing to the photographers at Number Ten and saying afterwards of the Prime Minister, 'She's so cuddly.' Neither the Prince nor the Princess approves of smoking and the Princess does not like small children being forced to talk to her if shy. She also much prefers a one-to-one chat rather than meeting masses of people, and 'has a talent for spotting the shy who are hanging back', Richard Aylard says, always making 'a point of singling them out'. Then for the final touches to a visit, the Princess, her equerry and lady-in-waiting will talk in her sitting room in Kensington with its dusty-rose sofa and family photographs, sitting by the marble fireplace filled with dried flowers.

Once an engagement is accepted, the detective and an equerry go off on a recce. In their dark navy suits they look like a couple of quiet businessmen as they talk confidentially over breakfast on an InterCity train to Leeds or Birmingham, as conspiratorial as if planning a bank robbery.

A final programme is sent to every department in St James's Palace and on the day of the visit is produced in miniature. The team has to think about rain – will the Princess mind carrying an umbrella? They plan the quickest route, where the cars will stop, where the Princess gets out, how she reaches the disabled in wheelchairs. Ideally a recce takes place about three weeks ahead of the visit; this way, Aylard says, people don't have time to come up with 'brilliant new ideas' so that the itinerary has to be redone.

Buckingham Palace handled early press inquiries but the need for their own press secretary grew apparent as the Princess of Wales rapidly became a world star. A harassed young New Zealander called Warren Hutchings was appointed and was later succeeded by Vic Chapman, an amiable Canadian *bon viveur* with a laconic wit and a tendency to lean against the mahogany Palace doors chewing gum while he considered some cheeky proposal. Vic died in 1988, the Prince and Princess having watched a remorseless cancer with dismay, as he lost weight and buoyancy. They liked him very much even if occasionally he was a bit too relaxed.

This could never be said of the present assistant press secretary, Mr Richard Arbiter, formerly a reporter with a small London radio station. Easily irritated, he may not be sufficiently phlegmatic or have the necessary political acumen when Prince Charles becomes King, when he will require someone of the calibre of the new man at Buckingham Palace, Charles Anson, who has a City background.

The Press Office is part of the Household's more rarefied atmosphere. Much more down to earth are the Staff, which includes people like the Princess's dresser Evelyn Dagley, also detectives, chefs and butlers. Even there you find snobbery and a hierarchy. One nanny would not travel with the dresser necessitating a cavalcade of five cars along the M4 to Gloucestershire.

When Fay Appleby, assistant dresser, was seriously ill with cancer, the Princess supported her, later went to her wedding and generally helped her recovery. When Fay gave birth to twins Diana drove to Devon with her own children to congratulate her. The butler, Harold Brown, is an upright Western Australian, one of the strictly religious Plymouth Brethren and carries his Bible everywhere, even on royal tours. In even the hottest climates the Princess is quite fussy about her food. 'Poor Harold, sweltering in a hut in Honolulu cooking them their beloved lasagne and jacket potatoes,' a Staff member recalled.

Apart from her dresser, who is confidante, mind reader and consoler, her detectives are probably closer to the Princess than almost anyone, and she is so jokey and relaxed that the role is a delicate one. There has to be a close bond between the protector and the protected, and it has been very difficult for the bodyguards looking after the Princess, with her youthfulness and lack of formality. She likes men about her who are funny, cool and young. Sergeant Dave Sharp seems to have struck the right balance. Her other two detectives are Ken Wharfe – the senior one – and Graham Smith.

The Princess finds security irksome. She tells friends, 'I feel guilty dragging detectives out shopping and jogging.' She loves giving them the slip. 'Hello chaps,' she said breezily, jogging through the gates of Kensington Palace in white running shorts and trainers. 'I've been for a run around the block.' They were appalled that she had been alone in Kensington Gardens and she was warned this must never happen again. In common with other leading members of the royal family, the Princess should always carry a radio-controlled 'panic' device. But with her sunny disposition and outgoing personality, it is hard for her to believe that anyone would make an attempt on her life.

It is not always easy to keep up with her. She loves to drive herself in her soft-top Jaguar sports car or a 154-mph silver-grey Sierra Cosworth which, according to Jim Walker, a softly spoken Scot responsible at Ford headquarters in Essex for supplying the Prince and Princess of Wales with many of their cars, is 'a sophisticated powerful sporty saloon with 220 horse power and two-wheel drive'. When she was caught speeding in High Street Kensington at seven in the morning in October 1990, it was her detective who was given a rocket. Her greatest embarrassment was trying to explain why she was in such a hurry, going through a pelican crossing red light at such an early hour.

In the summer of 1990 she experienced three security scares in a week, which left her nervous and rattled. A crude firebomb addressed to her was sent to Buckingham Palace but was spotted in the Palace post room. Now she is monitored by infrared cameras even when she walks in the gardens at Highgrove. An ambulance stands by on discreet alert and also a fire engine; a constant watch is kept. More than £500,000 was spent on security recently at Kensington Palace but that did not prevent Ali Kashabian, an Iranian businessman obsessed by the Princess, making repeated attempts to climb the eight-foot spiked fence surrounding the rose garden until smartly nipped by a police alsatian.

The quality newspapers and the BBC have already prepared obituaries on the Princess. Though this is normal planning it is a constant and chilling reminder for the ever-vigilant men who have the task of protecting her life, if necessary with their own.

The Prince and Princess send out a huge number of Christmas cards, remembering all the people who work for them, usually signing them on long flights. They hold parties for each Household, and at Christmas staff members are given £20 to buy a present which they wrap up themselves. They return these to the Prince and Princess who later present them with their gift.

There is no sentiment at the Palace. Once you are out you do not see the Prince or Princess of Wales again. Some have been hurt and dismayed, mistakenly lulled into a false feeling of security by being part of the fashionable Wales Household.

Acerbically the Princess once suggested to a departing member of staff, 'Why don't you read the weather; it only takes two minutes a day.'

CHAPTER 30

Very Much in Our Thoughts

———————◆————————

If there was ever an adjective that has been over-used when referring to both the Queen Mother and the Princess of Wales it is 'caring'.

'There is a quality of goodness about the lass,' a royal adviser will tell you. She succeeds in being caring without verging on the mawkish. The Princess is never pi, or patronising; her impact comes from the thoughtful gesture, the flowers, the surprise telephone call, the little present.

On engagements there is that buzz of excitement before her arrival, that expectant hush. Today she appears in a purple, pleated skirt, matching jacket and dramatic flat sombrero. Accompanied by the dignified, tall, silver-haired senior Church Warden in black robes, Trevor Turner, she takes her seat and looks for a while at the beautiful stonework of St Bride's, a Wren church in Fleet Street famous for its choir. The music would include her favourite Brahms 'How lovely are Thy dwellings', and the hymn 'I vow to thee my country'.

In the run-up to Christmas 1989, she is attending a service of celebration and opening of new assembly rooms in this historic City church built after the Great Fire of London. Traditionally St Bride's has been the journalists' church but they were only to be seen slipping in occasionally for a memorial service to a colleague who got away to the great newsroom in the sky. Now that their papers are based as far afield as High Street Kensington and the Isle of Dogs, it is a paradox that St Bride's should be busier than ever, due to the 'stir up' approach of the remarkable Canon John Oates and his programme of prayer and support for John McCarthy, the television reporter taken hostage in Lebanon.

The Princess met McCarthy's father after the thanksgiving and shook hands. 'It must,' she said, 'be devastating to face another Christmas with no news of your son. My family think of you every day and often pray for you.' She has always been deeply moved by the plight of the hostages and for the family of Terry Waite, the Archbishop of Canterbury's envoy, kidnapped in Lebanon while on a mission to try and secure their release.

'Who do we know called Diana living in Kensington?' Terry's mother Mrs Lena Waite asked. It was her seventy-sixth birthday and a huge bunch of lilies, carnations and chrysanthemums had just been delivered to her home in Lymm, Cheshire. The card said, 'You are very much in our thoughts. These flowers come to you for a very happy birthday. From the four of us. Diana (Wales).' The old lady was so touched she immediately telephoned the Archbishop of Canterbury to ask him how the Princess could possibly have known it was her birthday. Dr Robert Runcie replied, 'She just knew.' The Princess had planned to telephone but then decided flowers would be nicer.

The Prince and Princess talk about their engagements and share their experiences, which sometimes results in delightful surprises. Prince Charles took the Princess unexpectedly to Stoke Mandeville Hospital, Buckinghamshire, in August 1983. Almost apologetically, as though he had brought an extra guest to dinner, Prince Charles, who was expected on his own to open the new spinal injuries centre, explained, 'I was telling her about this marvellous place and she insisted on seeing it for herself.'

What the Princess enjoys is a mixture of engagements: one minute in church, the next dancing at a tea party for pensioners in High Wycombe in Buckinghamshire. Charlie Bristow, seventy-one, a Dunkirk veteran, will never forget asking her to waltz to Mantovani's 'My Diane'. 'Who set me up for this?' she asked, but cheerfully handed her bag to a lady-in-waiting, saying, 'I don't think I can do this,' which was a bit hard to believe. According to Mr Bristow, the Princess 'was blushing the whole minute we danced.'

Many of her visits are celebrations. On 18 November 1989 Sir Richard Attenborough, Chairman of the Royal Academy of Dramatic Art, paid tribute in his fulsome way both to the Princess, who is President, and also to the distinguished active eighty-five-year-old, Sir John Gielgud. 'We have venerability and wisdom on the one side and youth and exquisite beauty on the other.' Sir John joined RADA as a scholarship student in 1922 and the Princess succeeded him as President in 1989.

The power of the Princess of Wales to do good has sometimes surprised her, indeed frightened her. A child injured in a road crash in which her mother and uncle had been killed had refused to open her eyes in hospital. But when she heard the Princess's voice she smiled and said, 'Hello'.

Bringing ease and lightness to the stuffiest of occasions, the Princess does her homework and asks searching questions about complex issues, whether on the treatment of AIDS or cures for deafness. She sways to gospel music, telling a group of disabled black people in Battersea how much she, too, enjoys a game of poker. Before visiting the men's section of an Islamic centre she made sure she had a Muslim chadar so that she could go in veiled. By putting them at their ease, she becomes completely involved with people, eliminating 'compassion fatigue'. This pure Queen Mother gift of listening intently to what people say keeps the Princess lively instead of feeling exhausted and bored: 'How many more hospital beds to go?'

Approached by two hundred organisations all asking her to be Patron or President, the Princess was selective. Sometimes she said 'No' at first or, as she did to Relate, formerly the Marriage Guidance Council, 'No, but I will come and see the work you do.' She went to Rugby, was impressed and has now agreed. With the other charities under her patronage, the Princess never took the easy option but has thoughtfully selected difficult modern-day problems: AIDS, Help the Aged, drug and alcohol addiction.

Determined to be much more than a figurehead, she stressed at the beginning, 'I don't want to dive into something without being able to follow it up. Nothing would upset me more than just being a name on the top of a piece of paper . . . I just long to help in all sorts of areas.'

Somehow you do not think of her readily as a Colonel-in-Chief but again she has done her homework, is aware of the subtleties of parade inspections and also looks very good in the red mess kit of the Royal Hampshires. The last royal line regiment with a single county affiliation, they have the largest number of battle honours including Minden and Gallipoli. In the past they had a Colonel Commandant, Lord Mountbatten. After his assassination, the Princess was invited to become Colonel-in-Chief, a special honour to her and to Prince Charles who was so attached to Lord Mountbatten.

One of her early engagements after the marriage was visiting the regiment in Berlin. The Princess went 'straight to a welcoming parade inspection, then a *feu de joie* [a bonfire], had tea with the wives and a laugh in the Sergeants' Mess.' She ate smoked pork, danced with the subalterns and slyly in 'Princess of Wiles' mood, said to one of them, 'I understand you had a rehearsal?' aware that her stand-in had been a burly black sergeant-major. She also pressed a panic button just to see what might happen. They loved her because 'She was marvellous with the soldiers.'

To someone of her background and fairly limited education, the great folders of papers on defence issues she receives as Colonel-in-Chief of the 13/18th Royal Hussars and the Princess of Wales Own Regiment of Canada, and Hon. Commandant, RAF Wittering, are not always easy to tackle. Really she would prefer to be cuddled up with a glossy magazine. However, the brigadiers and wing commanders going along to Kensington Palace found plenty of blue pencil marks on their briefing notes and were distinctly impressed by the questions asked by their pretty Colonel.

As Patron of the British Deaf Association, the Princess took the trouble to learn sign language and made a faultless speech in July 1990. 'I'm pretty hopeless at that, but it is important to show them that you are interested and not just breezing in and out having seen them for a morning. I've got all my senses . . .' A lot of hard work went into that speech – years in fact. But the Princess was serious and the result was excellent. 'No fluffs, everyone understood,' said Mr Bernard Quin, Director of Information for the Association. They stood and applauded her.

The depth of care is genuine. Without it the Princess could not, as Patron of Relate, sit in at a marriage counselling session and have the couple open their hearts to her. 'It was,' the experts said, 'extraordinary for someone so young to be so good at marital counselling.' They forgot that she comes from a broken home and does not have the easiest of marriages herself. She was 'a very receptive person, intuitive and a very good listener,' thought David French, Director of Relate, who was with the Princess during the counselling, while his colleague Zelda Westmead has said, 'Experiencing a lot of ups and downs in her own life, the Princess has reacted not by blocking off the sadness completely but, in the best way, gaining by it. The Princess knows how it is for people badly affected by pain.'

Dr Roy Strong, former Head of the Victoria and Albert Museum, says, 'The Princess has shown compassion.' Rod Hackney, Prince Charles's architectural friend and adviser, endorses this. 'She has a warm and generous personality which is evident in her attitude to people, and is admirably suited to but unaffected by her royal position.'

Never the sort of Patron to appear only at annual general meetings, the Princess popped unexpectedly into Help the Aged headquarters in Clerkenwell early one morning, surprising everyone and saying, 'Hello, I have just dropped my youngest for his first day at school and thought I would come and see you all.'

Then she went to the receptionist. 'I've met you before . . . you're Jackie.' Blind since birth, what touched the thirty-six-year-old telephone operator was the way the Princess had remembered her after only a brief first meeting when she had been one of a crowd of three hundred standing in a reception line. 'I remember her touch too – how caring it was.'

Serious visits have not been without their moments of humour. When Les Rudd, a medical sociologist, was showing the Princess around Glenoaks, a mental health project at Worksop, he directed the Princess to a door which he believed led to the stairway. As he opened it, muttering, 'I'll follow you, Ma'am,' he found he was shepherding her into a dark cupboard.

The royal family love it when things go slightly wrong, feeling this is a chance to see normal life. The Princess was tickled when a fridge door was opened proudly at a residential centre for alcoholics at Camberwell. Instead of being clean and ready to use, it was full of 'manky old sardines'.

July 4 1990 was a day of torrential downpours and wind when umbrellas blew inside out and women clenched their teeth in the driving rain. London came to a standstill. The Patron of the Royal Academy of Music was trying to get to Marylebone to present diplomas; the traffic was so bad that she was almost late, but not quite; the Princess never is.

The prizegiving was being held in a pleasant old church in the Marylebone Road, a place where cars never go to bed and the noise is deafening. Sometimes the Princess can look a little fazed, as if she has just had a hair-raising experience or, as in this case, a traumatic journey. Her yellow and white linen suit looked slightly creased, unusual for her, and a little tight around the waist. Her hands were clasped a bit tensely, but the President got a shy smile from under her white Stetson when he complimented her for being on time. Perhaps it was a security scare. 'I never get used to them,' the Princess once confessed, 'they terrify me.'

Now in an artistic atmosphere of gentleness and charm, she began to relax. The President said, 'What a fantastic team we have here,' looking at the Princess who is very musical and then at the distinguished guests being honoured that day who included José Carreras and the conductor Claus Tennstedt. At first in a slightly abstracted way, she applauded very slowly but brightened up to give a special warm smile to the great Carreras who had conquered cancer, described delicately as a 'period of indisposition'.

Making the awards was hazardous and involved standing up each time, walking down three steps, handing over the diploma and then, after a few pleasantries, delicately reversing back.

'She is an absolute poppet,' John Bliss, Adminstrator of the Royal Academy of Music, summed her up.

The Princess likes a feedback on her visits to know how useful they have been and whether, in the case of charities, they are bringing new people in to help. She insists on sending very speedy thank-you letters. These are not the usual stilted, uncommitted couple of paragraphs which often follow a royal visit, but extremely warm.

'Her Royal Highness was delighted to have been able to attend such a marvellous service in such splendid surroundings; it was very special, and the music was magnificent,' signed Laura Lonsdale on behalf of the Princess, was the one to Canon Oates.

Personal letters the Princess does by hand, and she is not economical with adjectives. This buoyant up-beat approach is infectious and part of her secret.

During the 1990 Christmas and New Year royal family holiday at Sandringham, the Princess drove a hundred miles to Nottingham to see twenty-four-year-old roofer Dean Woodward, who had been in a coma after a road accident. It had been the Princess's voice, when she visited him three times in the hospital where Prince Charles was also a patient, that helped his recovery.

'Just keeping in touch,' the Princess said when she telephoned him, twice on Christmas Day, and she kept the promise made to Dean in hospital that she would call and see him at home. Not only did she cheer him up but also the whole family. Thirty relatives had gathered and there was lots of laughter when the Princess, with Dean's arm linked through hers, posed for photographs at his uncle's house. Dean's uncle Terry Woodward said simply, 'We think of her as an angel. She walks around with a halo over her head as far as we are concerned.' Afterwards she sent one of her happy, handwritten unselfconscious letters with a D and a coronet at the top and dated 2 January 1991.

Dear Terry and Linda,
    How wonderful it was to see you all today and I am over the moon with my beautiful flowers and the thought that went into them. This comes with my love to you both and my heartfelt thanks for making me feel so welcome today – I left your home full of very special memories.

CHAPTER 31

The Primitive Passport

If you happen to be strolling past Kensington Palace in the early morning when it is quiet except for the chauffeurs coughing, you hear the sound of music. It is often 'Work That Body' by Diana Ross and inside the Princess, in shorts or a designer Lycra leopard-skin leotard and exercise tights, is in the middle of a fast workout; not out of breath but with that jogger's 'can't stop now' look, unless of course it is Prince William or Harry. Sometimes she will watch a keep-fit video by Lizzie Webb, a TVam keep-fit expert. She also likes to jog in the park, but if it is raining has a two-mile walk on a mechanical treadmill, and describes it as like 'going uphill fast'.

Her day begins at 7 A.M. when she puts on a scarlet tracksuit and drives to Buckingham Palace for twenty lengths of the pool before dashing back to Kensington Palace for her workout. Then she likes a spoonful of Crabtree and Evelyn's own brand of honey before going for a run in Kensington Gardens at 9 A.M.

Cover-girl glamour the Princess certainly has, picking up hints from people she admires. In 1982 she met the film star Elizabeth Taylor and immediately began to copy her neat way of defining mesmerising eyes with sapphire blue pencil liner on the inside of the lower rim to great effect. But if she looks good it is because she works at renewing what Dame Edith Evans in her last years described as the 'primitive passport'. This was the elderly actress's view of natural beauty, which, without any real regret, she felt had eluded her.

Weighing 9 stone 7 pounds the Princess is passionate about keeping slim. After watching the British Fashion Awards, she enviously suggested to the top American models Linda Evangelista and Christy Turlington, 'You girls must all live on lettuce leaves and nicotine.' Even before the royal wedding, she invited her music teacher Miss Lily Snipp from West Heath to play while she cavorted on the 1830 Nash floor of the Buckingham Palace Music Room. Later they moved to the Queen's Throne Room after she had damaged the Music Room floor by her vigorous tap dancing.

The first royal to go to exercise classes, the Princess had weakened her back picking up children and went to stretch sessions at the Pineapple Studios in South Kensington. In October 1990 using the pseudonym 'Sally Hastings' she checked herself into a fitness club in an unglamorous corner of old Isleworth, Middlesex. For an hour she worked really hard in the gym under the instruction of the engaging Carolan Brown, the studio director. Later the Princess pleaded with Carolan to give her private tuition at home. The publicity surrounding the Princess's visit had made it impossible for her to enjoy club membership. Her £199 joining fee was returned and now Miss Brown goes regularly to 'KP' so that the Princess can get on with the strict programme of exercises in some privacy. She always prefers a woman personal trainer and would not even consider a man for the job. One of the exercises they do together is called The Step and is fairly exhausting. It involves stepping on and off a platform, looks deceptively easy but burns up the calories, the equivalent of running at seven miles an hour, but does not give you biceps like a boxer.

Pleased enough with her almost perfect 34–25–36 shape, she just wishes for an inch more on her bust. At the club they were impressed by how knowledgeable the Princess was about exercise and body rhythms. Over the years she has taken dance lessons with the London Festival Ballet, wearing her favourite pink leotard. She is almost excessively health conscious, an exercise addict, and a 'fitness freak'. Disapproving of alcohol and cigarettes, on her sitting room door the Princess has hung a large No Smoking sign. At Balmoral she put her sister-in-law Sarah through a punishing keep-fit schedule, persuading her to jog, swim and generally work off the extra pounds after Eugénie's birth.

In common with the great composers, Beethoven, Mozart, Liszt, Schubert and Brahms, the Princess has a stronger left side to her face while eighty-five to ninety per cent of the world's population is right-faced. According to Karl Smith, an American Emeritus Professor of Psychology, this makes her exceptionally talented musically. The Princess hates being photographed from the left side, feeling it exaggerates her strong profile and firm mouth. 'The only thing you don't know about me is how many fillings I've had,' she once laughed. She has perfect teeth, none capped.

The world thinks her beautiful but she dislikes many things about herself: her legs, the tiny mole on the left of her upper lip; her large nose and schoolgirlish hands; this explains why she tends not to wear many rings. Once she stood badly, with a slight stoop, but thanks to private hour-long ballet classes now her head is held high.

Her make-up only takes twenty minutes even for a gala and for daytime she makes sure it is done in daylight, sitting at an ivory tri-mirrored kidney-shaped dressing table. Her skin is excellent. She cares for it with Neutrogena or Simple Soap and a pinky moisturising Lilyroot and Marshmallow Lotion made by Boots. She does not need foundation; any tendency to pinkness is balanced with a green-based cream, then just a little topping of Clinique's hypoallergenic 'Buttermilk Cream' and a transparent buffer powder. Then, after deftly using concealer sticks and eye-lash combs she dips a sable brush in desert gold blusher to give her cheeks a flattering 'Dynasty' glamour quite different from her original slightly floury English rose. Wisely the Princess avoids strong red lipstick and always wears a soft pink gloss; she rounds off with a pampering spray of Floris or Diorissima. How different from most other royal women who would feel a little rose water and a light dusting of powder was enough. Blue eyeshadow and pink lipstick, 'all that stuff', were only for a ball at Windsor. The Queen Mother is a credit to this minimalist approach.

There are regular monthly or twice-monthly facials with the Yorkshire beautician Janet Filderman who believes in vacuum suctioning, 'hoovering' the skin, at her Albemarle Street clinic in Mayfair a skin already kept scrupulously clean with Milk of Roses every night. It may all cost a great deal but the Princess of Wales can afford to spend money on herself. Fastidious, pleasantly preoccupied, she is not, however, obsessed with looking good. Spending so much time on her feet for official engagements, she pampers them with Body Shop pink minty-cool peppermint lotion. Keen on keeping her beautiful body, she listens avidly to fashionable friends, drinking in the latest tips while toying with avocado and mozzarella for lunch, sipping water with a slice of lemon and gossiping about who has had a nose job. 'I'd love to have my conk fixed,' the Princess disarmingly says. 'It's too big. I consulted doctors but decided I couldn't go around for days with my nose bandaged. And what if it went wrong?' But somehow her nose does seem less obvious now.

If the Princess had not married the future King, as a rich young woman she would probably be spending even more on herself than girls around town with manes of blonde hair seen sitting on the bonnets of Range Rovers at the Cartier polo match or enjoying après-ski in Klosters and Val d'Isère. As it is she has aromatherapy with Daniele Ryman and swears by her Flight Comfort Kit which keeps jetlag at bay. It includes a tingling gel for the sinuses and, to help her sleep on flights, a little orange oil to dab on a small pillow.

Like Prince Charles, the Princess is a great believer in holistic medicine and has regular acupuncture and Shiatsu massage. This oriental therapy helps beat the stresses of public life and busy schedules. It has made her much calmer and helped her to stop biting her nails. Accompanying the Italian President Francesco Cossiga to an exhibition of paintings of Naples in London in October 1990 she flaunted long red nails to match a low-cut Grecian evening dress.

'I am very enthusiastic about acupuncture,' the Princess explained. 'It helps me to keep calm and relax.' During weekly visits an acupuncturist inserts special needles into her body to relieve pressure and deaden pain. 'I've been having it for a year and I really enjoy it. In my job I cannot afford to panic. I have it everywhere and it is great.'

On a quiet Sunday afternoon in January 1990 at about 4 o'clock a quiet car carrying two blonde girls swished through Hertfordshire country lanes past red stone, white-doored cottages and swung into Champneys Health Farm. Recognising the Princess of Wales, the estate manager doffed his cap.

Champneys is rather like a cruise ship; discreetly creamy, designed to be sybaritic, with colours and heavy carpeting to soothe fatty executives on stringent diets. Everyone looks much the same in towelling robes; a health farm is a great leveller. 'There was,' said one beautician, 'none of "Your Highness this, Your Highness that", but nor did we holler at her; instead we would go up to her and say, "It's time for your facial."' Gradually it dawned on people that the blonde girl who had checked in under the name Beckwith-Smith was the Princess. They could hardly believe their eyes as she scampered around in a high-street Dash pink tracksuit easy and relaxed.

A friend, Kate Menzies, had gone along too, making things even more fun over the three days. They stayed in the modern east wing rather than the chintzy old house. The two royal detectives played tennis and swam and thought their job some-times not all bad.

Health farms tend to be rather introspective places but the Princess introduced a levity amongst the publishers, polo-playing dentists, actresses, convalescents, footballers, tennis stars, rich women, acquisition dealers and models. In the dining room over-looking sweeping lawns where gardeners tried to keep their eyes averted as newly thin faces settled down to carrot, chervil soup and rabbit food, the atmosphere was one of serious restraint but suddenly a royal missile, a piece of cheese, was sent flying across the sunny room and the Princess was doubled up with helpless laughter. 'What a hoot!' Soon everyone was laughing; then the Princess skipped off to spend a few hours in the advanced dance class.

There were quiet times too when she had beauty treatments in a softly lit cubicle snuggled up in a blanket. Her beautician was

Lona who shares a cottage in the grounds with a blind masseuse who had just lost her guide dog through leukaemia. The Princess was quiet and completely relaxed for her Clarins Paris facial which works through the lymphatic glands and which only a few beauticians are qualified to give. The Princess's skin was flawless, a classic 12 o'clock type, not too dry, not too oily.

In the body steamer when everyone sits in a white zipped-up tub with hot air billowing round, it was not long before there were girlish squeaks. 'Oh, we are cooked,' the Princess laughed. Then, wrapped in huge white towelling robes, she and Kate Menzies were put in the rest room under apricot blankets and low lights for a compulsory lie down for fifteen minutes before the massage.

At the end of the day after saunas, swims, massages and steam, the Princess's skin felt like silk when a couple of ladies in white coats vigorously rubbed her with salt. These sturdy women, not unlike Black Sea beach wardens, had been given a lesson in protocol and thought they should curtsy. But when the Princess breezed into the spa, said 'Hi' and slipped off her gown, the ladies got down straightaway to her slender back with the grains of salt. 'You do your front yourself.' She thanked them and went into the shower.

The joy of those few days, an inspired Christmas present from Prince Charles, had not really been about beauty treatments at all, but a chance for her to enjoy 'normal, happy, giggly gossiping' with the other people, particularly women.' She picked her toe-nails, bit her fingernails and, when asked if she would come again, shook her head but added, 'My sister-in-law would love this place.' When it was suggested that they might come back together, she said, 'They'd never allow it,' nodding towards an imaginary Buckingham Palace.

Nothing could be further removed from softly lit beauty salons and ritzy health farms than Joseph Corvo's curious Bayswater flat in Cleveland Square with its tired straggly geraniums, china rabbits on the mantelpiece and peach sheets covering the sofas. You are shown into a small bedsitting room and Corvo, a gangling sandy-haired man in T-shirt, jogging trousers and beige shoes, sits on the end of a bed and hums and sings as he tweaks the Princess's feet vigorously for half an hour, chatting about gentleness and love and making her wince when he touches a bad spot.

Corvo, a former Yorkshire miner, specialises in Zone Therapy and claims to make people look ten or twenty years younger as he massages the nerve endings in their feet to relieve tension in other parts of the body. 'Joe the Toe' believes in a 'lifestyle diet' based on never mixing proteins and carbohydrates and recommends the Princess drinks eight large glasses of warm water every day to flush out damaging toxins.

Her choice of beauty products is informed and she does not fall into the trap of many rich young women who spend a fortune on a cream believing it to have magic properties but in reality are only 'buying hope', hoodwinked by the packaging. However the Princess has been attracted by the Erno Lazlo Institute and has a special personalised membership card. It is all terribly exclusive; a woman simply cannot buy a product over the counter. Her skin had first to be analysed by a Lazlo expert in a white coat. Only then was she allowed to spend a small fortune. However, the Princess has chosen one of the cheaper Lazlo beauty routines which involves splashing warm water on her face throughout the day.

There is a chemist's shop at London's Sloane Square called Bliss which specialises in health foods and has a window full of sponges. Before she was married the Princess was always popping in and Mr Raj Voara, one of the directors, has a flair for publicity and treasures a prescription in the name of Lady Diana Spencer. Today it is more likely that it will be one of her detectives who will collect the Princess's supply of royal bees' jelly. Kept in the freezer, it is taken with a tiny teaspoon to give her energy and stamina at a cost of £120 for a few months' supply.

The Princess's secret is that she has never settled complacently for a hairstyle or a look and consequently never appears dated. In the hot summer of July 1990, she had her hair cut much shorter by Sam McKnight, an international crimper who works with Daniel Galvin but prefers preparing models for glossy fashion shoots. Nobody could ever say McKnight lacked confidence. While her former hairdresser Richard Dalton might have been reluctant with the scissors, McKnight snipped off a good two inches all round, took away her heavy fringe, replacing it with a fined-down short feathery affair, and then jumped on a plane to Paris. It was all completely unexpected and that is what is so stimulating about the Princess.

McKnight is not the sort of hairdresser who would relish doing boring daily wash and blow or perms. A colleague who worked with him years ago says, 'Sam is the type of guy who likes doing crazy things with a model's hair – but only at the front. It will only last for a couple of seconds; he's not into the steady shampoo and set business.' Her haircut is very short and very trendy, a style which could be a nightmare for a milliner but the Princess is wearing fewer and fewer hats.

The Princess has admired the Duchess of York's smooth hairstyle and is now popping into Carey Temple McAdam in Hill Street, Mayfair for a £20 wash and blow-dry with their star stylist Ivor. Customers were shocked by the Princess's skinniness when she took her jacket off. 'My dear,' said one, 'she was so thin, her skirt was held in at the back with safety pins.' She is obsessed with being skinny and when she visited the Norwich centre of the Eating Disorders Association in November 1990 was especially sympathetic to anorexic cases. Pleading for more understanding of this sickness related to compulsive slimming, she said with feeling, 'It is not about women being silly.'

She likes to use a camomile Body Shop shampoo with a banana conditioner and, to counteract any bad effects from too much swimming, Shimmer Lights, a silver ultra-violet conditioner, stops her highlights turning yellow. Her hair colour is naturally dark mouse but over the years it has become lighter, a fun colour reflecting her own rather special chemistry.

The parting with Richard Dalton was amicable. This thirty-nine-year-old baker's son from Edinburgh first learned about hairdressing by combing his grandmother's long flowing hair and admiring the sleek elegance of women in old-fashioned Hollywood films. Dalton's critics thought he relied too heavily on backcombing and Infusium texturing hairspray. But so long as he kept his CFC (chlorofluorocarbon) hair products hidden – they are not allowed in the Palace – Dalton was allowed to trim and blow-dry the heir to the throne's own hair.

His willingness to put the Princess's hair up for her first State Opening of Parliament – and that was what she wanted – earned him eight years as royal hairdresser and a salon at Claridge's. He ousted her regular stylist Kevin Shanley at Headlines, South Kensington, who had refused to give her such a severe upswept style. Now Dalton is free to holiday with rich clients in Florida and the South of France. 'Working for the Princess of Wales,' he says, 'has been the most wonderful and memorable experience.' He has hilarious memories of trying to put a hat on the Princess's head while flying through turbulence: 'I was glad I learnt to roller skate.'

'The old style was too hot,' the Princess said, almost as an apology to Richard Dalton, but she knew people had begun to think her hair was 'safe and boring'. The new look had a gamine quality, almost boyish except it was not block cut at the back, being instead layered and slightly uneven to give a feminine look.

In 1991 *Hello* magazine readers – and it was no surprise – voted her the most elegant and stylish woman of the year. Runners-up included Princess Caroline of Monaco. *Harpers & Queen*, a more sophisticated glossy, put her on the cover as 'a model princess' with the comment, 'Her hair may change and so may the hats but the face remains exquisitely just the same.' A poll in *Today* newspaper decided the new haircut made the Princess look younger and more stunning. But not everyone liked it. One Throne Ranger remarked, 'I think short hair is frightfully common.'

At the Gala opening of the Cultural Centre, Hong Kong in November
1989.

Above: With Barbara Bush at the White House, 1990.

Below: Meeting Michael Jackson at Wembley Stadium, July 1988.

Above right: A droll aside with Sir John Gielgud. The Princess succeeded him as President of RADA in 1989.

Below left: The Princess played tennis with champion Steffi Graf at the Vanderbilt tennis club when she opened the Women's International Tennis Association European headquarters in June 1988.

Below right: A keen dancer herself with a strong interest in ballet, the Princess met Dame Margot Fonteyn at the Covent Garden Gala tribute to the famous ballerina, May 1990.

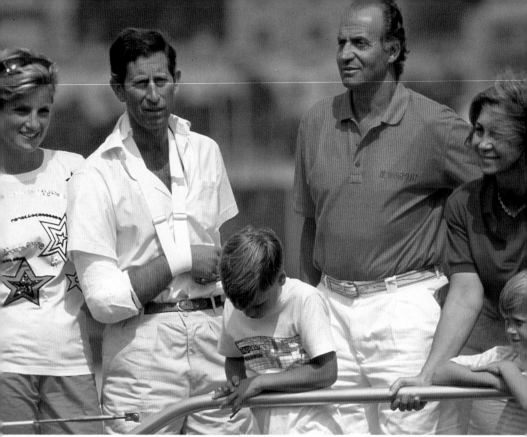

Above: Summer 1990 in Majorca with King Juan Carlos and Queen Sofia of Spain aboard the King's luxury yacht, *Fortuna.*

Left: At the Peto Institute for handicapped children in Budapest, Hungary in May 1990.

Above right: With Issa Ghanem al-Kuwari, Qatari Minister of Information, at the Qatar Camel Race in November 1986.

Right: As Colonel-in-Chief, the Princess wore a specially designed regimental mess jacket when dining at the headquarters of the Royal Hampshires.

Far right: The Princess was warmly applauded when she addressed the British Deaf Association's centenary conference in Brighton in July 1990 by signing.

Above: Carrying 'first lady' into Grandma's House, a home for children suffering from AIDS, in Washington DC.

Above right: With AIDS patients Derek and Paul at St Mary's Hospital, Paddington, December 1990.

Right: Making an informal visit to John Street Old People's Home, Newham, October 1990. The Princess is patron of the Guinness Trust, which runs the home.

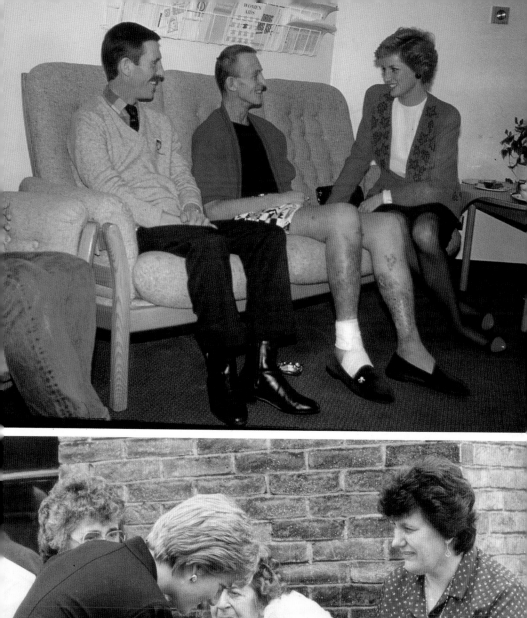

Meeting young homeless people at a day centre in Adelaide Street, London, February 1990.

CHAPTER 32

A Little Disinterest

---◆---

Everyone remembers the kiss on the balcony, the tenderness and the laughter that followed the marriage. The Princess tickled Prince Charles under the nose with a piece of scented white blossom in a lemon grove in Italy; they joked, clowned around in puppyish playfulness, enjoyed frivolous whispered asides, not unkindly or ignoring their hosts but in shared laughter and sweet exchanges.

He always had an old-fashioned courtliness and liked to kiss her hand and give her a fresh flower. In the Sistine Chapel in Rome, the Princess rested her head on his shoulder. They were mad about each other. The Prince teased her in public. In Canada he told the guests at a formal banquet in St John's, Newfoundland how much he regretted not having time to 'take my wife to a place called Leading Tickles'.

Then there were the loving notes when she came back from an official visit alone abroad, from Princess Grace's funeral in Monaco, the surprise presents. One was a window from Park House. The Prince had spotted Diana's childish signature on the white wooden frame and, in true kingly style, ordered the entire frosted pane to be delivered to Highgrove.

However this besottedness could not help the Princess cope with a centuries-old condition, post-natal depression after the birth of Prince William. She got tired, did not sleep at night, was scratchy. She grew thin and refused to let Barbara Barnes do too much for the baby, saying, 'A mother's arms are so much more comforting.' At Highgrove she was almost reclusive and used the back stairs which had been boarded up for twenty years rather than come face to face with staff.

Wilful, the newly married Princess always determined to look good insisted on keeping an appointment with her hairdresser on the evening of a ball at Althorp, leaving Prince Charles to go alone to face 'Mummy', the Queen, at the Chelsea Flower Show when both had been expected.

'I'm exhausted,' she told people quite openly. Achieving so much in such a short time, becoming a future Queen, producing a vital heir to succeed, took an emotional as well as physical toll, the worst combination.

Royal family holidays in Scotland or Norfolk were not the answer. They had one of their first rows at a pheasant shoot at Sandringham. When Prince Charles upbraided her for dragging her feet she snapped back, 'You know I didn't want to come in the first place.' He would quickly realise that this young girl, rich, socially creamy whom he had thought genuinely at home in the kale fields, would wilt peevishly when kept away from the bright lights. Soon the Princess was hopping off to London to be soothed by shopping sprees in the Knightsbridge Tiara Triangle: coffee in the General Trading, a look at a friend's wedding list in Peter Jones and then a few hours spent browsing and spending in Harvey Nichols.

Balmoral is fine if you shoot, fish or stalk. It made George V sad to wonder why his sons spent so little time at their Scottish home. It was left to James Thomas, outspoken Labour railwayman and Secretary of State for the Dominions and the Colonies, to tell him bluntly, 'The reason the Princes don't come 'ere is because it is a bloody dull 'ouse.'

For someone young and frothy like the Princess it was even more dismal; the weather was ghastly and once she had bought a few teatowels and sweets in Braemar the fun for her was over. Prince Charles, on the other hand, was in the bosom of the royal family, proud of his young wife whom everyone adored, completely happy. In a blithely masculine way, he was unaware of his wife's boredom and was hurt and then shocked when she flew to London. It was the first sign of her unwillingness to put up with anything she found impossibly dull in her own free time. There was enough tedium in her public life.

Even at Kensington Palace or Highgrove the Princess could still get tetchy. One evening, when Charles and his polo chums were enjoying tales of chukkas won and lost, instead of simpering and smiling, the Princess jumped up from the table, flung down her napkin irritably, 'I've never been so bored in all my life.' Prince Charles gave that sideways quizzical smile but it had been embarrassing.

'Over here, darling,' he used to call when they were first married, and would propel his wife towards the crowd, delighting in the pleasure given by a glimpse of that tall creature with a speedy walk and her look of surprise that anyone should want to see her. But when he called 'Over here, darling,' on the ski slopes two years later, it was humiliating. The Prince and Princess were trying to have a restorative few days in Liechtenstein, an icing sugar principality much favoured by the Queen for its privacy, old-fashioned charm and Franz Josef its elderly ruler.

Pursued by the media, the Princess had utterly refused to pose for even one photograph, pulling her woolly ski hat over her head so that Prince Charles was forced to plead, 'Please, Diana, don't do that. Don't be stupid. Please, darling, please.' Unwittingly, he gave the world a vignette of the relationship and of difficulties which until then had only been rumoured. 'Prince Charles is not a wimp. He is giving in to her a lot because she is so young and because of the children . . . he is a thoughtful husband but hardly henpecked.'

The skiing trip followed an unpleasant and potentially worrying tantrum when the Princess had refused to attend the Annual Festival of Remembrance at the Royal Albert Hall. This was when they had a particularly blistering row. Prince Charles slammed out and the Princess shouted, 'Don't you dare go without me.'

But the Prince did go on his own, excusing his wife: 'Diana's not well.' Then to her credit she suddenly turned up in the royal box, fifteen minutes late and, worse, arriving after the Queen. Prince Philip grimaced as if sucking a lemon. The Princess could well have asked, 'Is it better I make the effort or would you rather I stay away?' A glum Princess is better than almost any other member of the royal family except the Queen Mother. Prince Charles decided then that his wife needed a break. In her view, the Princess will tell you that she was entitled to a private ten-day holiday and that she had not planned to share it with the world's press. As a courtier said later, 'She was damned if she was going to have her picture taken.'

Asked if it was true that they had many noisy arguments on the ski slopes, the royal couple later denied that there had even been a problem. The Princess countered with, 'There was a total misunderstanding . . . We don't have arguments.' Prince Charles added, 'No, no, but occasionally we do.' The Princess disagreed: 'No, we don't.' Prince Charles then admitted, 'I go on longer,' and the Princess, bossily insisting on the last word, added, 'Yes, but I'm faster.'

It would be the worldly Sarah Ferguson, married to the Duke of York in July 1986, who, with her appetite for fun, would awaken in the more restrained Princess of Wales a feeling of isolation and the thought that perhaps she had been missing out for the last five years being the perfect wife and mother. Whatever the Duchess of York did in the royal family it seemed to be accepted. It was fearfully embarrassing when Major Ronald Ferguson was caught out in a massage parlour in London, but the Queen was sanguine about the ex-army officer's peccadillos and, unperturbed, turned to her discomfited daughter-in-law to ask, 'Sarah, what is your father up to now?' with a shrug that seemed to indicate, 'After all, boys will be boys.'

As a special seventh wedding anniversary surprise, the Princess presented Prince Charles with a video of herself dancing and singing to 'All I Ask of You' from *The Phantom of the Opera*. It was surprisingly professional. She had the help of *Phantom* choreographer Gilly Lynne and got a proper film crew; but Prince Charles might have been just as happy with a book on Byzantine architecture and a bit of peace and quiet.

Indeed he was turning away from his wife more and more. It

was ironic that now her husband seemed to be one of the few men not a little bit in love with her. Both were lonely in the marriage. A member of the royal family explained, 'It was terribly sad: the trouble is that Diana, though she is funny, absolutely sweet, could never match him intellectually.'

'I don't think the Princess would ever be a bolter like her mother,' mused a royal cousin, adding, 'and Prince Charles is far too moral a man ever to stray.' Asked if they still have laughs together, one of the royal family says today, 'No, and that's the real sadness.' Sometimes when the Prince and Princess are together she will look at him quizzically, kicking her foot, head on one side and almost sad as she listens to him enthusing about a favourite cause.

Neglect is a sure breeding ground for mischief. The Princess needed to have fun and missed her friends. Most of them were married and perhaps stuck in the country with a Filipino *au pair* for company and a growing baby.

One evening a friend of the Queen Mother's was walking through a fashionable part of Pimlico when the Princess, at the wheel of a black car, drew up alongside and asked him, 'What on earth are you doing so far from home?' Teasingly he said, 'I could ask the same, Ma'am.' Looking into the car he saw she was wearing 'very sassy' satin shorts. 'A dark good-looking fellow was cowering in the back, a detective sat in front.' 'I'm off to play bridge of course,' she replied airily and, without the flicker of an eyelid, she drove off.

'The Duchess,' remarked Lucy Acland, a perceptive twenty-five-year-old, the granddaughter of Sir Cyril Kleinwort, 'has given Diana a taste for the champagne lifestyle.' The Prince was being seen as a rather tightfisted reclusive figure who was dismayed by his wife's lack of intellect, and the Princess as a lonely whirling creature dancing alone to the music of Wham, slightly vapid, obsessed with her physical appearance.

Things were bad in October 1987; the clichéd seven-year itch had come early. The Princess, called 'Duch' by close friends, was becoming very keen on bridge, going dancing, enjoying lots of harmless horseplay at supper in friends' houses throwing cushions and not averse to mildly risqué 'Dame Edna Everage' jokes made by the actor Barry Humphries about the 'tip of his gladioli'.

She herself could be ingenuous. Once, twanging the Portuguese President's braces, she talked about the chill in the air. She was in evening dress and asked the blushing Mario Soares, 'If I get cold will you warm me up?'

Now she was being escorted around town to a David Bowie concert and a restaurant by Major David Waterhouse, a nephew of the Duke of Marlborough. 'We are childhood friends,' he said; and also by an amiable young man, Philip Dunne, heir to Lord Daresbury. A twenty-nine-year-old merchant banker, Dunne was the son of the Lord Lieutenant of Hereford and Worcester; his sister Camilla, 'Millie', a full-time organiser of the 'Help a London Child' charity, was already a close friend of the Princess.

Dunne had a longstanding relationship with Lord St Just's daughter, Katya Grenfell. Wild and attractive, thirty years old and working as a photographer, she had a reputation as a blueblood who refused to wear knickers. Formerly married to Oliver Gilmour, conductor and son of Sir Ian Gilmour, her book of photographs *Naked London* with captions by Greek boat person Mr 'Taki' Theodoracopulos was published in 1987.

The Princess was seen putting her head on Dunne's Old Etonian shoulder, nothing remarkable for this warm, uninhibited and uncomplicated girl. She would be quite capable of doing the same with any fatherly or kindly shoulder; but in her position, the only acceptable shoulder was Prince Charles's and that had been taken out of the country to Italy and his easel.

In June 1987, the Princess felt prompted to explain, 'Just because I go out without my husband doesn't mean my marriage is on the rocks.' About this time she could often be seen driving to the flat of her stalwart friend and adviser Anne Beckwith-Smith in Knightsbridge late at night, once in her nightdress under an overcoat.

A restless Princess would drive round London in the small hours with the innocence of someone who has always been protected but she was frightened when a group of Arabs chased her in Sloane Square. Having been taught anti-terrorist drill by the SAS, she lost them by doing an impressive handbrake turn at the wheel of her speedy turbo-charged Ford.

But it was the wedding of the heir to the Duke of Beaufort, the Marquess of Worcester, to the actress Tracy Ward early in 1987 which flashed the true Red Alert on the state of this royal marriage. Prince Charles left the reception soon after the dancing had begun but the Princess stayed on, dancing wildly, flying in her free-spirited flamboyant style. Some guests thought her 'out of control'; 'out of her dress' one suggested drolly. Teasingly she replied when asked if she had a lover, 'Yes, he's black and he's Catholic.'

In the past, the Princess was always a little jealous and watchful if Prince Charles paid too much attention to other women. 'Now,' a friend said sadly, 'she didn't give a damn.' Hurt in the early days by his apartness, a little disinterest had entered her soul, and there it would lodge until in 1990 they began to appreciate each other all over again. American couturiers even dreamt of her as a model gracing the catwalks once she was released from the tedium of her marriage.

On 15 October 1987, Prince Charles flew to London from Balmoral after thirty-three continuous days away to stay with the princes overnight. His wife was at a nightclub celebrating the Duchess of York's twenty-eighth birthday. The Prince had gone by the time she awoke the following morning. That night, when he got back to Balmoral, a new house guest, Lady Tryon, had arrived. Whatever riverbank or grouse moor being walked by the brooding Prince, often alongside him would be this cheerful Australian 'Kanga', 'the only woman,' he has said, 'who really understands me.' Over discreet picnics and hours spent at the remote Carabhallt Shiel Lodge, they talked, or rather the Prince unburdened his anxieties about the marriage.

The Palace was seriously worried when the Princess recklessly made an apparently unchaperoned overnight visit to Dunne's home in the country while his parents were away. The Princess, it was claimed, was simply learning to play backgammon. Her tutor was Mr Dunne. However Prince Charles felt compelled to intervene and forbade the Princess to fly to a party in Majorca with Dunne as an escort. Instead she would attend the Braemar Games. Her non-appearance at this Scottish outdoor meeting was unthinkable.

Friends of the Prince claimed he was losing his grip in his own home. Sinclair Hill, an Australian polo friend, put it simply, 'One thing he wants to do now is to keep wearing the pants in the family. You have to keep a woman in her place,' he suggested with Australian male chauvinism.

A royal servant who works for the Queen shook his head in disbelief. 'I read all this stuff about the marriage going wrong and we get upset because she is a lovely lady. She talked for ages to my wife at the Christmas party about the mess Christmas presents make. Anyway, I come to work and find the Prince and Princess laughing and playing in the gardens with the princes.'

But to royal advisers the Princess seemed strained, the bright smile was missing too often. Tense and pale, she was often preoccupied. Extremely thin, a skinny size 8 which had always been her ambition, she seemed to have very little substance. A picky eater at the best of times, she nibbled so little that at the end of a day she would collapse in a chair from total exhaustion.

Alarm bells rang seriously once more on an evening when Prince Charles was attending a service at Gloucester Cathedral and staying at Highgrove. The Princess, in a satin bomber jacket, purple trousers tucked into her boots, had swung out of Kensington Palace at 8.20 P.M. at the wheel of her Sierra Cosworth to drive to Kate Menzies' flat in South Kensington. Dismissing her detective, Sergeant Dave Sharp, telling him to come back at 10.45, the Princess went inside to play bridge with car salesman James Gilbey, one of the gin dynasty, and two other friends. When she eventually appeared at 1 A.M. she was appalled as a photographer leapt forward and wisely burst into tears, appealing immediately to his better nature. 'You don't know what this is doing to me,' the Princess blubbed miserably.

Leaning against a wall like some delicate trapped woodland creature, the Princess went on, 'I have so few friends. Kate has organised this; it was very sweet of her and this is the only time I've been out all week. This will make things worse,' she wailed. 'I've been working hard all week and I just don't get to go out any more.' Her kind heart and loyalty to her friends had apparently been the reason for this embarrassing evening. Mr Gilbey had been having troubles with his love life and needed the comfort of the Princess's sympathetic shoulder.

The world has an image of the Princess taking great care of herself with an intense beauty routine and going to bed almost as early as Prince Harry and Prince William but here she was in the early hours, pleading, 'I have to go to Wales tomorrow and I'm so tired I want to go to bed,' as she begged the photographer to protect her reputation. It was an unlikely scenario.

A month later, the Princess touchingly drove to Leicestershire for a day with the Belvoir to watch Prince Charles hunting, a sport she loathes but for his thirty-ninth birthday she wanted to make an exception. The only trouble was the Prince had not turned up. Staying outwardly cool, the Princess chatted with her sister Sarah McCorquodale who lives nearby in Rochford, Lincolnshire. The girls sat on a gate and talked intently for about an hour and then gave up. That day, most uncharacteristically, Prince Philip called off a shoot at Sandringham.

Earl Spencer, always the protective father, was forced to admit, 'They have their rows, what couple don't?' and then wistfully added, 'Diana would love more children.' A poll said that love in the Waleses' marriage was dead.

Leading such separate lives, Prince Charles leaving his wife to the four-poster while he prefers a single bed in his dressing room, another baby might come as rather a surprise to them both. Even so royal advisers feel that the Prince and Princess would like a daughter, while Germaine Greer says the Princess has shown 'a conspicuous independence' in the control of her fertility by limiting her family to two.

So accustomed to his own solitary life, thoughtful and at times ascetic, Prince Charles might perhaps have been better suited to not forming a deep relationship with any woman, let alone a young, vulnerable and volatile wife. He has worried constantly about their age difference. 'I'm sure it must be absolute hell living with some ancient old thing like me.' He had been used to the fleeting company of beautiful girls, there never was a shortage, but ideally it would not be for much longer than a weekend.

On his own admission he often has a desperate need to get away. His training has equipped him for solitariness. His retreat may be a crofter's cottage in the Scottish Hebrides or a Duchy of Cornwall farm near Dartmoor where he contentedly leads the life of a farmhand. In his earnest, soul-seeking way he would compare marriage to the Commonwealth: 'People tell me that the most successful marriages are the ones where you have to make an effort, that you cannot expect the whole thing to be lovely, rosy and successful unless you work at it.'

A psychiatrist at a leading London hospital who has watched the Prince and Princess over the turbulent years feels a great deal of patching up has had to be done and it has become a fairly sterile relationship. Nowadays he thinks the Princess is happy and fulfilled but, 'Her marriage plays a small part; she is involved with events.' He compared her to many beautiful women who are outwardly erotic and extremely flirtatious, but inwardly frigid. 'If you look at their interests,' he pointed out, 'Prince Charles is academic, ecologically and architecturally minded, pretty deep really, while hers are fairly superficial, but she makes sure she has lots of escape routes such as shopping and dancing.'

His critics say Prince Charles is a victim of old-fashioned Establishment upbringing. Never really comfortable with women, parted from his mother and sister at an early age, he went to public school at a time when girls were not admitted, then into the forces enjoying mess life in another boisterous male enclave and seeing women in a fairly simple light as 'goers' or revered like 'Ma'. A really close, tender loving relationship with a young modern woman these men find more elusive. Of course they make all the overtly romantic gestures and do the expected things on anniversaries. Prince Charles sent the Princess £50-worth of red tulips when she had four wisdom teeth removed in April 1989, but he has always found it difficult, like all the royal family, to talk about what is in his heart.

Mildly irritated by his wife's flying flirtiness, he publicly distanced himself from her in wounded dignity, almost deliberately inviting comment. It would be easy for him to arrange private space, an art at which his father has excelled in a very long marriage.

When things were obviously almost intolerable, the Queen just back from Canada called the unhappy pair to her study and told them how to survive. Running away and having fun, no matter how innocent, was damaging. Now they had two sons and for the Princess especially this must be an incentive to try harder. They put on a convincing show of affection on a tour of West Germany in November 1987.

Fully aware of her role as future Queen, the Princess would

never jeopardise the monarchy even if it meant sacrificing her personal happiness. So now she began to look at her life.

She would distance herself from the Duchess of York, though giving her all the comfort imaginable before the birth of her second baby Eugénie. But she worried about any repercussions on the boys at school of 'Aunt Fergs' with her slightly smutty hearty jokes. In a way the Princess has been fortunate in having the more extrovert Duchess as a foil. By contrast her own more dignified approach seems maturely wise.

In February 1989 Philip Dunne was married to Domenica Fraser at Brompton Oratory. It was a full Roman Catholic ceremonial, fidelity forever, no birth control and certainly no flirting with married ladies. The Princess was a guest at the wedding. Domenica, the daughter of Sir Ian Fraser, was a twenty-nine-year-old film-maker and one of the Bright Young Things at Oxford where she read Modern Languages.

The Prince will go on being bookish and, in his self-effacing way, continue painting, believing that 'it is good for the soul'. He will take pleasure in working late on abstruse plans and documents. He is a caring man, some think almost too much so, agonising over the world's unhappiness. The summer of 1990 when his smashed right arm was slow in healing was a time of enforced rest, and pictures of him recuperating in France, in the village of Le Barroux near Avignon, revealed a man clearly in pain, psychological as well as physical. The face of the future King had a haunted look, he was like a man in prison. He had been forced to spend introspective days often alone, unable to play the sport which serves to distract him from the future. However it was not all misery. He was being cared for by the attentive and svelte French baroness Louise de Waldemar.

When he came back after a spell at Balmoral he visited the Chalice Well in Glastonbury, Somerset, paid his 40p and went in to drink the holy water. The Prince may have had great faith in the powers of the metallic, earthy waters credited with healing blindness and deafness but when they were tested they disappointingly contained no special ingredients. He would have been as well off drinking tap water. Neither, however, was likely to help the incipient depression, when, as one courtier put it, 'For days he sits behind his bullet-proof window and reflects on what might have been.' The severity of the break was such that a close polo playing friend feared that the shock of seeing 'a bone sticking out horribly at the elbow' would bring about a clinical depression. At the best of times, the Prince is inclined, as he says himself, 'To worry about things too much.'

This vision of a sad dismayed prince brought home at least the possibility that the burden of monarchy could be too much in spite of having won himself a perfect future queen. Until recently he had not realised how she has developed and changed and before his accident really had not spared the time to notice. Now in the relationship she often appears the stronger. When he was taken to hospital after the fall, she rushed away from the opera at Covent Garden and drove a hundred miles to be with him. When he was in excruciating pain, she remained at the hospital all day and was eventually instrumental in persuading him to have further surgery at the Queen's Medical Centre in Nottingham. Here they fixed a titanium plate to the broken arm and took a piece of bone from his hip to help the fracture heal. The Princess stayed at a secret address nearby.

But in the autumn of 1990 the Prince appeared even more isolated, spending a great deal of time in Balmoral deliberately separated from his wife and children, and returning after thirty-nine days apart only for the princes' half-term. Then, duty done, he went back to Balmoral. He had been helped enormously by an Australian physiotherapist Sarah Key, who travelled with him to France and back to Balmoral before flying home to her family in Sydney. She spent weeks with the Prince helping him to get his arm mobile again. They went swimming together, the bouncy Miss Key shouting encouragingly, 'Go on sir, you can do it.' Meanwhile the Princess gamely went on with public engagements. At this time of his apparent frailty, which was not just physical, she was supportive and with an almost defiant confidence appeared on behalf of both of them at functions such as the dinner for the Italian President Francesco Cossiga in October 1990.

This long separation inevitably drew the kind of unwelcome speculation about their marriage which the Princess loathes. In Balmoral Prince Charles was surrounded by married women friends, Camilla Parker-Bowles, Patti Palmer-Tomkinson and a garrulous new friend Lady Sarah, the forty-five-year-old daughter of the Earl of Dalhousie and wife of the banker John Keswick. Outgoing, funny and informal, Lady Sarah is just the sort of person the Prince enjoys having around to cheer him up but there was a brisk icy exchange when she met the Princess of Wales in the Royal Box at Covent Garden. Voices were raised and companions tactfully tiptoed away. 'How can anyone call her coy? How can people believe all that sugary stuff about her?' a friend of Prince Charles asked, and added, 'The Princess is tougher than she looks. She has character.'

Another slightly older friend is the Italian marquesa Bona Frescobaldi, a leggy forty-nine-year-old Florentine who frequently visits London staying at Syon House with the Prince's good friends the Percys. He sends a car for her and they will have a pleasant supper together at Kensington Palace. For a while, friends thought that he was attracted to her daughter Fiammetta, aged thirty, but it is her mother he much prefers for her cultivated mind and knowledge of art. One of these women was quoted anonymously in an American magazine decrying the Princess's lack of intellect, saying, 'It so discourages Charles.' His mature friends have found that the Princess is diffident. Conversation can be halting. She will reply quickly enough and brightly but will never initiate a new subject and this can be heavy going. It is as if since the marriage she has become painfully aware of her lack of education. In seeking alternative company abroad the Prince of Wales is like his father who is a European royal. It is easy to see Prince Philip's eyes brighten at the approach of some sophisticated Italian, French or German aristocrat rather than her horse-loving English counterpart.

All the same his son has found one soulmate nearer home in Candida Lycett Green, the blonde daughter of the late Poet Laureate Sir John Betjeman. She is forty-eight and adores architecture and rambling round old churches and houses, while her father's engaging sense of humour makes her an ideal companion. The Princess has complained to friends that she finds so many people in her husband's circle 'unbelievably old', but it is not surprising that Prince Charles turns to women closer to his own age for more intellectual companionship and a sophisticated sense of fun.

In November 1990, clearly stung by criticism of him as an absentee husband, the Princess made a point of appearing with the Prince at an engagement in the Merchant Taylors' Hall in the City of London. She had not been expected but wanted to be at the Prince's side as he spoke about the problem of the homeless.

In addition to comments about these far too frequent 'avoidable' separations, the question has been asked, Does Prince Charles have a sophisticated Italian mistress? A man of unusual integrity, it is unlikely but he would always be extremely discreet.

Whatever their problems, the Princess seems to thrive on solo engagements and is not acting in the unhappy way her sister-in-law Princess Anne displayed before the breakup of her marriage. A courtier observed sadly, 'The Princess seems happier when she is away from her husband.' With her strong sense of duty, a little stubborn streak and gentle persuasiveness, she will hold the marriage together. It helps too that she knows no other way of life. 'Diana knows no different,' a friend explains and practically all her aristocratic friends have similar marriages. The Queen and Prince Philip do not share a bed; even the raunchy Duke and Duchess of York sleep separately. 'That is how Diana has been brought up. I don't think it hugely worries her.' What sustains her still is the idea of becoming Queen. She once fell in love with the idea of becoming the Princess of Wales, now she is more ambitious. On their tenth wedding anniversary the set of eight pillows bequeathed to the couple by an American millionaire will arrive. Sir Joseph Nickerson, who died in America at the age of seventy-five, had arranged that the Prince and Princess should be given pillows on their tenth, twentieth, thirtieth and fortieth wedding anniversaries. Perhaps this old farmer thought it would be an ingenious way of keeping the couple together.

Late in 1990 her devotion even extended to being at Sandringham for a shoot, her husband's first since his polo accident in June. She may not approve of blood sports but knew this was important for his morale. Acquitting himself well, wearing a pink eyepatch and using his good arm to shoot off his left shoulder, he brought down three birds in less than five minutes. On the following Sunday, they all appeared as a quite happy little family at Sandringham church with the Queen. However the concern is that the Princess is too young, too spirited for a merely polite marriage. She may tolerate it for several more years but there is a worry that the strain may be too much and there might be a collapse of that outward sparkling bounciness.

Most marriages benefit from a little separation from time to time and the bond between Prince Charles and his wife is founded on trust, respect and a love which now may have less to do with chemistry and physical attraction than belief in each other. Upper-class marriages always appear to allow much more freedom than is usual for the average couple. Money, land and several homes allow this enviable space.

As the Prince and Princess of Wales now enjoy an improved, serene and more adult relationship, there are fewer rows and chilly silences. The inflexibility of monarchy helps for it insists that their marriage must be forever. They are compulsory companions for life.

CHAPTER 33

Miss Polly Had a Dolly

———————◆————————

The Prince and Princess of Wales were in Hungary from 7 to 10 May 1990 on a first official visit by the royal family to an Iron Curtain country. The Pope was to go in 1991. The first free democratic elections had just taken place and the Soviet presence was down to a few soldiers.

It was a time when you could eat yourself silly on *pâté de foie gras* or goose; dinner for two was £12; you could enjoy a fifteen-mile cruise along the Danube for 70p; in hotels, porters called 'colleagues' who were usually young economic or philosophy graduates, carried your suitcase and gave a dignified nod. The antique shops glowed with Russian icons smuggled out of their homeland by the Russian soldiers.

In spite of years of repression, many of the neo-classical houses survived with their dusty frescoed ceilings but a little dilapidated. In the once formal gardens, decadent cherubs round dried-up ornate fountains held out chubby chipped hands as if in poignant plea for a graceful past. Gipsy violins still played in the cafés, and linden walks leading to ornate basilicas were green and cool in May.

This was an openly political visit and unusual for a member of the royal family. Prince Charles, who had always admired the Hungarian struggle for freedom, remarked, 'I could never see the Iron Curtain myself without feeling a sense of this amputation.' The last coronation in Hungary was of King Karl and his wife, Queen Zita on 30 December 1916. Their exiled son Otto, who is a European parliamentarian, had recently been given a pleasant homecoming to his native land. Talks were held about the restoration of the monarchy, but it was a notion which appealed neither to the seventy-eight-year-old Dr Otto von Hapsburg nor the Hungarian people.

Now in Budapest coffee houses elderly Jewish couples, thin as birds, ate Sachertorte or with bony hands picked the day's newspapers from their wooden holders, avid for news of this springtime visit by the Prince and Princess of Wales. An imperceptible smile flitted across the parchment features of an *ancien régime* aristocrat, 'Before our darkest days,' he said, 'we had visits from your royal family. Edward VII visited his lady loves in Budapest . . . why not? Princess Michael of Kent,' he added, with mock regret, 'is half Hungarian.' She hardly ever admits to her Magyar origins these days, but she is very typically southern Hungarian, full of emotions, and swings of mood from lowest despair to tears and laughter.

Behind the scenes in London there had been briefings for the Prince and Princess. Visas were needed even for the royal couple. The old bureaucratic machinery cannot be so easily dismantled.

An agitated messenger in statutory navy gaberdine mackintosh arrived at the elegant Hungarian Embassy in London, saying urgently to the young man behind the glass window in reception, 'I'm from the Palace, the Prince of Wales's Office.' But the receptionist shrugged: 'Oh yes?' and turned his attention longingly toward the small divan with an off-beige bedspread in the corner of the office.

'But,' flapped the big man, 'I have in here the passports of the Prince and Princess of Wales,' and a bit desperately he began waving the briefcase in the air. 'There is a queue next door.'

'Still you are going next door.' Wearily the receptionist showed him out, indicating a queue stretching down the steps of the

Eaton Place consulate and cluttering up the pavement of one of Belgravia's finer wide streets.

'I see.' The messenger shrugged, defeated. It had been a little cameo of eastern European inertia. There would be no royal priority.

Upstairs, benignly unaware, the Hungarian ambassador Dr Jozsef Gyorke sipped black coffee from an enchanting tiny Herend cup. The Princess adores this Hungarian porcelain and a collection of floppy-eared rabbits, parrots with wingtips in lime green and pale blue and endearing hippos with gold snouts decorates her sitting room at Kensington Palace.

From this vast room with tall French windows and great marble fireplace, the ambassador had helped orchestrate this royal visit eighteen months earlier. The Hungarians had really wanted the Queen, but it was suggested by the Palace that the junior but dashing royals should go first. The party would include Sir John Riddell, then Private Secretary to the royal couple; Laura Lonsdale, lady-in-waiting, a blonde clone of the Princess; the stalwart Evelyn Dagley, the Princess's dresser, and Helen Roach to assist the lady-in-waiting. Secretaries to the Household were Sally Hughes and Fiona Wilson who each day sent out a huge number of thank-you letters. Ronald Lewis was the baggage master and, almost the most important person for the Princess, was Richard Dalton, her hairdresser.

Lieutenant-Commander Patrick Jephson, then the Princess's equerry, a small man who looks like an amiable smart teddy in his dapper double-breasted grey silk suits and is a perfect troubleshooter, had gone with the Princess's bodyguard, royal detective Dave Sharp, on a recce to Hungary several weeks earlier.

The visit to this intellectually rich but materially poor eastern-bloc country was considered so important a press briefing was held not at Buckingham Palace but at the Foreign Office. In statutory Englishwoman's summer Liberty print, Anne Lewis, gentle and earnest from the East European desk, beamed. 'There could be no better or more exciting time for the visit.' Sitting alongside her in the whitewashed room with its clock ticking an hour slow was the Palace press team Kilhoran MacGregor and Dickie Arbiter.

There was a mild stir of interest when Prince Charles's blood links with Hungary were mentioned. 'He is one thirty-second Hungarian through his great-grandmother Queen Mary.' Her grandmother, Claudine Countess Rhedey, had married Prince Alexander, Duke of Württemberg, and their son Francis, a good-looking, impecunious young man, married Princess Mary Adelaide of Cambridge, a cousin of Queen Victoria, who had frankly given up all hope of marriage. Her lady-in-waiting thought her 'a purple plush pincushion', and Princess Mary herself was resigned to a life of simple pleasures savouring a 'capital hot lunch of chicken and rice, and beefsteaks and fried potatoes' on the Royal Train to Sandringham.

However this 'jolly and overweight old maid' aged thirty-two was married on 12 June 1866 to Francis, Prince of Teck at Kew. Their eldest child, Princess May, was born on 26 May 1867. Queen Victoria looked at the baby and thought her 'not as handsome as she ought to be' – unkind but true. She later became the wife of George V.

The briefing droned on. 'Hungary is famous for apricot jam, Tokay and honey . . . needs British investment. This is one of the main reasons for the royal visit . . . only forty-eight British businesses in Hungary compared with three hundred German.' 'Goulash Communism' was mentioned to interest the tabloids, but their representatives just stared at dirty marks on the walls where pictures had been removed.

The men from the *Guardian* and the BBC pressed on delicate subjects. 'What about the £25 million British loan to Hungary?'

'Isn't this all rather erudite? We are not used to all these serious questions.' From the back of the room came the unmistakable educated long vowels of James Whitaker, the *Daily Mirror*'s superior royal reporter.

'What I want to know is if there is direct dialling for my monkey?' The *Daily Mail*'s Geoffrey Levy's beard wagged in silent laughter at the bewilderment of the Foreign Office people, who were not to know that photographers are affectionately called 'monkeys' by reporters.

Ignoring the levity, the briefing continued. 'The Prince of Wales will meet Professor Ernest Rubik,' a man who enterprisingly became a millionaire in Hungary under the Communist regime with his maddening little puzzle game. 'The Prince will try his hand at the Professor's more recent inventions.' At this there was an irreverent chorus of 'Blimey, we'll be there all day,' and the briefing came to an end. Except for the man from the Palace who could reveal that it was so warm in Budapest 'Some of our chaps in the Embassy are in summer suits.' Mocking roars, 'Oh, thanks a lot, Dickie.' This was a typical piece of Palace press information.

Outside desultory chat about the last royal tour with the Princess of Wales: 'Wasn't Nigeria awful? Shit in the streets, public loos were just cardboard boxes . . .' Only people who do not go on royal tours think they are glamorous.

'Is there a black market exchange in Budapest? . . . Right, see you there.'

A hot afternoon, an air of boredom at Budapest's Ferihegy airport on Monday, 7 May, the only sound the photographers' aluminium ladders being dragged across the tarmac so they could be level with the top of the aircraft steps.

Children kicked their heels in the drab VIP hall and stared moodily at the bouquets of roses and orchids they were to present to the Princess. In true Marxist tradition, they had been elected by school ballot. There were no crowds. It seemed an unpromising start, with none of the usual air of expectancy before a royal visit. Hungarians, appreciating the freedom of not having to turn out as they did in the past to welcome some fat commissar and his wife from the Soviet Union, assumed today's visitors would not be exciting either.

The Prince and Princess of Wales's gleaming white, blue and red plane, the Royal Standard flying, touched down forty-five minutes late. The Prince, a sprig of yellow mimosa in the buttonhole of his double-breasted pale cream suit, was at the controls. In polka-dotted tie he had a nice light Urbino touch of the sun. The Princess had picked him up on the way out in Italy, where he had been on a sketching holiday and launching an exhibition of fifty-seven of his paintings.

She looked like an E. M. Forster 'raj' heroine in a pale cream silk pleated dress, matching cream silk hat, long pearls, coffee-cream co-respondent shoes and clutch bag. Her clothes tended to be sensitively low-key in a country where women had little money to be fashionable.

Gracefully, with a contrived hesitancy, she stood back demurely cool. The timing is an elegant pavane between the two as Prince Charles moves to meet Hungary's newly elected first non-Communist leader, Dr Arpad Goncz. An academic, he made light of a gaol sentence for his part in the 1956 uprising, and his struggle against the forty-year Russian presence in his country. He spoke beautiful English, learnt, he told the royal couple, from reading the diaries of Winston Churchill in his prison cell.

During the long and hauntingly sad Hungarian anthem, his wife Mrs Zsuzsa Goncz, aged sixty-four, a homely figure, wept soft tears which fell on the lapels of her navy pinstriped suit. The Princess reached out and held her hand, a moment of delicacy and skill.

The Princess manages to be tactile, with a light touch to a child's head or an old person's arm, and this instinctive warmth and impulsiveness distinguishes her from the rest of the royal family. The President noticed and was appreciative, thanking her publicly for her 'very warm personality' which . . . 'has made it all very special for us.'

In a country where most people have three jobs a day to make ends meet, there were indulgent smiles as the royal Bentley F725 KMB drove the couple to the modern Government Guest House in Budapest. 'Horrible,' said the architecturally aware Prince Charles, looking wistfully from his bedroom at the old mansion in the grounds. 'I hear the Prince thinks the guest house is awful,' Mrs Goncz teased the Princess who bit her lip in mock horror: 'Oh no, did he say that?'

But he loved the pure and original architecture in the Castle district, the crumbliness of the ochre mansions with their heavily carved doors and riotous rococo shells and curves. But 'How can they do that?' he asked his hosts, appalled, and pointed to a modern grey concrete hotel by the banks of the Danube.

Old countrywomen sitting on the cobbled stone steps in Castle Hill selling their handmade lace from Transylvania nodded and smiled as they overheard the Princess say, 'Hungarians are elated to be free. I can feel the excitement among the people here; it's almost spiritual.' Church bells were chiming and hundreds now could flock openly to the neo-Gothic rose-windowed church of King Matyas tucked behind the pale stone ramparts of the Fishermen's Bastion.

In the Government Guest House, as her dresser Evelyn Dagley laid out the shimmering white evening dress, the Princess picked up the telephone in her room. The Prince and Princess like to have a bedroom each with a connecting corridor. She wanted to speak to William and Harry in London as soon as they got in from school in Notting Hill Gate, but pulled a momentarily sad face as she put down the receiver. 'The first thing they ask me is "When are you coming home?" We have only just arrived.'

That night there was no hint of this motherly fretting as the Princess shimmied through the ornate gold-painted Parliament Building, modelled on Westminster, to the President's banquet in just a simple white dress, except it made the most of every single curve. A tube dotted with seed pearls, with a slit up the back, it revealed just a hint of suntanned calf.

This was real glamour. Her skin had a lightly golden patina. Round her neck she wore a whopping necklace with a huge blue sapphire clasp. The gaunt stone of the building, the statues, the palms and the carved gold figures of Hungary's traditional artisans, made a perfect backdrop. Hungarians have always liked to dress up, an old-fashioned formality which they never lost even during the Russian occupation: 'Our departed guests.' The women wore red velvet and dramatic black and white; the men dressed up too, some in diamond-studded skullcaps.

The President was beaming and drinking champagne. 'No,' said the Princess, refusing a glass from a silver tray. 'Water please . . . just water for me.' She laughed. 'Oh, you'll need sunglasses,' she remarked as her host blinked under the glare of television lights. During the banquet she picked at her strawberry dumplings and spent more time admiring the lace placemats embroidered with roses.

'Viva Diana,' they cried next day in the huge covered market in Dimitrov Ter. Ancient Hapsburg traditions came flooding back, prompting unlikely men to bow low and kiss her hand. As the Prince and Princess met the people, stallholders with celebrated Hungarian names like Balogh, Novak, Merzog and Esterhazy, reached out and gave her single pink roses or offered her jars of plums and walnuts and sunflower honey the colour of lemon curd.

Brightly embroidered drawstring blouses with blue, yellow and red flowers fluttered over wooden shutters. Old couples with shopping bags who had been prowling around crankily looking for cheap peppers stopped, crinkly faces brightening as they saw the Princess's blonde head bobbing above the crowd.

'Where is he, where is he now?' She always keeps an eye, but Prince Charles was spending an inordinately long time at the Hunah stand with its long strings of spicy garlic sausage. The Princess shrewdly ducked this photo opportunity with its ribald potential as her equerry hissed in her ear, 'The press are behind you, Ma'am.'

'Diana, Diana.' The Princess looked up and smiled at a sea of children's faces peering down at her through a balustrade, then waved and was gone. A flash of pink and purple, a magic moment almost spoiled by a fat porter in a T-shirt who shouted, 'F . . . the monarchy' in imperfect English.

On the third day, after the drive to the wonderful Hungarian plains famous for wild horses, fruit and wine, the Princess felt distinctly queasy, too much goosefat perhaps. The royal Bentley had bumped along the country roads from Budapest to Bugac for an hour and a half though the way had been cleared by outriders, who took a certain pride in leading the Prince and Princess after years of shepherding unglamorous tinpot bureaucrats.

They had a flamboyance, like conductors, bringing traffic to an immediate standstill, raising themselves up in the saddle, arms elegantly extended right and left, a motorcycle ballet. But one or two of the royal party still thought fondly of a royal tour in Canada and of Frank, a senior outrider from the Royal Canadian Mounted Police, who wore a gold helmet, chewed gum and would call out, 'Okay fellas, let's boogie' as he led off the royal procession.

Before any introductions could be made at Bugac, the Princess in her eau-de-nil silk dress, clutching her stomach, waved her hands in the air and rushed away. When she reappeared after ten minutes, Prince Charles asked solicitously: 'Are you all right, darling?' Playfully she took a piece of the bun he was eating, but refused a sip of his plum brandy.

A musician in soft leather boots sitting on a painted chair began to play a hurdy-gurdy. The Princess, now almost fully recovered, but still flushed and not feeling as cool as she looked, stood with her feet at the ballet position and rested her hands on her hips, watching the folk dancers quizzically. As the white lacy figures hopped round hollow logs full of geraniums, she whispered to her husband: 'Do you think this is a warm-up?'

The last thing the Princess needed was perhaps a ride in an open carriage, but she kept cool with a peacock fan. It was all rather romantic as she and Prince Charles, almost alone, meandered along charming dusty lanes, ribboning through unspoilt meadows scarlet with poppies. Both country-lovers, they appreciated the purple and yellow wildflowers, while as an ecologically minded landowner the Prince loved the simple farms, the depressed years in Hungary perhaps bringing a 'green' bonus in the absence of costly pesticides.

Grannies with dark red and blue rose-sprigged dotted scarves tied picturesquely round their heads, a legacy from the days of Turkish rule, stood outside whitewashed thatched cottages smiling uncertainly at the royal couple and, hiding shyness, shooed away the fat ducks and somnolent hens sitting in feathery contentment round kitchen doors. Their buxom daughters, loading the family Lada cars with cauliflowers and radishes, covering them with red-and-white-check teatowels for the market in Budapest, stopped and waved.

Freshly baked homemade bread was pressed on the skinny Princess at a farm. Over an alfresco vegetable terrine and salmon lunch, the royal couple watched butterflies hovering in the lilac and asked about a wreath of corn on the branch of a tree, the farmer's sign for a good harvest.

A nearby farmer's wife proudly took the Princess to show her a pregnant sow. 'How long is the pregnancy?' the Princess asked. 'Three months and three weeks.' 'Lucky her,' she said ruefully, and quickly put a restraining hand on the woman's arm as she tried to prod the pregnant pig into attentiveness. 'Oh no,' the Princess said with feeling. 'Please don't. If I were her, I wouldn't want to move,' with a reproachful laugh.

The afternoon ended with a display by Hungary's wild horsemen. 'Quentin, more rope.' Dickie Arbiter, the Press Secretary, barked at the rather quiet and studious First Secretary at the British Embassy, who was beginning to wonder whether the gruelling Foreign Office exams had really been all about tying the world's press behind some string on the Hungarian plains.

'Where do these horses come from?' the Princess asked; the diamond clasp of her necklace glittered in the brilliant sun as the nomadic Magyar warrior tribes galloped by, sometimes astride, sometimes standing up on flamboyant Hungarian half-blood greys. But she was more interested in finding out where the horsemen got their ornate soft leather boots. In a far corner, foals ignored the thudding hooves and cracking whips, the swirling and wheeling, and rolled on their backs, fetlocks raised to a blue sky.

That evening they went to Budapest's elegant old theatre to see a performance of *King Lear* by the Renaissance Theatre Company, starring Richard Briers as the unhappy old king. Barely trying to hide her boredom, the Princess studied her programme and sat well back in the box, hiding her head in her hands during the bloody scene when Gloucester's eyes are gouged out.

But Prince Charles loved it all. 'Wonderful stuff, great stuff,' he said afterwards backstage. 'You've got to live life a bit to understand Shakespeare.' The Princess blushed, admitting, but not very convincingly, 'Oh, I love Shakespeare . . . It's just that at school, you know . . . so much Shakespeare . . .' and her voice petered out into a little embarrassment.

She would not be protected from the grisly side of Hungary's recent history when she was taken to film studios outside Budapest to see a film being shot about the Hungarian uprising in 1956. When the Princess arrived she seemed tired, stretching her leg as if she had cramp. On the damp lawn of the Embassy earlier, as the actress Emma Thompson had taken off her shoes, the Princess had said, 'How I envy you.'

On the film set they put her in a smoky cellar, where she seemed a slightly outlandish apparition, surrounded by black-bearded actors playing the part of student rebels. 'It must have been a horrifying time,' she said to the young cast, after watching the re-enactment of the execution of a student who died on his eighteenth birthday. Her distress was obvious, and the equerry, realising her horror, reacted swiftly like all good courtiers and cut the visit by ten minutes. But not before the Princess, always sensitive to others, had talked to the leading actor. 'People think acting is very glamorous,' she said understandingly, 'but there is the strain.' Of course, she was referring to herself. 'My role,' her voice faltered, 'can be . . . is an act too.'

It was on the last morning that the Princess really came into her own. Until then she had been decorative and charming, but now Hungarians would see her compassion. At the Peto Institute, which stands high on a hill above Budapest and offers hope to children disabled at birth by cerebral palsy, her lightness of touch made despairing parents more cheerful than they had thought possible. It is run by a small, birdlike woman, Dr Maria Hari, dedicated to the 'tough love' approach of physiotherapy which encourages the active parts of the brain to take over from the damaged and help free children from the tyranny of their handicap.

In addition to royal approval, the Institute was being given a gift of £5 million from the British government for modernisation which the old place badly needs. It is not much changed since the death of its founder Professor Andras Peto in 1967. A difficult and brilliant man, he said his hobbies were 'slow eating and drinking' and singing with his 'little patients'. He never said 'hello' when he came to work or 'goodbye', believing in a rather charming metaphysical notion that this ensured his presence was always at the Institute.

Several of the children appeared, wobbling on the steps and wearing 'Welcome Diana' T-shirts. In a simple navy and white dress and jacket, just the right colour and style for the day, a smiling Princess hurried inside. She had to fulfil an important mission from the Queen, to pin a gold medal on its pale pink ribbon on the shoulder of the ascetic Dr Hari.

'It is the Queen's wish that I give you this Order of the British Empire. She hopes that my being here will help the Institute,' the Princess said softly.

The doctor, of course, was appreciative, but for her perhaps the greatest reward that day was seeing nine-year-old Dawn Rogers, with her cheerful, swaying windmilly gestures, climbing the steps unaided, arms flailing until she reached the top where the Princess was waiting.

'That's a pretty outfit,' the Princess said, kneeling down to talk to her at eye level. 'We are colour co-ordinated,' she added, pleasing Dawn very much as she admired this spirited child's sailor dress. Three years earlier, when she was brought from Nottingham in a wheelchair, Dawn had been unable to move her head, sit straight, feed herself or use her arms.

Taken into one of the rooms where the children were singing 'Miss Polly had a dolly who was sick, sick, sick', the Princess sat on the end of the slatted wooden beds where they lay on blue rolled duvets, many unable to sit up. She talked earnestly to the conductors, as the staff are called, and asked questions. 'How long is the training? How many years? Does the treatment differ?' But all the time the Princess kept gently tickling the children's feet. She tried hard not to show how moved she was, some of the children made infinitely touching by the way they held their heads on one side, sharing that obvious vulnerability of the blind.

'Anyone here know the Muffin Man?' the Princess asked in the international room with children from Austria, Brazil, England and Poland. They chanted a little United Nations chorus of 'yes, yes' as the Princess stroked their heads and hands, her eyes extra bright. She met the parents, some of whom had mortgaged their homes in England to give a sick child a chance. 'It is,' she said, 'heartbreaking but wonderful work they are doing.'

A little girl was struggling to hang on to bars on the wall as the young conductor tried to get her to walk. The Princess was helping too; but then reluctantly had to move on. With a wistful backward glance she looked at the child: 'Oh, I want to take her home with me.' Real compassion makes a nonsense of royal restraint.

The good doctor is not given to flowery sentimental words but she thought the Princess was exceptional with children, and 'would make a wonderful conductor.' A veteran of royal tours exclaimed, 'Wherever we go they say she would make a wonderful pilot, lumberjack, prime minister. People just fall in love with her.'

A chubby fairhaired woman from Somerset, Mrs Angela Smith, blurted out, 'When are you going to have a little girl?' Perhaps when you have a child as frail as her son, five-year-old Jacob, you suffer no tongue-tied hesitancy in front of the royal family, but the Princess reeled back in mock horror. 'Give me a chance; don't rush me. I've got fifteen more years in which to have children yet; I am not a production machine.'

One young pale English mother, Debbie von Malachowski, had just arrived at the Peto with her three-year-old child Holly. Holding her daughter tightly in her arms, she said, 'The Princess really listens to you; she cares and she understands.' The Princess twiddled the ribbon on Holly's hair, how difficult a gesture that would be for the Queen, Princess Margaret or even Princess Anne. 'Have you got other children?' the Princess asked. 'Yes, a son, John, he is at home.' She laughed. 'Oh, he'll be spoilt rotten . . . no discipline,' and bit her lip in that appealing way, as if he was about to become a handful for her too.

After the emotionally draining morning so beautifully handled, the Princess was in the mood for a lunchtime cruise down the Danube on this shimmery warm day when even the shabbiest old tankers hooted approval. She took her jacket off and later, as she stepped ashore, her look in her sleeveless straight dress was pure sixties. Instinctively she is fashionable, with a talent to anticipate a trend long before the print in the pages of *Vogue* is dry.

The President spoke and said he hoped the royal couple had 'felt the love of the Hungarian people.' Then before flying home they caught a tram and hopped off in the main Vigado Square for an old-fashioned cheery walkabout. The dear phlegmatic Hungarians went wild as if they had suddenly realised that this blonde Princess, pinkly glowing in the crowd, was with them for only another half-hour; like the starving guest who has time for only a few spoonfuls of soup. There had been practically no publicity for the tour in Hungary; now the people were determined not to let these precious moments slip away.

They kissed the tips of the Princess's schoolgirl plain unvarnished nails – nowadays they are cherry red and elegant – as she charmed them with her softly spoken 'koszonom', handshake and smile, her hello a subtle way of convincing everyone she was delighted to see them, a joke, a lightness. Waiters wiped their hands on large white aprons and stood still outside the coffee houses. Shades of Christopher Isherwood's thirties Berlin, a city slowly coming to life, grey faces in grey office blocks lighting up; in the square a Bohemian-looking artist did a sketch of her which made her laugh.

Prince Charles once told her how people talked wildly when they met the royal family; now an Englishman in the crowd told the Princess he would be flying home the next day but not in her style, 'in Club class'. 'Oh yah, we know all about that,' she replied. Another told her he had tried to arrange a tennis match for her. Tennis had not been so vital; she managed to swim every morning at the American Club in Budapest.

'Mind not too many jetés, don't work too hard,' she told Sean Hounsell from the Canadian Royal Winnipeg Ballet. 'Oh, you are skinny,' the Princess said admiringly to another dancer. 'You can talk,' the girl replied. 'You are skinny yourself.'

Prince Charles said he would definitely be back. The red trams were almost at a standstill. These crowds were here of their own free will, stirred by this young couple.

Even if you are a beautiful princess married to a future king, with children, jewels, houses and untold wealth, you want to be of value. After this visit the Princess telephoned her father, Earl Spencer, and told him how much they had enjoyed Hungary. But most important were her final, delighted, astonished words. 'You know, Daddy, it was one of the best trips ever. We really felt needed.'

CHAPTER 34

Uptown Girl

'There can be terrible loneliness,' a friend says. 'I still remember those whispered calls from Balmoral: "Hello, it's me, just wanted a chat." They have to let their hair down,' and that is exactly what the Princess does.

Although the Princess thrives on being busy she also relaxes in lots of ways, curling up on a sofa to watch the BBC 'Clothes Show', or the popular soap opera, 'Neighbours', intrigued by the adventures of Charlene, Scott, Des and Madge in an Australian suburb. 'I've gone off "EastEnders",' the Princess says; 'I now prefer "Brookside".' Addicted to chat shows, the Princess says she prefers the host Jonathan Ross to Terry Wogan, saying, 'I've sat next to him twice at functions and I think he's wonderful.' On being told this Ross responded, 'I have to say I prefer the Princess to Terry Wogan.' Nobody can guess how much she enjoys television programmes which give her a glimpse about other people's lives; as for 'Spitting Image', she calls it 'an absolute scream' although it makes her seem a little bossy.

Another release for her may be an afternoon of helpless laughter with William and Harry at the Cirque du Soleil watching a clown

paint her detective's tie white, or shopping for 'notions' near the
Palace in 'Kensington Di Street'. In a bookshop she thought it
very funny when she asked an assistant, 'Did you see me on
television last evening?' and he replied, 'No, there was something
better on the other side.' The Princess giggled and hurried away
with her copy of Judith Krantz's novel *Scruples*. Once when
telephoning for tickets to a Rolling Stones concert, the Princess,
who is a great fan of Mick Jagger, especially when he sings
'Satisfaction', explained, 'I've persuaded Charles to come along
as well. But even if he changes his mind because of the crowds,
I'll still be going.'

She loves buying fun presents for the children and for Prince
Charles, perhaps a sweater with a message which says, 'I'm a
luxury few can afford,' or dancing along the piazza at Covent
Garden in the early morning throwing oranges at friends and
enjoying the image of herself as Bernard Shaw's Eliza Doolittle,
the flower girl who did well for herself tutored by Professor
Higgins, a much older man. Maybe she will enjoy a trip to her
local Odeon cinema in Kensington High Street, where she may
well queue and even buy tickets for herself, but always, for
privacy, in the back row. She loved Dustin Hoffman in the
Oscar-winning *Rainman* and has been to *The Phantom of the
Opera* four times.

The Princess also appreciates a vigorous game of tennis or a
fast drive. She fell in love with a £60,000 Mercedes convertible,
a gift delivered to Kensington Palace. Loving its power, she took
the princes for a run round the Gloucestershire lanes. 'It looked
like she was enjoying herself,' a local remarked, after seeing her
at the wheel of the 150-mile-an-hour red convertible. The Princess
drives well and fast but Prince Charles made her give back the
German roadster because the royal family drive only British cars.

Lunches with girlfriends have always been important but, they
complain, 'So much has to be cancelled; her work comes first.'
Looking completely relaxed, she often enjoys girly lunches at The
Caprice, Green's and other Mayfair haunts where they are used
to celebrities. For birthday treats she will take the children to
Smollensky's Balloon opposite the Ritz in Piccadilly, where she
arrives separately, pink with excitement, racing downstairs with
balloons to join William, Harry and a nanny already sitting at

the table longing to order hamburgers followed by incredibly rich chocolate cake and fudge sauce.

Lately the Princess has had the confidence, when in need of a treat, to skip off alone with her mother or a girlfriend. While the Queen was cruising round the Western Isles of Scotland wrapped in warm woollens, a tartan skirt inadequately protecting her knees from a whipping wind, her daughter-in-law was being serenaded by the cast of *Aida* on a warm night in Italy. 'It was absolutely marvellous . . . really unforgettable,' the Princess told them. 'I was so profoundly moved.' Her hostess Countess Guerriera-Rizzardi, who gave a party for her, later embarrassingly carolled 'Diana', an old Paul Anka number, when the Princess appeared.

A psychologist, Dr Jane Usher, approves. 'This was a very relaxed atmosphere compared with the life the Princess leads at home.' The caring does not stop; she merely comes back to her public life refreshed after a highspirited release of tension.

In centuries past, if a Princess of Wales got very tired or stressed, a lady-in-waiting might sing to her or play a madrigal. When Queen Alexandra was Princess of Wales a letter from the Palace in Denmark might soothe with family news. Queen Mary as Princess of Wales found it relaxing to feed personally a royal pet a dog biscuit each evening. Once when a bishop came to dinner, she denied herself this treat and handed the biscuit to the prelate who promptly sycophantically ate it, watched mournfully by the dog, while the Princess, who rarely smiled in public, was at her imperturbable best.

In common with the Queen who has been heard to say, 'No more big books for me, I only have time for small ones,' the Princess is not a reader and does not long for a moment to get her hands on Professor Stephen Hawking's *A Brief History of Time*. Instead she prefers *Vogue*, her equivalent of the Queen's *Sporting Life*, which is delivered on a silver salver.

Recognising the need to unwind is important. 'I'm a great believer in having these wherever I go,' she says of her Sony Walkman. 'It is a big treat to go out for a walk with music coming out with me.' And, the Princess says defensively, she is not always listening to the Rolling Stones or Duran Duran. 'I tend to listen to an enormous amount of Grieg, Rachmaninoff and Schumann

. . . I love it.' But then she comes from a background where every well-brought-up girl is taught to play the piano and not allowed to give up until sixth grade. Prince Charles has had some influence and she enjoys impromptu visits to Covent Garden, perhaps with Viscount Linley in a minibus to see *The Nutcracker*. Accompanied by one of her BFs, Kate Menzies, she attended a recent performance of Rossini's *The Barber of Seville* which is about a woman forced into a loveless marriage. They deliberately chose to sit in the Dress Circle rather than the more formal Royal Box.

The Princess is keen on shopping, a well-known therapy for women. She uses the fashionable part of London like any other wealthy bright young thing, sometimes leaving her XJS green Jaguar on a yellow line. She goes to Covent Garden for Paul Smith sweaters; Bond Street for Ralph Lauren separates; and fashionable Butler and Wilson jewellers in Fulham Road for fun accessories. Buying a huge spidery clip and earrings, she came back the next day saying, 'I liked them so much I want to give them as presents' and bought lots more. 'My friends will think they are a great joke,' she said. Even a pair of flowery trews bought for fun give a tremendous lift.

Tennis is another release for this loosebodied, agile Princess. The joy of the Vanderbilt tennis club is that it is in an unprepossessing part of London's Shepherd's Bush, secluded and ideal for a princess arriving unnoticed along a little street of red brick artisan houses. The Marquis of Douro's wife, Antonia, introduced her to the 'Vandy' three years ago, when she paid her signing-on fee of £650 and £500 annual subscription. Often she has a lively game with Julia Dodd-Noble, otherwise known as Crown Jewels because of her friendship with the Queen's two daughters-in-law. Charles Swallow, the club's old Carthusian director, an ample fellow with a hint of the cat with a saucer of Jersey cream, is godfather to Camilla, a sister of Philip Dunne, and has coached the Princess with schoolmasterly authority. Her game improved so much she gave him a hand-knitted sweater with a tennis racquet design. Now Prince Harry and Prince William are learning to play with small rubber racquets and a 'slaz', a Slazengerball.

If the Princess chooses Number One court with its German carpeting, this is for 'show-offs' and she has no privacy. But she enjoyed a much publicised match with the tennis champion Steffi

Graf who was impressed by her speedy footwork. Number One court attracts spectators. Lean balding men, dentists, dealers, property developers and blondes with dark skins, they watch the game through glass windows before dashing off in sky-blue BMWs. Well-brought-up, well-groomed young Fulham and Chelsea wives leave their shopping baskets to one side, change into unmonogrammed tennis skirts – slogans are thought vulgar – and are far too polite to even glance towards the Princess; others shamelessly savour her speedy game. Afterwards she may have a quick carrot juice and if in need of a further treat, a chocolate croissant.

'Shall we have lunch?' and a few hours later her chauffeur-driven car draws up in a little cul-de-sac between Gloucester Road and Kensington High Street in Launceston Place, near Frog Hollow.

Her preference in restaurants still tends towards her father's taste. Because of her glamour and because she is so modern, it is easy to forget that at heart she is unchanged, and is unlikely to be found sitting on the floor of an ethnic restaurant eating sweet potato and yams in north Kensington while listening to bongo drums. However she enjoys Chinese food and goes to Mr Wings in South Kensington.

She takes friends to Launceston Place because it has a private room atmosphere, with its dark, creamy sage green walls and old portraits. The Princess likes brill with vermouth while an escort may prefer more hearty calves' liver with red onion marmalade. Nearby an elderly banker entertains a young girl with long hair who flatters him. 'Oh, I do want to hear about your love life,' and the tale begins. 'Well, it was a house party, one of those weekends . . . along the corridor, you know,' knowing smiles, *Les Liaisons Dangereuses.*

These jaunts to restaurants; to Luigi's in Covent Garden; La Poule au Pot in Pimlico, Green's in Mayfair or The Golden Chopsticks near St Mary Abbot's off Cromwell Road, are all important to the Princess. As she explains, 'While Prince Charles and I have many friends in common' – she is believed to adore Sir Laurens van der Post – 'obviously there is not always the time, especially on a weekday, to see them. My husband goes to a lot of dinners where the wives aren't required.'

Beauchamp Place, a pretty jewel of a street filled with antique silver in bow windows, has two of the Princess's favourite designers, Caroline Charles and Bruce Oldfield, and this is where she loves to shop. 'It is,' she says, 'nice to go out shopping with a girlfriend who wants to buy something and wants me to come along.' The Princess sounds like a matronly adviser up from the country for the day, whereas she is actually leading the way to Present Affairs and other fun shops searching for jokey notions.

Full of energy and bounce, she has a capacity for fun. It may be teasing a disc jockey on Capital Radio who had been complaining of perspiring palms early that morning: 'But your hands aren't sweaty at all,' or asking for a request to be played by telephoning as 'Disco Di from Kensington'. At Rory Scott's wedding she swept the bridesmaids up in her arms and danced with them, and then, to the envy of others in the buffet queue, fed two of the guests, Lord Harrington and Captain Patrick Drury Lowe.

Her lunches are not always with girlfriends and sometimes the Princess slips into Groucho's with the dancer Wayne Sleep or goes to his Mediterranean-style studio in South Kensington which is like an art gallery with its white walls and black and white room. They sit at a trestle table. 'I cooked her something simple, no great roast, but avocado and trout then strawberry gâteau'; and the talk is about dance.

'I could keep dancing all night,' the Princess told Kid Creole and the Coconuts at a London party. When eventually they stopped playing at one o'clock she pleaded with them to continue, saying, 'You see, I get so few chances to go out dancing and there is nothing I love more.' Sometimes she dances quite happily on her own.

Sleep appreciates her passion for ballet and has probably had more intimate contact with her than most – 'I danced with the future Queen' – and although he thinks of her as a friend, there is always that distance: 'You never forget she is royal, though after lunch she did help with the washing up.' The royal family love washing up; it is one of the Queen's greatest treats in Balmoral or Sandringham, like a little girl playing house.

Wayne Sleep helped to orchestrate her dance début at Covent Garden. 'I'd love to do a number and surprise my husband,' the

Princess said, and asked if he would choreograph a four-minute piece for her. For his help, but above all for his discretion, this diminutive dancer may well be rewarded one day. Ambitious friends are careful to be reticent and watchful, fully aware that in time the Princess will have strong influence at Court. It could even be: 'Arise, Sir Wayne.'

Sleep, one of Britain's finest dancers, sat in his dressing room after a hugely successful performance in *Song and Dance* dressed in a T-shirt that said 'Monster'. He recalled how when the Princess suggested the idea he had slight misgivings. After all, his reputation was on the line. 'Dance has been my life,' he said as he took a sip of Perrier.

But the Princess was so determined – 'She's no fool and is never out of her depth' – that he agreed, and they had secret rehearsals at Kensington Palace. 'There was no barre, we just held on to the Chippendale,' hoping not to be spotted by Prince Charles.

In leotard and leggings the Princess danced to Billy Joel's 'Uptown Girl', 'rather appropriate really', and went over her routine without a moment's hesitation. Sleep was surprised by her jazzy steps. 'They were sensual, sexy.'

The Palace had worried about the propriety of it all and full credit goes to Sleep for his discretion. Rehearsals could have been tricky. What do you say? 'Your Royal Highness, a little to the left if you would be so kind,' and then a courtly bow? 'Oh no, it was much more, "Princess, over here . . ."' as Sleep directed her. 'Arch your back,' he would say, and both would laugh as he joked, 'What do you think I am, a forklift truck?' as he raised her in his arms. 'We had a lot of laughs; you don't ever expect her to be that funny.'

On the night, the Princess was totally professional, sitting backstage chatting to other dancers from the Royal Ballet.

'I came on first,' Sleep recalls, 'to fool them, and they were applauding anyway and I thought, Just you wait. Then the Princess walked out and there was this huge gasp, an amazing buzz. Charles was speechless. Then she danced and it was stunning.' There has been a very special friendship between the Princess and Sleep ever since. He appreciates her need to dance.

Secretly the Princess thinks she would have loved the life of a dancer. She has a certain showbusiness flamboyance about her and loves to surprise. In France she did a showy solo at a French château, astonishing Prince Charles who had been enjoying a spirited fan dance performed by the French hoofer sixty-three-year-old Zizi Jeanmaire wearing very few clothes and giving her best for the Prince des Galles.

The old guard at the Palace were not amused by the future Queen's soft-shoe shuffles and high kicks. It made others wonder whether the Princess had ever really been all that shy, for it takes colossal nerve to dance on stage at Covent Garden.

CHAPTER 35

Wills Could Take His Teddy

———◆———

It is 3.20 P.M. on 15 May 1990 in a bosky square of tall cream houses in London's Notting Hill. Pink chestnut candles are dropping making people sneeze, the pollen count is high on this hot still afternoon. Young mothers, their hair held by Alice bands and dressed in bright T-shirts and flowery skirts wait outside Wetherby, the £800-a-term preparatory day school, for their little Alexanders, Ruperts and Freddys.

Suddenly the red door opens. The boys sit on the stairs in pairs, but are counted out one by one as, heads bent, they concentrate on carrying their tadpoles and plants out carefully. Some are still munching cakes. Outside there are a couple of motorcyclists and at least four police cars, two with engines softly running, others wait like panthers. Several plainclothes men speak into their walkie-talkies, prowl about and look irritated when a child holds up the royal getaway. But the tall solicitous headmistress, Mrs Blair Turner, bends down in flowing denim; her responsibility is for all her charges, to hear more about a cut lip, to soothe and ask, 'Is Mummy here?'

Just then Prince William appears, his satchel on his back. There is a moment of extraordinary tension as, cap pulled down, not looking right or left, the little sandalled grey-socked feet plunge down the steps, anxious as, lower lip tightly drawn over the top, he races to the waiting car as if running for his life. Two detectives jump in beside him and he is driven away at high speed. A mother turns away. 'I've never felt so sorry for anyone in my life.'

The royal detectives guarding the princes are kindly, fatherly men but, like the SAS, crack shots. Now they go into the school again to give it another scouring. A few minutes later Prince Harry appears, reddish hair in tufts. He looks even more vulnerable as he too rushes down the steps, not quite as anti-kidnap fast as his older brother, and climbs on to the school bus which has had several last-minute checks by detectives.

The other boys are already on board and the door is slammed shut once the detectives are inside. The bus is followed by a red Ford Escort, a green car and a motorcyclist. The uniformed policeman on the beat says into his walkie-talkie, 'Three-thirty P.M. The princes have now departed.'

The rest of the boys trail home with their mothers; one asks, 'But Mummy, why can't we go to his house?' 'Well, you see darling, he is a prince and . . .'

The princes were happy at Wetherby, not far from Kensington Palace, which was chosen partly on Princess Michael's advice. It has helped Prince Harry gain a little in confidence, no longer always outshone by his older brother.

In the autumn of 1990 they were parted, and everyone except Earl Spencer felt it would be good for the development of both boys. A bit of an old softie, he said, 'They have been so happy at Wetherby and had lots of friends there,' as if sad to think that they might need any higher education. Prince William is not precocious but already an assured little boy who had the self-confidence, when he heard he was going to a new school, to pick up the telephone and book a table for two, for himself and the Princess, at her favourite San Lorenzo's in Knightsbridge. Wills is particularly partial to their salmon fishcakes.

In September 1990, looking smart in long trousers and a hacking jacket, Prince William went as a boarder to Ludgrove preparatory school at Wokingham in Berkshire. He gravely shook hands with Mr Gerald Barber, one of the joint headmasters, as he stepped out of a chauffeur-driven Bentley. His new life would mean less attention from 'Mummy' every day, a 7.15 A.M. start, learning French, history, music, art and geography, fencing, playing soccer and seeing nothing of Trigger, his pony. Returning from Ludgrove that evening the Princess said, 'Wills was very happy but I wept.'

The Prince and Princess had a parents' feel for the place and were pleased that there is no caning and that Wills could take his teddy as his father always did when he was at boarding school. There had been tremendous jockeying by social-climbing parents to send their children to this Berkshire prep school. Ambitious mothers already buying couture clothes were hoping to catch the Princess's eye. But the Princess, depending on how she feels, may turn up in drainpipe trousers, bomber jacket with an eagle emblem on the back, baseball cap and imitation leopardskin flatties, as she did when she took Prince William to a motorfair in October 1989. Many thought she was the best exhibit.

The security at Ludgrove is intense; some seventeen detectives discreetly roam the school. If all goes well there, from being a 'squit' at the £2,350-a-term school which includes Lord Home and the Duke of Kent amongst its old boys, the Prince will become a 'squirt' in his second year – about the time when he will begin to realise fully that he is different. Prince Charles was about that age, around nine or ten, when it began to dawn on him slowly 'that people were interested in me . . . and I got the idea that I had a certain duty.' He understood the difference even more when he was having tea with schoolfriends and some cake crumbs fell on the floor. They were astonished when Richard Brown, his eighteen-year-old manservant, knelt down to clear them up. 'Why haven't you got a Richard?' asked the puzzled heir to the throne. By the age of three he had as well his own footman, private detective and chauffeur.

Prince William is quite an assured little boy, who stands with his hands behind his back like Prince Philip and, egged on by his smiling mother, will often make a little parting speech to a member of staff going to another job. 'William is my flower boy,' the Princess might say. One of the Queen's staff who watched Prince Charles grow up thinks Prince William already knows his destiny.

Around this time nanny Ruth Wallace decided after three years and at the age of forty-three, that she was no longer needed in the Kensington Palace nursery. It was an amicable separation. She gave the Princess even more notice than is usually required, so a replacement could easily be found. For although there is now only one boy at home, the Princess still feels the need, as she is so busy herself, to have two nannies. Full time, on £6,000 a year after tax, is Jessie Webb in her early thirties, who lives in at Kensington Palace; and at Highgrove there is a reliable middle-aged relief nanny, Olga Powell, for weekends.

It was not only Prince Harry who missed Prince William terribly, but also the Princess. Children are her passion. The Princess braved a blizzard to visit ten mothers whose babies had died from cot deaths: 'I couldn't get here fast enough.' She found her own two 'utterly adorable', especially when they were about three and mischievous, calling them 'my two little thugs' and saying in amused exasperation to her youngest, 'My dear Harry, what do you think you are doing?' She is also very protective of the boys and when she won three goldfish at a funfair at Tetbury, was glad of another so her sons would not be jealous.

Ask this doting mother if she would like a girl and she almost takes this as a slur on her boys, as if they were not enough. 'I don't want a daughter,' she tells you defiantly. 'I'm sticking at two.'

Prince Harry, the apparently gentler by nature, has always made the Princess overly protective. It was he who was plagued by chicken pox, then he had a mystery virus and later an emergency operation for an undescended testicle though the Palace insisted it was a hernia. He was taken to Great Ormond Street Children's Hospital where the urologist Patrick 'Issoo' Duffy from Belfast operated. Outspoken and abrasive, Duffy was standing in for the main consultant. He is known as Issoo because 'My father was so delighted by my arrival that he sat by my cot with a Guinness burbling "Issoo, wuzzo a little pet?"' Now Mr Duffy was operating on another precious youngster, the third in line to the throne, and not helped by ribald colleagues teasing him about the crown jewels and the damage he could do to the royal line. The Princess stayed in the hospital overnight and admitted next day she had 'hardly slept'. But the operation was a success.

Months later, sitting in a Gloucestershire cottage garden, ruddy in the sun with his psychiatrist wife Zara whom he calls 'Pet Lamb', Duffy, in a Miami Dolphin T-shirt, was full of praise for the Princess. 'She struck me as being a terrific mother; she asked all the right questions.'

A young, unstuffy royal mother, the Princess skittishly enjoys playing 'bulls and matadors' with the boys, trailing her blazer. When Prince William was home for his first half-term she planned a series of treats and seemed to be having even more fun than her sons when she took them to Alton Towers fun park in Staffordshire. Refusing complimentary tickets, the family queued with everyone else and squealed with them, too, on the Log Flume and Rapids Ride. They all sat happily in the Teacup Roundabout showing no sign of queasiness and cheerfully getting soaked. There were jokes about this single-parent outing but in his position Prince Charles could really not be drenched in a fairground having a go on the Flailing Octopus with its tilting high chairs.

The Princess took the boys shopping in Cirencester, where she treated them to favourite KitKat fingers and muffins. A watchful mother, she once picked up a soft-drink can which had just been drained by Prince William, read the list of ingredients with intense concentration and banned it for containing too much sugar and artificial preservatives. She insists they eat fertiliser-free vegetables. However she does not always stick to these strict dietary principles.

On the way back to London from Sandringham, if Wills is being very good his mother may take him to a roadside café on the A1 at Astwick, Bedfordshire. In late November 1990, after a weekend at Sandringham, she and Prince William stopped at a Happy Eater where she ordered a burger and chips and Coca-Cola for her son, a mineral water for herself. After the twenty-five-minute stop, she paid the £8 bill and left a £2 tip. 'The biggest I've ever had,' an astonished Cathryn Morse, their waitress said later.

In London she may dart out early in the morning to Kensington High Street to buy their favourite food, standing in the check-out queue dressed in jeans and paying cash. 'I just wheel my trolley along,' she says; 'no one takes any notice of me,' and smiles not really expecting you to believe her. The boys loved these expeditions for their three-pack school socks at £3.50 and five-pack of boys' underpants, £4.99. Their Pepe jeans cost around £22 and fashionable 501 Levi's are from about £25. Shoes from Russell and Bromley are Startrite. When they were younger they were sometimes dressed as twins, snazzy in navy and white pinstripe with crimson sweaters.

A treat was going to a café in Kensington High Street for orange juice; otherwise it was back to the Palace where the Princess, not a great reader herself, used to switch on a *Jungle Book* cassette or an Eric Hill *Spot the Dog*. She also likes the boys to read a comic called *The No-No Kids* which warns children against the dangers of drugs.

The Princess does not like spoilt brats but she is an indulgent mother. The princes have Walkmans, cuddly toys and miniature £10,000 Aston Martins, copies of their father's James Bond style car. In October 1990 they raced out of St Paul's to see the blitz fire engines parked outside after the Princess had taken them to a service commemorating the bravery of wartime firemen.

Prince Charles has always stressed that he wants his sons to be 'honest, tolerant and, above all, well-mannered'. His great-great-grandfather when Prince of Wales had no heart for the disciplining of his children. When their son George behaved badly in the dining room, he was ordered to spend the rest of the meal under the table. But it was his parents who were humiliated when he was told to come out to apologise and emerged completely naked. This was the future George V, in later life the epitome of rectitude.

Manners, Prince Charles feels, will help William as both Prince of Wales and King to have some understanding of other people . . . 'and even if they proved not to be very bright or very qualified, at least if they have reasonable manners, I believe they will go much farther in life than by not having them.' Rather a statement of the obvious but undoubtedly setting a good example to the nation's parents.

With this training in mind, the Princess earned her first black mark in the summer of 1990 when she gave the wayward Prince William a light cuff on the backside when he refused to answer her call during the school sports day in Richmond Park.

Barefooted and flushed, the Princess had just come third in the

Mothers' Race and was not pleased, she is very competitive. Three years earlier, arms outflung, she triumphantly breasted the tape to win. Now cross and tired, it was the last straw when she called 'Come here' and Prince William ignored her. Hearts went out to him getting a mortifying slap in front of his friends. Child experts were disapproving.

But he had been nicknamed 'Bill the Basher' and annoyed other boys by talking about 'When I am king' and 'Grandma's castles'. He had been a little overbearing: 'You can't come past me. I'm Prince William,' to which staff might retort, 'And I'm the Queen of the May.' His favourite words were 'soppy', 'boring' and 'yuk', picked up from his mother. When he heard about Prince Andrew's first child Beatrice his only comment was 'Yuk, a girl.'

However after his public disgrace, the Princess made sure he had a special eighth birthday. They went shopping at Party for streamers, funny hats and balloons; she escaped Ladies' Day at Royal Ascot and took him to the zoo, shuddering as he cuddled a large python called Belinda. There was a touching moment during the Olympia showjumping championship in December 1990, when Prince William with a determined hand turned his mother's face round to him and gave her a squashy kiss.

Time with the children at Highgrove is treasured. Here in deepest Gloucestershire the boys entered gymkhanas under assumed names as Masters William and Harry Cox. Their instructor Marion Cox cannot persuade the Princess to take up riding seriously again. 'I wish I could,' the Princess says; 'but I can't' as she watches her jodhpured children going through their paces. 'The business of riding scares the life out of me. I lost my nerve following that accident years ago when I was lucky not to suffer permanently.'

Prince Harry, who has always been a bit accident prone, only four weeks after his father's polo accident in the summer of 1990, fell off his own pony at Highgrove on to his head. The accident was almost a replica of his father's but much less severe. Prince Charles rushed him to Cirencester but the X-rays showed just 'a bump on the head'. Father and son were seen quietly together afterwards comparing aches in the grounds at Highgrove. Gentler pursuits have always been shared by Prince Charles with his younger son as he takes him by the hand round the garden at

Highgrove telling the little fellow, 'Harry, you must always be kind to flowers and remember they are gentle too and will never hurt you.'

A loving father, Prince Charles revealed, 'Funny, I never realised, when you have children of your own, you only then discover what fun they can be.' When they were much smaller, by the time he got home at 6 P.M. they were usually asleep in their twin beds, curled up with their Snoopy dogs. This was the time when the Princess did some sketches of both boys, thought charming by art experts.

Prince Charles took the boys cycling with Harry in his back basket or would play games with them throwing a handkerchief over his head. But he seemed awkward, unrelaxed, smoothing back his hair as if about to attend a tricky meeting with some disgruntled Commonwealth minister. The formality is always there.

Then he began to distance himself from them and in his absence the princes' detective, Dave Sharp, became such a father figure, and the children so attached to him, that he had to be removed. He was not demoted but transferred to the Princess's personal security team. About three years ago things got worse; Prince Charles seemed to be spending a great deal of time away; but the Princess made sure the boys spoke to him every day, explaining, 'Papa has very important business in Scotland,' and Prince Charles wrote loving letters to his sons.

In an odd way, the Prince's accident was a bonus for this small family. His sons have seen more of him than ever they might normally. They raced up the hospital steps in Nottingham to be at 'Papa's bedside' while the Princess followed more sedately with a game for her husband called Manager about running a football team.

The sport the boys adore is polo. They already have their own tiny polo sticks made from Indian cane and costing £27.50 each from a Sussex polo shop and love watching their father play what the Princess disapprovingly calls this 'reckless exercise'.

Prince Charles's arm was painful and even after a second operation there was a danger of infection; he walked with the aid of a stick as a piece of bone had been taken from his hip to help the shattered arm. The Prince could not keep any of his public engagements and had to slow down. He found two small sons at a crucial point in their lives and needing him. It was a precious interlude for all three.

Last Christmas, Prince Charles made up for moping neglect during the summer and spent time with the children. Prince Harry was seen proudly sitting on his father's knee in a green Range Rover at Sandringham and attempting to steer. He also took the princes out on their ponies.

Such is her devotion and anxiety to look after the future interest of Prince William and Prince Harry that the Princess joined the beaters – farmhands and estate workers flushing out pheasants at the first shoot led by Prince Philip over the 1990 Christmas holiday. After the last drive of the morning, she emerged from the undergrowth with an arm round William's shoulder; he was clutching a miniature stick given to him by Prince Charles. Whatever the animal liberation groups may achieve, the Princess, with her background, realises it is important for the boys to understand the protocol of these essentially Establishment pastimes. They may not appeal to her but as a good mother training a future king, she can overcome any distaste and is aware that the Queen shot her first deer when she was sixteen. Besides, coming from such a background of hunting and shooting at Althorp, it really is second nature to her and she loves the socialising, the fresh air making the most of her complexion and being admired by a large number of men.

Each day the Princess gives thanks for her 'two very healthy strong boys' and says, 'I realise how incredibly lucky I am.' Prince William has a strong look of his Spencer grandfather, while the younger Prince Harry has a sweetness, with a hint of his mother's early diffidence and his father's thoughtfulness. He has always appeared the more sensitive of the two though staff find he can be quietly mischievous.

'We want them,' the Princess says, 'to have as normal a life as possible.' They are trendy and have joined the *Teenage Mutant Ninja Turtle* craze. 'These cult characters have taken over our home,' the Princess remarked indulgently and found time in her own busy schedule to learn the special turtle terms.

CHAPTER 36

Bobbing and Curtsying

Although the Princess would dearly love to create Christmas at home with her boys, the festival must be spent with the Queen. After one royal Christmas she sent her mother-in-law a cheeky card. On the outside it read, 'Like you, one will be spending one's Christmas with the family, and one will be very pleased . . .' Inside it said 'When they all go home.'

The Queen did not think it very funny. She loves these seasonal get-togethers and is deeply attached to the immovable rituals of her great-grandfather Edward VII's day. The royal migration is relentless for the Church festivals of Christmas and Easter as the Court moves to Windsor or Sandringham.

It is rather charming. The Queen really believes this is when they are just like any ordinary family. They drink vintage Krug from Waterford crystal, eat Beluga caviar served on pretty gold-trimmed Danish Flowers porcelain, toy with peaches from the Windsor hothouses and pull expensive Tom Smith crackers which hold not the usual boring whistles and Dinky lorries but leather notepads and amusing costume jewellery.

On Christmas Eve, presents are piled up in the Red Drawing

Room, warm with pink and white cyclamen and banks of red poinsettias, and are handed out by Prince Philip. This Danish custom dates back to Queen Alexandra and leaves only Christmas stockings for the big day. Flashy, expensive presents are considered bad form. 'It is not quite oven gloves,' a member of the family suggested, 'but perhaps a book for the Queen, a compass for the Duke of Edinburgh.'

The Princess's presents are witty; she has shopping expertise: soaps shaped like corgis for the Queen as well as something more serious like a pretty personalised enamel box. For her mother, Mrs Shand Kydd, who shares her sweet tooth, a £55 box of Charbonnel et Walker's irresistible chocolates is sent to Scotland.

Everyone is up around 7.30 A.M. on Christmas morning, when the Queen and her family take Communion in the Saloon. 'We don't have a minute,' a young royal explained. 'After communion there is breakfast then off to church again, this time at St George's, then drinks with the Dean before Christmas lunch.'

Then the family, with a flurry of corgis and posse of excited children, the 'nursery party', racing ahead, move to the Crimson Dining Room. Footmen in scarlet waistcoats and black tailcoats almost stand to attention as the Norfolk turkey is carried in by the Royal Steward. The chef carves the bird and is applauded by the Queen and her family. They all wear funny hats and then sit down to watch the Queen's Christmas broadcast.

At five o'clock everyone goes to the Grand Saloon for tea, Christmas cake and mince pies. Then William and Harry with the other royal children say goodnight to 'Grandma' and, marshalled by a flurry of nannies, reluctantly go to bed. 'Lights out, Wills, by 7.30, please.'

Meanwhile parents are hurriedly changing into evening dress – the Spencer tiara for the Princess – for the traditional 'Exiles Night', a glamorous dinner party for de-throned European kings, queens and princes. It is probably one of the most amusing nights in the Windsor calendar and nobody goes to bed before midnight which is late by royal standards.

Normally after dinner at Sandringham or Windsor it is time for the old-fashioned parlour games beloved of the Queen Mother and Princess Margaret. Fortunately the Princess is accomplished in the drawing room, plays the piano well and is a good mimic.

One year, both she and Prince Charles were quite convincing when they shuffled in, the Princess in a filthy old suit, big heavy boots and beard and leaning on two walking sticks, while Prince Charles dressed as a widow woman in a raggy old frock and cardigan tottering alongside her.

In happier days he once bought her a jokey false bosom; the Princess had been complaining about the reduction in her own after the birth of the boys. On Christmas night she wore this new accessory over her evening dress and tried to debag Prince Charles in a bucolic romp watched by an amused royal family.

But when the Duchess of York tried to liven up the tedium of a family Christmas by inviting everyone into the Waterloo Room to watch the Princess and herself doing the can-can, there was a decided frost. Charades are one thing but high-kicking daughters-in-law showing off their legs was, the Queen felt, taking things too far. After Boxing Day, young members of the royal family can decently get away, driving off calling out 'Happy New Year' as footmen shut the car doors with experienced precision.

Those who complain about the length of time it takes to have renovations done may find it a comfort to know that the Queen is having to wait seven years for Windsor Castle to be rewired. This is extremely inconvenient because Christmas and Easter must now be spent at Sandringham where there is only room for close relations, although to the Princess's regret there is unfortunately room enough for her and the boys. Unlike Princess Michael of Kent, the Gloucesters and Sir Angus Ogilvy and Princess Alexandra, she is not excused this royal get-together. Presents were opened in the gold-edged ballroom round a huge tree from the Sandringham estate. Each child had a silver tree in their bedroom and another in the nursery.

The royal New Year is always spent in bleak fenland country at Sandringham, the monotony of following the guns broken by huge classic teas when cucumber sandwiches, homemade short-bread and chocolate cake are carried in on silver trays. Dinner follows just a few hours later at 8.30 P.M.

The *longueurs* are lightened by the Queen Mother with her fund of stories. A favourite arose from a banquet to mark her ninetieth birthday. When the French waitress asked if she would have beef or lamb, she replied in her impeccable French, *'Boeuf'* but unfortunately the waitress returned with both lamb and beef for the best-loved person in Britain. Films are shown in the ballroom and rarely end before midnight. The royal family sit on green canvas chairs and tend to enjoy derring-do films like *Memphis Belle*, about the crew of an American bomber in World War II.

Dressed in baseball cap, sneakers and jeans, the Princess, who is marginally obsessional about her body, paid £195 for her membership of the Knights Hill Health and Leisure Club at King's Lynn near Sandringham and another £60 each for Princes William and Harry so they could swim with her. On New Year's Day she grinned at Dave Boy Green, the former European welterweight boxing champion, better known as the Fen Tiger, when she saw him at the club, saying, 'You look a bit the worse for wear.'

Whatever the anxieties about the marriage, at a family discussion the Queen proposed a huge family party at Buckingham Palace to celebrate the Prince and Princess of Wales's tenth wedding anniversary. Prince Charles was not that keen. The Princess, for once not looking like a bewitching tsarina in fur hat but in a headscarf and wellingtons, drove alone in a Land Rover to Snettisham beach to walk for forty-five minutes, leaving her seventeen royal in-laws, especially the Queen Mother, excitedly planning an event she viewed with doubtful pleasure. Her mini escape caused a rolling of eyes amongst the Royal Protection Squad.

The Duchess of York escaped to the ski slopes and wearing an Aspen Colorado cap was photographed gambolling in the snow at Lech in Austria with two-year-old Princess Beatrice. The Queen was not pleased, thought it too early for her second youngest granddaughter to learn to ski and considered it highly embarrassing that one of her family should be publicly holidaying when the country was on the brink of war in the Gulf.

A frequent royal guest admits that 'Staying with the Queen can be a pantomime of buttoning and unbuttoning, zipping and pinning, combing and hoping. You change your clothes a lot.' It is a sweater and skirt in the morning, trousers for walking, shooting or stalking, something neat not gaudy for tea and then the big number for dinner.

The Princess is a quick-change artist like her mother-in-law and also singularly lacking in vanity. She can reappear in minutes looking sensual in a *Dolce Vita* slinky Valentino or sexy Gianni Versace. Italian designers she knows have a subtly sensuous way of making the best of a slim shape. But for many of the women guests looking good takes more time.

During the Ascot week house party at Windsor it can be a nightmare. While everyone is having a pre-dinner drink, the Queen will be glued to her video; she likes a post-mortem on the day's racing and nobody can go up before the Queen. At about 7.37 P.M. she will say brightly, 'Shall I go and tidy myself?' and is back before 8 P.M. ready for dinner, looking immaculate while everyone else is slightly pink from the sprint to and from their guest suites in the remote King Edward III Tower.

The men in the royal family wear 'Windsor uniform', an evening coat of royal blue with red cuffs and distinctive gold buttons. New arrivals in the family must prove themselves before being allowed this evening kit designed by George III. In the dining room you sit in a different place each evening, keeping an eagle eye on the Queen who, after each course, turns her head to talk to the person on her other side. The whole table must follow suit if there are to be no wallflowers and this ritual seems often to have the makings of a Ruritanian musical.

Balmoral is where the royal family enjoy a rare chance to be together, and husbands and wives can feel excluded. The thought of going abroad for holidays is abhorrent to the Queen; to her there is no place more wonderful than Balmoral, to the Princess of Wales nowhere more ghastly. Touchingly the Queen has just installed a swimming pool in the hope that this may help the Princess to enjoy the baronial house in the Grampians more, but she still finds the old place 'unspeakably boring'.

Adoring sun and sand, after their summer week staying with the Spanish king, Juan Carlos, she finds the Queen's Highland home seems even more uncompromisingly tartan. In Majorca they have a suite with a king-size double bed with lemon bedspread and matching cushions overlooking the Palma yacht club. The Princess loves the feel of the decorative tiled floors of the Marivent Palace under her bare feet as she pads back in a pink bikini for another novel to read beside the pool – very unlike Balmoral's cold tartan lino and gloomy stag heads so loved by Queen

Victoria. The Princess hates all the heartiness and endless climbing in and out of muddy Land Rovers to join the guns, but, she jokes, is detained at Her Majesty's pleasure.

It can be a strain too on the children. Prince William and Prince Harry are expected to behave, as are the adults. From 8.30 A.M., when they are woken by a kilted Pipe Major playing, 'Hey, Johnnie Cope, are ye wauking yet?' everyone is unnaturally polite. After the Queen appears it is, 'Ma'am this and Ma'am that' and a good deal of 'curtsying and bobbing and falling into the furniture'. One guest with arthritic knees complained, 'I spend the whole morning anxiously waiting for the Queen to appear round a corner so I can get my daily curtsy over.'

The Duchess of York, on the other hand, is happy in Scotland leading the 'smalls' out on their ponies until, puffing, she joins the other royals in the heather to listen to Prince Philip talking about the population explosion as he fries sausages or 'Prince Charles banging on about the environment.' It is serious conversation and will fascinate until it is time to go back to the fishing or stalking.

The Princess secretly checks the times of shuttles from Aberdeen to London. There are always a few sly smiles amongst her staff when invitations come in for late August, September and early October. They are accepted with alacrity, giving their lady boss the perfect excuse to escape from the in-law holiday.

'You've got to have something to say for yourself at Balmoral,' says a royal cousin. 'What has really destroyed Prince Charles,' who loves to get into his threadbare green jersey and Argyll boots immediately he arrives, 'is that Diana hates the place. The trouble is he does enjoy serious conversation and this isolates her more.' Balmoral is all about self-reliance.

The Princess finds there really is nobody amongst the younger royals who shares her interests in tap dancing, ballet, aromatherapy and shopping. Princess Michael, for all her supposed faults, is good value; but she is never invited to Balmoral where undoubtedly she would look stunning and maybe frighten the birds on the 11,750 acres of grouse moor.

CHAPTER 37

The Precious Continuity

———◆———

The Prince of Wales has always understood his destiny. It is only the mischievous who enjoy a picture of him in lethargic gloom waiting for the Queen to die so he can be King, but racked by guilt for such unworthy thoughts.

The most enlightened and original future King for centuries, over the years he has been baited and mocked. He tries to fill the time productively, worries that moral and spiritual values are in danger of being eroded by the pressures of 'the lonely crowd', especially in the dense inner cities. In this age of ghetto blasters and fear of quiet, his need for solitariness is seen as eccentric and reclusive.

The time he took, almost six months, to recover from a badly shattered arm was criticised, even his reliance on painkillers and a light tranquilliser while he coped with the post-operative depression. He is seen as complex and stubborn, coldhearted towards his decorative young wife. She says, 'Like most men, he does what he wants. He's doing what he shouldn't do half the time.' But she is referring to the Prince's longing to play polo again rather than any addiction to French contesses and Italian contessas. Both he and the Princess have learnt to live with a curious mixture of avid adulation and prurient curiosity. If the Princess gets too thin, she is anorexic; if she is seen kissing an old friend like the Duke of Westminster on the cheek, she is having an affair.

It is to their credit that they have not become cynical or disillusioned. Both are refreshed by the ordinary people they meet and optimistic about the future. Each has a strong wish to serve. It is because they have been so effective as Prince and Princess of Wales that it is assumed they are longing to be on the throne, but that is newspaper perception.

There is a Palace adage: 'In the royal family, we have beheaded monarchs, usurped monarchs, but we do not have retired monarchs.' The parliamentarian, Enoch Powell, puts it more poetically. 'Monarchy is emotional, symbolical, totemistic and mystical.' Prince Charles for his part has always understood hereditary monarchy. No grinning crone sat by his cradle whispering malevolent Borgia plans to topple his mother from the throne as soon as he came of age.

The Queen does not feel it is for her or any mortal to decide when to stand down. Sure-footed, phlegmatic, full of common sense, with those bright quick eyes she looks at her son and they smilingly agree that it must rest in the hands of the Lord as to when Charles succeeds. The Queen will stay on the throne until her death and, as Lord Denning says, 'The ladies of our royal family are traditionally long-lived.' The Queen regards her destiny as God-given. The very fact that Prince Charles is still only heir apparent at forty-two is a symbol of Britain's precious continuity of hereditary monarchy. It has been broken only once in ten centuries during the eleven years of Cromwell's Commonwealth. Prince Charles understands better than anyone that if a King or Queen could retire whenever they chose, the whole spiritual essence of monarchy could be destroyed and the role, described by the constitutional lawyer Walter Bagehot, of 'listening, counselling and warning' diminished. As they will tell you at the Palace, 'Good God, you don't give up so your son can have promotion!'

Tom Paine, in his eighteenth-century classics, *Common Sense* and *The Rights of Man*, was scornful about hereditary succession, seeing it as a farce, a burlesque on monarchy. 'It puts it in the most ridiculous light by presenting it as an office which any child or idiot may fill; it requires some talents to be a common mechanic; but to be a king, requires only the animal figure of man, a sort of breathing automaton.'

If anything should happen to Prince Charles and the Queen while Prince William is still a child there would be an immediate council of regency which would include Prince Philip, Prince Andrew and Princess Anne. The Princess of Wales would of course make a marvellous regent, a skilful mother of a future king, steering him gently but effectively like all the great matriarchal figures in history.

Tom Paine would be surprised by Prince Charles, probably the most educated heir to the throne ever. Much of the credit goes to his own determination: 'I've had to fight every inch of my life to escape royal protocol. I've had to fight to go to university. I've had to fight to have any sort of role as Prince of Wales.' For all his *embonpoint* his great-great-grandfather Bertie was an intellectual lightweight and not for him the benefits of a university education. Charismatic and sociable but quite indifferent to constitutional history, he had to be given a crash course in Bagehot when he was a twenty-eight-year-old Naval officer. The Prince will go on learning, as he puts it drily, 'in the way a monkey learns – by watching its parents.'

Mother and son are close, and Prince Charles has seen the toll on her private life. The Queen may be the richest woman in the world – her wealth is 'incalculable' – but she is never free of state papers. Twice a day the red boxes arrive at the Palace by horse-drawn carriage. Prince Charles shares these state papers and makes comments. His own come in an ancient maroon leather box but he has never been diligent about paperwork and remains reluctant to settle down to Cabinet reports.

He seemed at one time to drive himself to the limits, so much so that when the Queen saw him staggering round the paddock at Kempton Park with blood streaming from his nose, she forbade him to go steeplechasing again, an edict which had his wife's wholehearted support. He has always liked dangerous sports, which provide him with the sort of excitement he felt lacking in his life. Believing in the Nietzschean principle of 'Live dangerously',

Prince Charles admits, 'It helps you appreciate life.' Although he saw his friend Major Lindsay killed in an avalanche at Klosters, he went back two years later in 1990 to do the same Wang run; a driven skier, he succeeded.

These are some of his best years; he is too perceptive to long for the day when the last scrap of privacy is eroded, and shrewd enough to know that as Prince of Wales he has a freedom to express his views which as King would be impossible. His voice is heard on his favourite causes: the environment, architectural carbuncles, ecology, the joy of talking to flowers, homeopathy and organic bread. No Prince of Wales has ever been so outspoken, committed or caring. He understands and manipulates the media, vital for the survival of the monarchy and it is noticeable that he tends not to make a speech about an important issue when the Princess is with him in case her very presence steals all the press attention.

He is amused by the media and rarely loses his temper with them. Sampling tea in Kenya he spat into a spittoon, then turned to an adviser and said, 'Tomorrow's caption has got to be "My Spitting Image".' He was right.

When the Queen took over at the age of twenty-five royal public relations were bad and throughout the fifties, criticism of the monarchy was rife. Information from the Palace came in the Court Circular, collected by two Court Correspondents reverently dressed in black jackets and striped trousers. Today royal tabloid correspondents wear Armani and Ralph Lauren, thanks to the saleable glamour of the Princess of Wales.

Prince Charles says of his destiny, 'I didn't suddenly wake up in my pram one day and say, "Yippee . . ." This . . . just dawns on you slowly . . . you get the idea you have a certain duty and responsibility.'

From an early age he has known that once anointed by holy oil at his Coronation – he is hoping to bring some made from his own roses at Highgrove – he faces a life of sacred duty and will symbolise a fixed point in a changing world. The difficulty has been finding the right work for him until that day. He appreciated the outspokenness of a Qantas flight attendant who said to him, 'What a rotten boring job you've got.' The Prince repeated this exchange at dinner with the Prime Minister and some Labour ministers. They looked aghast but the Prince said, 'You don't understand. She was right!'

He has presented well-thought-out, persuasive documentaries on television, surprising his critics by his awareness. It has been too simple to call him a crackpot because he supports causes which make people uneasy and are sometimes ahead of their time. One of his interests is alternative medicine and he has urged doctors not to close their minds to long-neglected complementary medicine. He has been accused of being eccentric, slightly dotty because he talks to flowers. Now every gardening expert will tell you this is the right thing to do. And that you must hiss at weeds.

Fingers twitching, wincing slightly, seated on an apricot silk sofa, the Prince describes being royal as 'not a job, it is a way of life . . . you do what you think right and fit.' He has genuinely agonised over inner-city riots, pronouncing them 'rites'.

He has the Queen's earnestness, but then we do not want a grinning heir to the throne. The monarchy in Britain has always been distinguished from that of the rest of Europe by its good sense. It has been easy to laugh at the European cousins, the flaky monarchs in exile or Princess Caroline of Monaco at one time and her distrait tomboyish sister Princess Stephanie. But we, too, came dangerously close to becoming a Gilbert and Sullivan haven for 'modern major-generals' as the monarchy became slightly tinged by the activities of some of the fringe relatives. One, a girl with a sweet pudgy face, was called Marina; another was Viscount Linley, the Queen's nephew who went to court to prove he had not been a lager lout in a pub called the Ferret and Firkin; then there were some indiscretions from the House of York. The royal family was being nudged a little nearer the Eurotrash slide. The nubile charms of Lady Helen Windsor captured on the verandah of a Greek villa getting in some topless sunbathing earned the Sunday paper headlines 'Topless royal melons' . . . 'Queen shocked' and 'Grab an eyeful'.

The Prince's solemnity is balanced and diluted by the charm and gaiety of the Princess, who will sometimes look at him quizzically as if strangely fascinated. But he laughs and has a line in self-mocking humour. When asked about his interest in black magic and spiritualism he explains he does not spend every waking hour 'over the ouija board or trying to get in touch with Lord

Mountbatten'. He has vision when he talks about the plight of the elderly at the annual meeting of the Abbeyfield Society and suggests, 'Old age is not the postscript to the long letter of life,' urging the retired '. . . not to withdraw into the anterooms of society, often doing little or nothing, stagnating and wilting visibly.'

Of course the future weighs on him. He gets lampooned: Charles the Hermit Prince, Charles the Mystic Loon, and this really stings him. In the ninth century, there were emperors called Charles the Bald and Charles the Fat. In the twentieth for a while we had a cranky prince but today we have Charles the Anxious . . . the Caring. Always a defender of George III, he has been compared to this slightly potty ancestor who talked enthusiastically to flowers and shrubs and grew a knee-length beard. A fervent admirer of Arthur Koestler, he was instrumental in saving a bequest, made by the distinguished scientist and writer who committed suicide, for a Chair of Parapsychology, a subject considered in this country a little avant-garde, suspiciously close to the spooky and paranormal. Eventually the far-sighted dons at Edinburgh University took up the offer.

According to Sir Laurens van der Post, the Prince 'realised early that monarchy is no repeat performance'. Each king or queen must extend the boundaries, and certainly the Prince of Wales likes to give the impression of being radical, suggesting the royal family should live on earnings from the Crown estates. But in many ways he is quite conservative. He pays lip service to the need for racial harmony but there is still a yawning gap in the royal Household where no black faces are to be seen either pouring the coffee or writing speeches. There was once a token black secretary in the Prince of Wales's office, but somehow that did not last long.

Prince Charles can irritate with his green attitudes; yet the inconsistency of flying his helicopter across cities and farmland to get to a hunt meeting does not seem to occur to him. By January 1991, six months after he had shattered his arm on the polo field, he was able to ride out with the Quorn to enjoy a full day. He can be a little tactless, saying on French television that he abhorred the Channel Tunnel: 'I feel it represents a defilement of the state of Great Britain as an island.' But the caringness of this often troubled prince is attractive. Norman Tebbit, a caustic Privy Councillor and well known for his advice to the unemployed in Britain to 'get on their bikes', attributed the Prince's soulfulness to his being out of work: 'no job'. But he does work – in intangibles.

It is only human nature to compare the Civil List payments against the number of engagements carried out by each recipient of this wage. Recently the Queen's Civil List payment has been upgraded from £5.09 million to £7.9 million, but will not now be reviewed annually, being set for the next decade: no more increases even if inflation sends up the cost of a pint of milk to a pound.

The Prince and Princess of Wales, who are amongst the hardest workers, get nothing from the Civil List. This is the Prince's own choice, and it still leaves him a tidy sum from the Duchy of Cornwall estate, an inheritance dating back to Edward III and his son, the Black Prince. In 1978 the annual profit from the Duchy was £280,000 of which he paid half to the Treasury. By contrast in 1989 the profit was £2,515,925 of which he paid 25% back to the government. This apparently generous gift to the Treasury is more than £377,000 short of the tax which would be demanded of other millionaire landowners. But they probably have their money in tax havens too.

A good landlord and a caring farmer, the Prince, who took over in 1969, has paid more attention to the Duchy than any previous Prince of Wales and has made startling improvements to his inheritance. The 125,000 acres which stretch from the Cornish coast through Dorset, Somerset, Gloucestershire and Wiltshire, some of England's loveliest counties right up to the Oval cricket ground in London, are a credit to him. His inheritance also entitles him to two greyhounds, a grey cloak, a bunch of herbs, 300 puffins, a pair of gilt spurs, oysters galore from the river Helford and first refusal of any porpoise washed up on a Cornish beach. He also has a Stock Market portfolio valued at £20 million.

An accountant, Mr Michael Peat, has been appointed as Director of Finances and Property Services with the Royal Household. This setting up of the Royal Family PLC is unprecedented. The Queen is a considerable landowner and has large slices of prestigious property in Manhattan, in London and about 250,000 acres in

Britain altogether. Her personal fortune is about £7 billion, making it all the more endearing that she is extremely frugal, always switching off lights. Even her beloved horses are expected to lie on newspapers instead of straw. Once when one of her dogs killed a hare, the Queen picked it up and told the kitchen staff, 'We can eat this.' Her eldest son has inherited this sense of thrift. In his bathroom he keeps a silver clamp for the bottom of his toothpaste tube. Embossed with the Prince of Wales feathers, it is a typical royal Christmas stocking filler.

As barriers in Europe disappear, jingoistic fervour may be less fashionable, but after two World Wars it is still popular to mimic Queen Victoria or Edward VII speaking English with a German accent and it was only during the First World War that George V was persuaded to give up the German family name of Saxe-Coburg Gotha, changing it to Windsor on 17 July 1917. So it was important for Prince Charles, who has 56.2% German blood and is only a quarter British, to bring home a perfect English bride. The Princess is 90.6% English, Scots and Irish, and as we go into Europe we are envied by the French, the Italians, the Germans and the Americans for this British girl. Even in Russia, a picture of the Princess helps ease the hardships of queueing for a tired cabbage.

In the hands of this Prince and his Princess the future of the monarchy is hopeful and assured. The Princess with her newly acquired devotion to duty – and a courtier will tell you it did not come easily or naturally – is our greatest asset for its survival.

CHAPTER 38

Happier in Pearls

The Princess is not a very jewelly person, happy enough with her gold chain with the letter 'D', her Russian wedding ring, gold earrings, a silver bracelet with hearts on it and the seed pearl necklace with a pendant in the shape of the Prince of Wales feathers in diamonds and emeralds. Even her gull's-egg-size sapphire blue engagement ring was not specially designed. But like many blondes she really feels happiest in pearls and looks good in a single-strand necklace. She also has a weakness for fun modern gold jewellery and likes to pop into Tiffany in Old Bond Street.

Prince Charles has now been persuaded by the Princess to wear a small gold wedding ring under his signet ring; it is engraved with the Prince of Wales feathers. Prince Andrew does the same. A very European custom, this is not seen as quite the thing in royal circles. 'Gentlemen certainly don't wear wedding rings,' a royal expert sniffed. 'Of course there are exceptions. The Pope has a very large ring on the fourth finger of his right hand.'

The only acceptable ring for a man has been a signet ring with the family crest. It is traditionally worn on the little finger of the left hand leaving the right hand free for sword play, but some of those who ape this tradition have some difficulty in calling up a family crest. An estate worker at Highgrove was summoned by the Prince's Private Secretary and told that he must never again wear his signet ring. It had been a birthday present from his parents who had saved £100 to buy it, but it had feathers not unlike those on the Prince of Wales's crest.

The Princess, always inventive in fashion, enjoyed a spell of wearing diamond earrings with 'joke' sweaters decorated with several white sheep and one black. Shortly after her wedding she got off a plane in Aberdeen with diamond and ruby pearl drop earrings dangling above a woolly cardigan against the chill of Balmoral. This went totally against the upper-class English attitude which insists on understatement. In the daytime little pearl or gold studs are the most a woman of good background wears. But nobody would have been surprised if she had worn Prince Charles' major wedding present on the grouse moors – an antique emerald and diamond bracelet. He had taken the Queen Mother's advice in choosing this, but it was a little heavy and old for his youthful bride.

The Princess is not terribly keen on tiaras either; somehow they symbolise a certain restraint and economy of movement. At the time of the marriage she had soft fly-away hair cut in a sporty bob not ideal for the first gift of jewellery from her mother-in-law. It was a delicate tiara with a lover's knot of diamonds and nineteen creamy dancing white pearls below. Today, with her layered hair, a tiara would be even more difficult to wear.

The Queen's gift, which she had inherited from Queen Mary in 1953, is pure French Belle Époque with its charming eighteenth-century bow knots and the Princess was intrigued by its strong flavour of the Russian Court in St Petersburg. It is worn on what the royal family call a 'big dressing day'. At Kensington Palace the Duchess of Gloucester, Princess Michael of Kent and other royal women may sit at nursery tea in cashmere sweaters and tweed skirts with tiaras on their heads, practising for the long procession at the State Opening of Parliament.

It is an irony that one day the Princess of Wales will inherit the mouth watering royal family jewels when she is not at all acquisitive and quite happy with stylish modern pieces. 'All her friends are very into paste and glitter,' a close observer has said, and indeed the Princess may well be happiest with glittery costume jewellery. For years she wore the sturdy almost mannish watch seen in the engagement pictures but later she graduated to the thin gold watch of all jetsetters. It is quite simple except it is studded with sapphires.

She brought nothing of note to her marriage in her jewel box but insisted on wearing the Spencer tiara, which is charming with delicate diamond fleurettes, to hold her wedding veil when she could have had her pick of wonderful sparklers from the royal vaults. Her earrings were borrowed from her mother. Indeed the Spencer family, especially the three daughters and their grandmother Ruth Lady Fermoy, enjoy operating their little jewel pool.

For the visit to Wales soon after the wedding, the Princess appeared in another Queen Mary jewel, a necklace of cabochon emeralds circled by diamonds, the Queen's personal wedding present to her daughter-in-law. It is possible that these emeralds were part of the Romanov jewels – the acquisition was kept rather quiet at the time – and the Queen had personally selected this special necklace from the vaults. It was handsome and sat well on the throat of old Queen Mary, but it was a little solemn for this young Princess with her easygoing manner and short hairstyle, and somehow heavy emeralds might have looked better on a darker girl. Prince Charles, appreciating the gift's importance, tried to make the necklace look lighter by buying the Princess an Art Deco diamond and emerald bracelet to match.

Among the Princess's favourite jewellery is a pearl and diamond necklace. At the preview of the Gonzaga exhibition at the Victoria and Albert Museum she wore this seven-strand pearl collar with a diamond clasp and although she does not really like bracelets, one made up of three different strands of pearls. On other occasions her long neck and good cleavage complement a favourite gold and white eighteen carat flower necklace set with cabochon sapphires.

The Princess is given scrumptious jewellery by friends. One gift was a three-rope pearl and diamond bracelet made by Nigel Milne and costing £2,200 which she wore to the first night of *Miss Saigon*. She loves little Russian trinkets and, of course, is not alone amongst princesses in having a weakness for Fabergé eggs.

The Princess is rarely seen wearing brooches but she does have a rather nice giant sapphire clip which guests at a Hampton Court banquet found quite compelling. More than most of the royals she likes to show off the clasps on necklaces, creatively turning them to the front.

Some of the most elaborate jewellery given to the Princess came from the Crown Prince of Saudi Arabia, who presented her with a sunburst pendant necklace of sapphires so stunning that the Princess immediately ordered a blue velvet dress to match and trimmed it with some of Queen Victoria's antique lace kept at Balmoral. The Saudi gift also included a becoming choker necklace of diamonds which the Princess wears on a black velvet ribbon. This suite of jewels, with sapphire earrings, ring, watch and bracelet to match and even a second spare choker necklace, arrived in an ornate green malachite box with gold palm trees, crossed swords and four huge butterflies.

In 1984 a camel was added to the other gifts. It was gold and carried spices inset in palm trees. While Mrs Simpson would wear panthers and snakes in diamonds, the Princess is rarely seen sporting this natural animal of the desert kingdom. Some presents of jewellery from the Middle East may be even less convenient. A watch, for example, may be inset with the ruler's face so that whenever you look at the time, a sheikh beams back at you with sapphire eyes and ruby lips.

In public you sometimes see the Princess in grand diamonds and pearls but privately she usually prefers fun jewellery often designed by her husband and full of sentimental meaning. Other private tokens of the Prince's are a necklace of grey and creamy baroque pearls and a rather heavy gold powder compact, the sort of thing the Queen might appreciate more.

Their personal jewellery is something secret between them, except for a delightful diamond necklace with a heart in the centre which was a present from the Prince after the birth of their first son. He has also had some charming pieces made for her but is cautious about cost. Apart from the gold wombat charm for her bracelet, which he gave her for her birthday in Canada, almost as special is a gold medallion which reads 'William' in the Prince's own handwriting and shows what a romantic man he can be.

CHAPTER 39

Going Solo

———————◆———————

'I'll be going solo on these trips. My husband is too busy with his own organisations.' This matter-of-fact announcement by the Princess early in January 1990 of her plans to go alone to backward countries to help underprivileged children slightly startled her normally imperturbable team at St James's Palace. One or two looked up and rather quickly eyes went down again to doodles on their pads of recycled paper.

It is true. The Prince and Princess are going on fewer public engagements together. The Princess says, 'I know what people are thinking, but inevitably we are going to be frequently apart; it's the nature of the job.' It has been noticeable that the Prince of Wales cut down on public engagements in the period from January to April 1990, doing only twelve in the first four months. But it is perhaps unfair to assess public value in this way when he is so effective and knowledgeable behind the scenes.

A member of the royal Household shook his head in admiration. 'She is strong. In the old days it was all "Let's do things together." Not any more.' Now he saw a young woman confident enough to forge ahead on her own.

Her mother will tell you that she 'always was self-reliant and resourceful from a very early age.' Perhaps it is Mrs Shand Kydd, spirited, poised, humorous but with an iron resolve hidden by beautiful manners, who is the best clue to her daughter's development.

'In the beginning,' the Princess explained, 'I wanted to get my act together . . . I had so many people watching me and the pressure was enormous, but as the years go on it gets better. But you are still learning all the time.' She admits that at first it was difficult to adapt; and really she had no idea of what she was taking on. But now that uncertainty is a thing of the past as each day she appears even more glossy and assured.

She gets it right, never makes you cringe. 'There is far too much about me in the newspapers, far too much,' the Princess says crossly, adding, 'It horrifies me when there is something more important like what is going on in the hospice, or there's been a bomb or something, yet they'll put me on the front page.' It is remarkable that there is no hint that this success is going to her head; she remains 'ungrand'.

'Ahem, with the greatest respect, Ma'am, isn't that the Princess Royal's speciality . . . deprived children . . . Third World?' a restraining note. The young woman at the centre of the table was firm. 'I am not too concerned if feelings are hurt. I must do what I can for those poor children.'

The Princess tells you she has the greatest admiration for Princess Anne, and of course there is absolutely no sense of rivalry with her sister-in-law. 'I'm her biggest fan . . . I just think she is marvellous. What she crams into a day I could never achieve.' Her voice is soft, never raised, light but firm. But you are in no doubt she is in charge and is a perfectionist.

Can this be the same girl who years ago demurely suggested, 'My role is supporting my husband, whenever I can. I have always been behind him encouraging . . .' all said with a downward flutter of the eyes and a deceptive coyness? One wonders whether the shyness was always partly a cover for a smart girl taking to the royal life with relish. She made a neatly mocking remark about her own intelligence when a milliner's fitter remarked that she had a relatively big head. The Princess laughed almost in parody of critics who point to her lack of academic achievement. 'Yes, but there is not much in it,' she said.

Is this the same Princess who would host, alone, a £5,000–£10,000-a-ticket Birthright charity concert in the ballroom at Buckingham Palace, when Prince Charles had to cancel because of his broken arm? She would even put guests out of their agony by announcing the latest on England's performance in the World Cup. A great roar from the servants' hall had echoed into the ballroom and prompted envious shifting about on the gilt chairs. So between the Vivaldi and Mozart, the Princess thoughtfully announced the result of the penalty shoot-out, though the 'I'm reliably informed that Pearce and Waddle missed,' sounded rather comical coming from those ultra-feminine glossed lips.

This was the evening when the frantic flashily dressed Mrs Ivana Trump, the estranged wife of American entrepreneur Donald Trump, desperate for social esteem and wearing earrings the size of cannonballs, elbowed her way to a small group surrounding the Princess. 'Yuk,' was the Princess's aside to Mrs George West, her lady-in-waiting for the evening.

She never allows the royal cocoon to isolate her from real life. 'Forget the helicopter,' the Princess remarked crisply on the eve of an exceptionally busy day. 'Let's take the train.' Next morning – and it gave her a real kick – she raced along the platform to catch the 10.20 A.M. British Rail InterCity from Paddington to Oxford, paying her £29.60 first-class day return. She had to sprint to catch the 3.15 afternoon train back to London, with her lady-in-waiting and detective in tow. Passengers blinked and smiled, then, being British, retreated behind their newspapers.

In October 1990 she flew by Concorde for a twenty-two-hour fund-raising trip to Washington DC and to visit Grandma's House, a home caring for children with AIDS in one of the most depressed areas. Close to tears she picked up a three-year-old black child dying of the disease and said to her, 'You are a lovely little girl and I am going to tell my two sons about you.' She held the child in her arms for most of her visit, and when the child asked, 'Please, can I have a ride in your car,' the Princess replied, 'Of course you can.'

The child tugged at her heart and even detectives were close to tears when they gently lifted her out of the green car. Then the

Princess gave the little girl a quick hug and they parted. The Princess knew that she would never see her again. The child was known as 'first lady' because she was the first baby brought to the home, when she was three months old, and would be the first to die.

That night the Princess, who has a chameleon ability to change with her surroundings, wore a slinky red dress for a fund-raising dinner in aid of the London Festival Ballet in Washington. Tickets cost £1,325 each or £1,850 for a private meeting but wealthy Americans grumbled about the cost and shunned the banquet though they are besotted by the Princess.

Even the President's wife Barbara Bush stayed away to express her disapproval of the cost. However, there were plenty of X-rays, socially ambitious women, slim to extinction and cruelly described by Tom Wolfe in *The Bonfire of the Vanities*. They have no substance, mentally or physically, whirling in a social vacuum with bony knees and bonier elbows.

The US Transport Secretary, Sam Skinner, whispered, 'You are a wonderful caring person and we are lucky to have you here,' as they whizzed around the ballroom to the sound of 'It's the wrong time, and the wrong place'. The burly minister had clumsily interrupted a dance the Princess was about to have with the British Ambassador to Washington, Sir Antony Acland. 'Excuse me, Ambassador, can I have this one?' Skinner said as he grabbed the Princess by the arm. The next day she had tea with Mrs Barbara Bush and giggled over *Millie's Book*, allegedly written by the Bushes' spaniel.

Today, after a decade, the Princess has possibly achieved as much as any other member of the royal family except the Queen Mother. This learner Princess is possibly the most famous woman in the world, the most publicised. People are endlessly fascinated by her style, her looks and youthful sophistication. The hint of shyness is still there; a controlled blush gives an added appeal and vulnerability. But there is also a self-confidence, a speedy elegance, an unspoken air of being royal. And motherhood has done nothing but improve her, as physically and mentally she revels in responsible parenthood. Had the marriage been better, perhaps the Princess might not have soared to such starry heights.

What is so refreshing is that she still has a quirkiness and *joie de vivre* which have not been squeezed out of her. Royal advisers may be a little dismayed by their glamorous Princess, even disgruntled, but they cannot complain. Everything is done with flair, commitment and a sense of fun. 'I don't have to introduce myself,' she explains going into a hall packed with people, 'they all seem to know who I am,' making it all seem enjoyable exactly as the Queen Mother has done, as if laying a foundation stone were the most delightful way of spending an afternoon.

The Princess is treasured and they compare her with the cruelly nicknamed 'Duchess of Yuk' who is despised in the tabloid newspapers for her chummy female equivalent of blokeishness. The British public likes the royals to be a little distant.

The reward for being willing to think more of others has resulted in a quick but not cumbersome maturity. She may not have been to university but she has been meeting the best informed people who head her forty charities and has absorbed what they have to say. This is the best education in the world, earning her an enviable degree of humanity. She seemed close to tears when, on a visit to the Foreign Office, she saw some of the letters sent by wives and daughters to their husbands and fathers held hostage in Iraq by Saddam Hussein. She talked about possibly paying a visit to see British troops in the Gulf and said she listened all the time to the latest news bulletins.

So the Palace should look back thankfully. This girl took advice and, before their astonished eyes, raised royal duties to a new unheard-of high profile. It was almost more than the old guard could stomach, but her admirers say, 'Now look at her. The head has come up; she has good bearing, has found her feet. From being vacuous she is maturing well; she does things ebulliently and is much more forthright now.' And they pay a compliment to her effortless securing of the dynasty: 'Bloody hell, she got it right twice over with those two boys.'

But the more experienced political courtiers who have been with the Queen for years will always tend to think of the Princess as 'lightweight . . . a little shallow; she does not work things out logically or intellectually,' which is true.

'All the same, I'd much rather,' said an old friend of the royal family as he walked through St James's Park, 'talk to the Princess than be nudged in the ribs by Fergie.'

Unlike the Duchess of York flailing about goodnaturedly, the Princess, though not really born to the role of duty and public life, listened to her husband and to some of the best advisers in the world. You cannot be constantly exposed to challenging new ideas and stimulating arguments, whether about politics, diet, architecture or music, and still wonder only whether to wear blue chiffon or satin shorts for dinner on the yacht.

The marriage gave them both confidence. In the honeymoon photographs of them in Balmoral, he looks slightly immature, not much older than his child-bride. A good sprinkling of common sense helped the Princess slowly to take on causes where she felt she could help. But no matter how she developed or how the world praised her, it seemed to bring little cheer to a miserable-looking Prince sitting disconsolately on a yacht in Majorca while his suntanned wife buried her face in a peach.

Nobody would have criticised her if she had done far less, emerging only occasionally from a privileged cocoon to appear prettily beside her husband. She knows she has been given a diamond-studded spoon but she has also been influenced by her husband's spiritual questing: his asceticism and her own feeling shared with a good man of a debt to society.

Had she married a young landowner, it is hard to imagine her charitable work being much more than smilingly shaking a box for the blind in the old market square or opening the family country house garden to the disabled once a year. After all, there is no reason to suppose that she is naturally inclined towards good works. But now, coming up to her thirtieth birthday, she begins to look almost like a glamorous Mother Teresa figure, a modern saint doing far more than could ever be expected. She goes into a room and bowls people over with naturalness and gaiety, then leaves them feeling good. But she is humble enough too to learn from everyone she meets.

This exemplary Princess who has chosen some unpopular causes has her critics. The late Patrick White, the great Australian bachelor writer, once described her as 'a waxwork figure'. Others say her good work is sublimation provoked by a lack of warmth in her private life. They also claim that anyone can be good with children. This is not exactly right. Children are intuitive, instant barometers; her natural affinity with them is not something given to all the royal family.

In April 1990 she fought her natural diffidence and made a punchy speech when she opened the annual drugs conference of Chief Police Officers in Lancashire. In white polo neck and tartan jacket she stepped bravely to the microphone and forgot any nervousness in her personal plea to 180 senior officers to save children from drugs and the evil pushers: 'Catch them in the classrooms before the dealers catch them at the school gates.'

'I am deeply embarrassed,' she says, 'when they put me on a pedestal.' And indeed there is nothing phoney or gushing about her as she kneels down to chat to an old person, no hint of 'Here I am, look at me, being awfully sympathetic,' while secretly thinking, 'The sooner I get away from these old bores and into my evening bomber jacket . . .' Hers is a quick intuitive way with crowds – she works them with jokiness and warmth. She is disarming and shows tenderness, her approach right every time.

Words often used most about her are 'caring', 'so understanding'. One of her advisers in the Household once complained, 'If I hear the word caring again, I'll scream.' He did and he left, no longer wanted on the voyage of this Princess.

CHAPTER 40

To Brighten Our Days

———— ◆ ————

Chosen to brighten our days, this 'girl of charm and sweetness' was blessed by the President of the Immortals with an appealing sweetness and a gift for caring. Standing in Nobottle Wood on a cold winter's day, dressed in a check chainstore shirt and green wellies, she caught the eye of a future king. As in fairy stories he found himself strangely attracted, his search for a wife ending unexpectedly in this ploughed field.

Plucked from schoolgirl obscurity, she became princess, wife and mother before she was twenty-one. Against all expectations, this airy young aristocrat made the uncaring think, the sour cheerful, the rich deliver, the hedonistic unselfish, the callous giving. Above all she made us laugh, for she has two of the world's greatest gifts, compassion and humour. It is doubtful if she goes to bed thinking about being Queen, yet much of the future of the monarchy depends on her. When the time comes she will take it in her stride.

Appealing, she is also desirable. 'You lot seem to like seeing me in a skimpy bikini,' she teased a group of young men at a Soho hostel who had pin-up photographs of her on the walls in

316

her minimalist red bikini. She can even make the homeless feel more at home.

The public side of her marriage may seem less than perfect, but her loyalty to her husband is unquestioning. When the late Armand Hammer, businessman and philanthropist, told her he had so much confidence in the Prince of Wales 'that, if he asked me to jump through the window there, I think I'd jump,' the Princess smiled and replied, 'Well, I'd jump right after you.' She loves her man in the real sense, is a match for him, but is also protective. They go their own way, but perhaps one day they will rediscover each other and be pleasantly surprised.

Child-bearing has not been easy for her and anyway hope of a sister for Prince Harry and Prince William is slight. Once when invited to pay a visit to the Royal Academy of Music six months ahead, the Princess laughingly asked, 'What if I am pregnant?' to which John Bliss engagingly replied, 'Ma'am, we'll take you as we find you.' A true Cancerian woman, her family matters most.

In the royal family there is guarded respect all round. They may wish she were not quite so starry but cannot fault her. She understands them perfectly. Utterly modern, she wears royal jewels with lightness and originality: an emerald necklace round her hair like a jewelled laurel leaf crown for a goddess. By sheer luck she was christened Diana, Goddess of the Moon, Artemis.

Patric Walker, the brilliant astrologer, studied the chart for her birth on 1 July 1961, and says, 'I was thrilled to find a wonderful combination brought about by the Moon and Jupiter in Aquarius. A child of the moon, she is the perfect Consort, a lesser luminary; she gets her light from the Prince of Wales, a typical Scorpio, a man easily bored and introspective. She has Voltaire's "best of all possible worlds" and everything is possible. I feel very optimistic about her. It is the moon her ruler which allows her to get things right. Hers is a water sign, sensual, vulnerable, generous, impulsive, determined. A tender plant, she is easily hurt, can be emotionally introverted and defensive but has that Cancerian ability to bounce back. Cancer is the most naturally female sign, and the reason Cancerians can cope so well is that they are perceptive, instinctive, almost clairvoyant. Only by giving do you become stronger, so that her reaching out to AIDS victims becomes a way of strengthening herself.'

In public life she has made her role seem easy. But that should not diminish what she has achieved: never any downturning of that soft mouth, none of the crotchetiness of Princess Anne nor overdone chumminess of the hit-and-miss Duchess of York. We are lucky in this Princess of Wales. She has about her a natural spirituality, a lightness which has nothing to do with being seen in church. Ask the Princess about her work, particularly for the charity Turning Point which deals with drug addiction, and the answer is simple, 'Because I care.'

Her sensitive letter from Kensington Palace early in 1991 to the British troops in Saudi Arabia preparing for the war with Iraq was typical. It began: 'A message written to the thousands of you in the Gulf from the safety of my home in London can all too easily sound remote or condescending. But I do want you all to know just how much you are in our thoughts . . .'

The wonderful thing is that she is as we see her, an example of how extraordinary ordinary can be. With each appearance she enhances the monarchy. Behind her softness and strength lies that great gift: 'Know thyself.'

She has come into an often dreary world with a happy power greater than herself, a goodness which surprises her constantly: the way she can make sick children smile and old people think it worth living a little longer. An icon, she outshines the most celebrated and has made our monarchy the envy of the world, yet is aware of both the elusive 'magic of monarchy' and its fragility.

Nobody sees her as a sacrificial lamb and that is perhaps the greatest compliment, for typically she has kept a sense of gratitude. By her seamless transition from plump *ingénue* to glossy performer she has become a fantasy of hope for millions of women around the world. Yet beneath the patina of style and confidence lurks the same skittishly endearing girl.

Index

319